Portrait of Chopin by Rubio

IN SEARCH OF
CHOPIN

BY

ALFRED CORTOT

TRANSLATED BY

CYRIL AND RENA CLARKE

GREENWOOD PRESS, PUBLISHERS
WESTPORT, CONNECTICUT

Library of Congress Cataloging in Publication Data

Cortot, Alfred, 1877-1962.
  In search of Chopin.

    Translation of Aspects de Chopin.
    Reprint of the ed. published by Abelard Press, New
York.
    Bibliography: p.
    Discography: p.
    1. Chopin, Fryderyk Franciszek, 1810-1849.
  I. Title.
  [ML410.C54C603   1975]   786.1'092'4 [B]   74-33504
  ISBN 0-8371-7971-8

927.8
C54c - T

Library of Congress catalog card number 74-33504
ISBN 0-8371-7971-8   *78-8957*

Printed in the United States of America

CONTENTS

1

SOME PORTRAITS

HEIGHT FIVE FEET SEVEN INCHES, a round chin, an oval face, a medium-sized mouth. These details are contained in a passport issued to Chopin in Paris on July 7, 1837. In this same document his parentage is stated to be French. He had accompanied Camille Pleyel on a short visit to England during that year. A passport was a necessity; red tape was as abundant then as now, hence the false statement concerning his parents.

If one accepts as accurate the only precise information given in this casual official description, he was slightly below normal height.

For all who came near him his appearance was characterized by an indefinable "resilience." A deceptive impression, engendered perhaps by the fact that his weight was well below average. In 1840 it was ninety-seven pounds.

As if to defend herself from the whirlpool of gossip that would attend the first sign of any cooling off in her notorious liaison with the composer, George Sand confirms this impression for us. In her provocative novel, *Lucrezia Floriani,* she sketches Chopin in the guise of Prince Carol. "Delicate in mind as in spirit, his face has the beauty of a sad woman." Careful to omit no detail that will fix the identity of her model, she adds, "pure and slender of form as a young god from Olympus and to crown the whole, an expression at once tender and severe, chaste and passionate."

Liszt gives an equally poetic description of the personality of this man, whose genius was to inspire some pages of remarkable aesthetic insight. "His appearance formed a harmonious whole . . . his blue eyes were more spiritual than dreamy, his gentle, delicate smile held no trace of bitterness. The fineness and transparency of his complexion bewitched the eye, his fair hair was silky, his carriage distinguished, his manners so instinctively aristocratic that everyone treated him as though he were a prince. His gestures were full of grace and freedom, the tone of his voice was muffled to the point of being stifled."

It is apparent that Chopin's contemporaries were incapable of remaining on the level of material reality when speaking of him. Liszt continues, ". . . His whole appearance reminds one of the unbelievable delicacy of a convolvulus blossom poised on its stem—a cup divinely coloured but so fragile that the slightest touch will tear it."

Charles Legouvé carried away from their first meeting the impression that he had just encountered "such a son as Weber might have fathered had the mother been a Duchess."

Finally there is this appreciation by Moscheles:

"What is Chopin like to look at?"

"His music."

In spite of its abruptness, it is not far from being the most penetrating and suggestive description we have of the poet of the Nocturnes.

Diligent research and an occasional unexpected piece of luck have enabled me to acquire several interesting portraits of the composer. The artist's brush confirms the writer's attempts to describe an incomparable art.

In the sentences that follow, it is my intention to compare these portraits with the prose sketches I have quoted. The writers' unanimity of opinion bears the hallmark of truth. It is in no way augmented by the addition of the writings of Delacroix, Heine, or Berlioz, which do little to bring him more clearly to life.

I hope that the description of these pictures, so far unknown or ignored, may add to the small body of material available for us to draw upon in the documentation of Chopin's outward appearance, and help toward a more intimate approach to his personality.

In the portrait that was once in the possession of the historian, Charles de Mazade, before coming to me, Chopin wears the expression George Sand describes when she picks out his essential characteristics.

Emaciated, melancholy rather than sorrowful, the delicate features bear the marks of a relentless disease.

His eyes, more gray than blue,* eyes which, we are told, could fill will laughter over childish pranks, look rather set and distant as though clouded over with the film of fever.

The mouth and chin remain those of a boy, the lips bloodless, and the shape of the chin indicates an almost feminine fragility.

Only a proud Bourbon nose, the object of so many jokes on his part, a feature which in anyone else might have been considered sensual, defies the menacing symptoms of his illness and give some indication of his burning vitality. With a quite unexpected realism it contradicts the immateriality of his character, which is shown so clearly in his pensive likeness.

Although several of his biographers describe his eyes as being brown, this detail is confirmed by the description in the passport and by Liszt's memories quoted above.

One might almost say it is prophetic of the ghost destined to remain a legend for all time.

Less dramatic than the stormy Delacroix in the Louvre, but with a more intense expression than the elegiac Ary Schetter, of which only the Dordrecht copy now exists, lacking the impersonal rigidity of the Kolberg in the Warsaw Museum, this picture shows him to be such a person as his music would lead one to imagine him to be. In feeling it comes close to the tenderness which his brief and sad existence inspires in us—a feeling halfway between an irresistible need for confidence and an instinctive shrinking from disillusion.

So far, all my efforts to identify the artist with the necessary guarantees of authenticity have been in vain. Personally, I think it is permissible to attribute it to the Italian painter, Luigi Rubio.

In a lithograph of the pianist, Gottschalk, and in a portrait of Franchomme at the age of six, perched on the end of a grand piano with his violin, the Princess Czartoryska, that great and faithful friend of Chopin, at the keyboard, Rubio employs a technique undeniably similar to that used in the painting to which I refer.*

Other reasons, which follow, also seem to justify my supposition.

A young pianist, whose name, Vera de Kologrivoff, leads one to assume that she was of Russian extraction, was Chopin's pupil and later an assistant tutor for some of his aristocratic students. From 1842 to 1846 she was constantly in his society. She became, until Mlle. de Rozières felt herself called upon to supplant her in this role, the involuntary recip-

* *One cannot believe with any certainty the recent assertion made in Poland that this picture can be ascribed to the painter Kwiatkowski, of whom I shall have occasion to speak later.*

ient of his more intimate confidences. She was probably the
first to be aware of the uneasiness which began to creep into
his relationship with George Sand, an uneasiness which, in
the face of daily shocks of disillusionment, was not long in
reaching an irreparable break between these two victims of
misplaced affection.

In a letter to Chopin, dated 1843, she informs him that she
has spoken to M. Rubio about a portrait. To save Chopin
the effort of climbing stairs, Rubio has for this once consented
to depart from his normal practice and come to him with his
palette and brushes. Rubio is determined, she adds, "to finish
the little portrait in oils in two sittings." She ends by begging
Chopin to agree to the project because she wishes there to
be in existence "a portrait that is a likeness." Since three
years later she became the wife of the young painter, her pre-
judice in favor of Rubio's talents was, no doubt, due to considerations other than those of a purely aesthetic nature.

Writing to congratulate her on her marriage, Chopin refers
to the imminent departure of the newly married couple for
foreign parts. In point of fact, after living in Geneva, Milan,
and Venice, they settled in Florence, where Rubio became
Professor at the School of Art, and where his wife died in
1882.

There is, therefore, nothing to contradict my supposition
that Charles de Mazade, a great admirer of Chopin, through
the Princess Czartoryska who was his friend and whose portrait Rubio had also painted, should have acquired the portrait
(which was subsequently to become my property through the
great kindness of his heirs) before the young couple went
abroad.

The signs of illness, which the artist's penetrating and ob-
servant brush has delineated, support my view as to the date

when the portrait must have been painted. It was a period in Chopin's life overshadowed by moral torment as much as by physical suffering.

The gradual withdrawal from Nohant, the increasing off-handedness of Maurice's manner toward him, the atmosphere of suspicion, caused by the intrusion of Clesinger into Solange's affections, coincide with this period. These depressing circumstances were added to by purely material anxieties; anxieties which led him after some months of unhappy solitude to look on the fatal trip to England, which was to hasten his end, as a kind of salvation of the spirit as much as a release from material necessity.

The ravages of twenty years of suffering, the piteous fixity of his gaze, clearly that of the visionary of sound, who has taught us with what penetrating intensity he could search the secrets of all dreams, the unexpressed stirrings of that longing for home, which will not be silenced, the superhuman confidence apparent in every page of his work, are all faithfully portrayed by this artist.

The idea of a Chopin-Ariel, of a Chopin-spirit, of a Chopin without physical substance, detached from all reality, is in no wise contradicted by this portrait. The inner significance of his work leads irresistibly to such a likeness.

And if a personal predilection has led me to dilate on the merits of a portrait which seems to me to be a singularly exact translation on canvas of the unhappy face of a beloved composer, this is not to vaunt its quality as a work of art, but rather the expression of what it has meant to me by its presence in my home. It gives me the illusion of being in intimate daily contact with that sublime personality from whom came those subtle, nostalgic musical utterances which were to transform the fundamental essentials of piano music. In this, for me, lies its great value.

While I was traveling in Belgium, I discovered another canvas, this time signed and dated. Less penetratingly observed and technically more conventional, it has, however, one special feature. Alone of all known portraits of Chopin, it shows him standing. I came across it under rather peculiar circumstances.

The artist, Louis Gallait, a native of Tournai and a painter with a firmly established local reputation, had, so it is said, been in Paris during the year 1843. There he had arranged with Chopin for some sittings. The picture was later to become part of the Bishop of Ghent's collection.

It was a strange coincidence that within an interval of several years I was to become the possessor of two portraits of Chopin, both painted in 1843 and both unknown to the master's biographers.

The artist makes no attempt to reach the hidden personality of Chopin, and, in speaking of this portrait, I cannot do better, since it best describes is pictorial value and the deliberate academic treatment, than quote the catalogue itself.

"The celebrated Polish composer is shown standing, three-quarter length, in a romantic landscape embellished with mountains and a medieval castle. In his right hand he holds the rolled manuscript of one of his works. At this period at the height of his fame he does not as yet show any sign of the illness which was to prove fatal a few years later."

One hesitates to add to or alter the exposition I have just quoted. To complete the description, however, I must mention the presence of a stone column and balustrade in the foreground. The latter enables Chopin to lean against it and to take a pose careless and confident, as though he had won a first prize or had just received his diploma.

It goes without saying that such a stilted composition does not, could not, compete with the portrait by Rubio. It contains no hint of understanding the personality or of making spiritual contact with the person portrayed.

No glow comes from this accurate, lifeless face. No freedom is allowed the figure limned against the artificial background. Instead, one's attention is directed to the meticulous care taken over the details of his clothes—the high threefold cravat, the white waistcoat, the very obvious watchchain, the carefully draped frock coat; in short, everything that mirrors the fashion of the period. Only the hands come in for a slightly less impersonal treatment. No doubt, for the honest Belgian artist it was of the utmost importance to depict the physical details essential in a famous virtuoso. In his eyes, this aspect probably far outweighed in immediate importance the less tangible attributes of creative genius.

To sum up, it is a factual portrait, from which any hint of psychological interpretation is deliberately excluded, but which, nonetheless, cannot but find a place with the other portraits of Chopin.

The two medallions of Liszt and Chopin, struck in 1837 by the sculptor Bovy, were the subject of a long and careful search before they were finally added to my collection. That of Liszt I bought for a few lira from an antique dealer in Pisa, where I found it while poking about in a heap of the most unlikely pieces of old iron; that of Chopin I bargained hotly for at an auction sale in Paris. The bidding developed into a struggle, lacking neither verve nor obstinacy, for more than one appetite had been whetted.

All of Chopin's pupils—Mathias in particular—joined in

praising the veracity with which Bovy's expert chisel had caught the facial expression of their master, especially the details of the hair and nose.

In bronze, the profile is in high relief and produces an effect of urgency and perfection of line. In this it is distinguished from the highly stylized interpretation with which Clesinger chose to ornament Chopin's tomb at Père-Lachaise.

It shows off very clearly the light tuft of side whisker, which Chopin lightheartedly mentioned to his parents in a letter from Vienna during July, 1831: a detail that is not to be found in any of his likenesses dated after 1839. In this letter he remarks jokingly that he only proposes to wear one side whisker, on the right, since the left-hand side of his face is not exposed to the public eye. Incidentally, the passport of 1837 mentions this hirsute ornament, stating vaguely and laconically: "Fair beard."

From another letter, written to Gryzmala from Marseilles on his return from Majorca, and dated March 17, 1839, we learn of its final disappearance.

These details are of secondary importance, but nonetheless serve to fix with a certain degree of accuracy the dates of several portraits and photographs, to which I shall again have to refer in the course of this study of Chopin's physical appearance.

Bovy, with scrupulously accurate modeling—based perhaps on the style of David d'Angers—has reproduced the expressive features of the young musician of twenty-seven: he, who has just written in Marie Wodzinska's album the *Valse de l'Adieu,* so full of the melancholy rhythm and undying echoes of an unhappy love affair; he, whose fingers bring surging forth from the piano the tumultuous rhythms of the tragic Scherzo in B flat minor; he, for whom Destiny is preparing

the imminent encounter with George Sand, the consequences
of which are to have such a deep effect on his character and
genius during the eight years of a liaison which, though not
without some bright moments, was devoid of any real happiness.

Here is Chopin on the threshold of the two most important
events in his emotional life. One look at that gentle, aristocratic face, with its affectionate and childlike expression, its
instinctive delicacy, is all that is necessary to know that in his
struggle against any of the great tragic realities, his physical
being would be bound to confess defeat, and that "Madem-
oiselle Chopin," as he was called, would find himself in permanent disagreement with that virile and robust creature
"Monsieur George Sand."

Contemplating the two original sketches made by Kwiatkowski at Chopin's deathbed gives me the feeling of humble,
tender contact with the ghost of the beloved master. But before turning to them, I would like to draw the reader's attention to a curious picture, which, though not unique, is
nevertheless almost unknown. I refer to a daguerrotype, which
was taken in Paris during the last months of Chopin's life.
The original, for a long time in the possession of the music
publishers, Breitkoff and Hartel at Leipzig, now the property
of the Chopin Institute in Warsaw, gives an aspect of his
appearance previously overlooked or unknown by all those
who have concerned themselves with the problem. One must
take into consideration the technical imperfections of the
process, then in its infancy, if we are to justify the strange
result. What still remains surprising is that here the expression
and even the structure of Chopin's face are quite different
from the characteristics shown in his other portraits.

The strongly marked flat surface is stamped with serious

ness and anxiety. It does not suggest the distinguished melan-choly seen in most of his portraits. Rather it hints at an aloof concentration, as though by instinct he had refused to be caught by a technique unable to interpret the emotional, spiritual aspects of his personality.

Weariness shows in his pinched features, an ennui which might equally indicate extreme reserve. The expression is hard, almost malevolent, the lips are pursued. Any sort of freedom or spontaneity is absent. It cannot be denied that the detail in this picture is exact. It has to be admitted that the principle involved in this method of portraiture must, by its very na-ture, catch the physical details of the face at the moment of taking. Herein lies the inherent weakness of the process—its lack of psychological penetration. The sensitive plate has caught but a fleeting glimpse of a human being. The deeper truths of the personality are absent. It has caught a face, but the soul is missing.

The two drawings by Kwiatkowski, sketched at Chopin's deathbed, during the night of October 16-17, 1849, are to my mind far more expressive of that tragic moment than the prose description by Graefle. These drawings, a few manu-scripts, ten letters or so, a lock of hair as fine and fragile as the hair of a sick child from which the life-force has vanished into thin air, these form the collection of souvenirs with which I am privileged to surround my worship of the master, a wor-ship that has always proved rewarding.

In profile, limned by a sensitive pencil, the two sketches show both sides of that pathetic face which is known to have been curiously unsymmetrical. The one showing the left profile has been underlined, as it were, by some touches of pain. Both are signed and dated that memorable night. Kwiatkow-ski, a compartriot of Chopin's, gave one of them to his friend, the architect Viel, as a souvenir. From memory he painted a dramatic version of the poet-musician's last moments, surrounded by his friends. He also made several rough sketches of Chopin during his lifetime. Quite pleasing to the eye, they are without any deep psychological significance. It is in the two profiles, drawn under the stress of a deeply felt bereavement, that the artist scales the heights of genuine feeling. The mystery and absolute stillness of death, a stillness like that of the images of Khmère, a contemplative serenity in which Chopin seems to reign unchallenged on the threshold of an unknown infinite, all of this has been captured by the artist and gives these pictures their eternal value.

Though death makes an essential change, Chopin continues to show through all its rigidity, in spite of the haggard features due to his prolonged illness, that indefinable power of attraction which was inherent in his nature. George Sand has attempted to define this essential characteristc, describing it as "a mixture of tenderness and sincerity, of passion and chasity." La Fontaine defined it as "a personality infused with the gift of charm." When Chopin was alive no one could resist it.

2

THE HAND OF CHOPIN

THE HAND OF CHOPIN. To the laymen, these words mean nothing more than the purely material fact they represent. To the imagination of the pianist, they invoke visions.

I would be content if this hand were no more than the indispensable link between creative thought and music, the means whereby the needs of thought and inspiration are satisfied through their realization in sound.

It was certainly not the hand alone that originated those nostalgic, those vibrant melodies, heroic and capricious rhythms, harmonies as yet unheard by any ear. In the depths of a personality continually in process of giving birth to music, it was the inner voice of the soul that dictated.

The mission of that hand was solely to translate into physical terms the expression of emotion and to adapt it to the keyboard. A cast of it is before me as I write. It has other virtues than blind obedience to the limitations of the pianoforte.

Spatulate fingers, developed by practice, tendons in relief, with a skin through the pores of which everything ignoble has evaporated, this human mechanism serves the ideal. All the poetry of delicate caresses, all the magic of half-tones, of those faintly heard accompaniments which did not interfere with the penetrating accents given to the articulation of the essential melody, all awake at his touch on an instrument, the very tone of which underwent a change when he came in contact with it. His thumb was placed in accordance with the instruc-tions laid down in manuals on piano playing. This gave him, we are told, an exceptional stretch, a physical feature in keep-ing with the exacting demands of a music full of fresh pos-sibilities of tonal combination.

With a caressive suppleness, well separated from one another where they join the hand, each well endowed with its own individuality and a miraculous agility, these fingers instinctively support his virtuosity. As ready to receive his flashes of inspiration as a branch of a tree bends to the last breath of wind or rejoices in the fanciful twinings of the honey-suckle or convolvulus.

"Velvet fingers," as George Sand loved to call them.

This almost immaterial touch was due to the unusual combination of an exceptional suppleness of the joints, capable of every delicate shade of movement, plus a well-knit bone structure, which, in the words of his pupil, Georges Mathias, was "that of a soldier."

Karazowski asserts that, like Schumann, Chopin as a child had considered having a machine constructed for increasing the length between the first and second joints of each finger, to be used while he slept. I find it difficult to believe this, since, in a letter to Fontana, written from Calder House on August 18, 1848, that is to say, about a year before his death, Chopin, half jokingly, half seriously complains that, to his chagrin, he had never been able to overcome his two worst enemies, "A huge nose and a disobedient third finger."

His interest in technique was governed by a basic principle. This involved the postulate that each finger was of a different strength, and that the strength diminished in the following order: thumb, little finger, first finger (the pivot of the hand), second finger—the weakest of all—with its Siamese twin, the third finger.

He appears to have encountered little difficulty in acquiring an astonishing degree of virtuosity.

Although the exaggeration of an admirer overcome with admiration is apparent, Stephen Heller tells us that in spite of the smallness of his hand, Chopin was able to stretch over a third of the keyboard. Exaggeration apart, this facility of stretch must have been of a spectacular, almost an abnormal character, to have excited a fascinated admirer to exclaim: "But this man has the hands of a snake."

However strict the exercises which Chopin imposed upon himself, which gave birth to those two volumes, the first items of which were published under the deliberately utilitarian title of "Etudes," one has to concede that this immortal collection of masterpieces, dedicated to the enrichment of piano technique, would never have been dreamed of if Chopin's hand had been other than what it was, Nature's princely gift.

Technique, although it must always take second place to creative inspiration, which directs it and gives it life, is nonetheless entitled to that place, and is of that much importance in the elements that go to the making of Chopin's genius.

Chopin was not only the most music-minded of pianists, he was also the most exceptionally keyboard-minded of all composers.

3

CHOPIN THE PEDAGOGUE!

THERE ARE CERTAIN combinations of words, which are as repellent to the mind as certain juxtapositions of color are to the eye.

Immediately I thought of associating the two words which indicate the subject matter of this chapter, I felt an instinctive revulsion.

Chopin a pedagogue? Chopin professor of the piano? Chopin lecturer on some subject or other?

Once it comes into contact with such a pedestrian phrase, the aura of idealism seems to fly off into thin air, and the legendary atmosphere which has surrounded the composer for several generations vanishes.

But facts are facts. Chopin did sometimes have to spend the best part of the day seated at the piano beside the young heirs of the aristocratic, moneyed families who formed the greater part of his clientele. Again, how inappropriate the word "clientele" seems when used in connection with Chopin!

Nevertheless, he corrected his pupils' faulty fingering, and was careful to point out any incorrect method of positioning the hands on the keyboard.

With difficulty, beneath a strained politeness, he disguised the tortures he endured. Every wrong note was like a knife thrust.

Hours devoted to efforts he knew to be valueless. Wasted hours spent in an atmosphere of bored resignation. This, added to his day-to-day difficulty in dealing with an existence already threatened by an incurable disease, must have been a heavy burden.

Hours denied to the outpourings of his genius, hours sacrificed on the altar of necessity.

From the moment when he set foot in Paris, he refused to accept any further help from his parents. His drudgery was the unavoidable price that had to be paid to secure a precarious independence.

He regarded Paris as a mere steppingstone on his journey from Vienna to England, but he was destined to remain on the banks of the Seine for eighteen years.

In that very worldly society that was Paris, a society which gave him flattery rather than financial support, he had to rely solely upon his own efforts. He took pride in doing so.

The concerts he gave were few and far between, and then, for the most part, on a friendly basis or in aid of some charity.

The receipts from his published works were no greater help in paying his rent or his servants' wages. Publishers stole the copyright of his works without hesitation, paid him a miserable price for them, and made enormous profits for themselves. Five hundred francs for one of the Ballades or Polonaises, a thousand francs for the Preludes; sums that didn't pay for his cab fares, his daily pair of clean white gloves, still less his constant generosity in discreetly helping his more unfortunate compatriots.

He had no choice, therefore, but to endure the drudgery of teaching for a living.

The price we know was twenty francs an hour, and the

hour was generally prolonged, without charge, in the case of promising pupils.

Never in his whole existence was there a period when he was not at the mercy of the necessity of earning his daily bread. He accepted this humdrum existence uncomplainingly and with the dignity of an aristocrat.

Except for his dealings with his publishers, with whom he was punctilious, he avoided the financial problems which threatened his independence. He sometimes showed, from shyness or casualness, an astonishing indifference to matters of this sort. There is, of course, the generous action of Jane Stirling in sending him 25,000 francs when she learned from a third party of the precarious state of his finances. But he was not aware of its arrival until several weeks later. He had not troubled to open the sealed envelope which contained the treasure that was to prove his salvation.

Here again we meet the Ariel myth, so satisfying to those who imagine a Chopin lost in dreams and remote from any contact with reality.

But when we examine the humdrum details of his life, we are moved to pity for this man around whose being romance has spun so many illusions.

The greater part of his joyless existence was spent in deal-ing with the day-to-day problems of his fight for existence. They weighed heavily.

All in all, Chopin's life as a teacher was drab and lusterless.

With a few rare exceptions, his pupils were drawn from a class with no professional musical ambitions. Amateurs, whose surnames were to be found in d'Hozier, could hardly be ex-pected to enhance the reputation of their master as a teacher or to display that enthusiasm for his artistry that would carry the public with it. No, compared to Kalkbrenner and Stamaty,

Chopin cut very little ice as the leader of an Academy. Pianists were anxious to add to their technique by studying with a famous artist. Liszt kept the Altenburg of Weimar filled because of his great European reputation. No such stream of international virtuosi passed through Chopin's rooms in the Rue Tronchet or his little house in the Square d'Orléans.

So far as a career as professional pianist is concerned, a very short list covers all of Chopin's pupils who were destined to leave any trace of their existence.

The most remarkable of these, and the only one to give promise of a spectacular career, was Charles Filscht, who died at Verrières in 1845, aged fifteen. Liszt heard this young boy, and remarked to de Lenz, who tells the story, "When that child starts touring I shall shut up shop."

As for the rest, they were no more than mediocre, remembered for being conscientious teachers rather than performers of any outstanding ability.

Karazowski made an approximate list, which can be condensed as follows: Among the women, Miss O'Meara, afterward Mme. Camille Dubois, who, in spite of her great age when I was privileged to meet her, had not forgotten a number of factual details given by Chopin concerning the interpretation of certain passages in his works; Mlle. Frédérique Müller, who later, as Mme. Streicher, collaborated in the production of the edition of Chopin's works, undertaken by Mikuli, and to whom the Allegro de Concert is dedicated. Vera de Kologrievof, the future wife of Rubio, to whom I have ascribed the touching portrait of Chopin which graces my home. She was chosen by Chopin to assist him with his pupils, a choice and an honor she shared with Mlle. de Rozières.

As regard the men, his young pupil, Filscht, apart, I must mention Gutmann, the genial German giant, of whom Chopin was very fond, in spite of his doubtful gifts as a pianist; de Lenz, author of the famous work on Beethoven and those satirical accounts of his occasional meetings with Chopin and George Sand—scraps of information that cast a curious light on the behavior of the two actors toward one another in that famous affair; Lysberg, whose compositions in an elegiac style found favor with the melody-mad middle classes, and who became incumbent of the Chair of Liszt at the Conservatoire of Geneva in consequence; the Norwegian, Tellefsen, who helped Mikuli with the preparation of the careful edition of Chopin's works, the particular value of which lies in the notes regarding the fingering of those pieces he had studied under the Polish master. Then, again, there is Georges Mathias, for many years professor at the Conservatoire in Paris, where his teaching was reputed to be based on the "secrets" of Chopin's playing. While I was still an unsophisticated youth, his kindly encouragement gave me the vivid impression of having come in direct contact with some of the ideas of the musician I had dreamed so much about. Like Filscht, Paul Gunsberg died very young. Finally we have Wernick, who settled in St. Petersburg, where little more was heard of him; and Gustave Schumann, whose activities in Berlin gained for him a certain reputation as head of a school.

It can be said with certainty that Chopin's feminine admirers brought him more honor and glory than any of his professional pupils.

Foremost amongst this band of enthusiasts was the Princess Marcelline Czartoryska, compatriot of the composer and a faithful friend, who was at his bedside when he died. Accord-

ing to Sawinski, she was able, by her phrasing and accentua-
tion, to recapture the master's playing in a most vivid manner.
Contemporary notices of the charity concerts at which she
occasionally played for the most part confirm this flattering
opinion. From every point of view she seems to have been
the most exceptional of Chopin's pupils, and the most faithful
interpreter of his style.

Since Chopin dedicated his Nocturnes and Waltzes to
them, the Princess de Chimay, the Countess Potocka, Mlle.
de Noailles, Mme. Petruzzi, the Countesses Kalergis, d'Est,
Branicka, Esterhazy, and the Baroness de Rothschild must be
mentioned. Though they have less claim to fame, they undoubtedly had talent.

Although restricted to a limited social circle, it is certain
that Chopin's reputation as a composer owed more to the
contagious enthusiasm of this band of elegant young women
than to the advertisement it received at the hands of professional virtuosi.

Except when played by Clara Schumann—and even then
only the shorter pieces that Chopin did not greatly care for—
and from time to time by Liszt and the master himself,
Chopin's music did not appear in the program of Paris
concerts with any frequency. It was among his friends, and because of the discernment shown by some of his aristocratic
women disciples, who consented to play his music in their
salons, that an authentic tradition of interpretation became
established. This intimate personal style moved Balzac to say,
"It could only be the song of a soul that was struggling to
achieve consciousness."

My generation knows of a number of pianists and professors
who have attempted or, in some instances, made a career based

on the false claim that they were one and all "Chopin's last pupil."

While admitting that some of them were privileged to have an audition, a privilege granted by Chopin on account of some recommendation or other, the matter generally ended there. The claims of these bogus heirs to a style and technique that were quite inimitable, and the advertising of his work for their own ends, have in the main proved disastrous.

The worst of it is, they set the ball rolling. Now a whole hierarchy of virtuosi, taking their cue from them, subscribe to the idea that it is impossible to begin to interpret Chopin unless all sorts of violence is done to his music. The views of these bogus heirs are quoted in support of the war they wage against the regal dignity of a music that refuses to capitulate in the face of exaggeration.

In such matters it is best to refer to the views of the master's own disciples, whose one desire it was to interpret him correctly, to get to the bottom of his intentions rather than to produce an imitation of his method. His style was one of complete spotaneity, the tender song of a nightingale dreaming at night and, like the nightingale, quite free from any preconceived formula or arbitrary musical conventions.

From what follows, it is made abundantly clear that he was exacting to the last degree in his regard for the technical details of execution. Once this rigorous physical discipline had been conceded, he desired above all things to arouse his more talented pupils to an imaginative approach: the delicacy of expression and touch which endowed his own performances with a quality unknown before his time, one which, adapted to the interpretation of the works he made them study, enriched them with a poetic quality. Convincing evidence can be brought in support of this view, which perhaps may be defined as "expressionist." It led him to advise Georges Mathias to imagine that "an angel was crossing the sky" at a certain point in Weber's Sonata in A flat. Listening to an interpretation that was at variance with his own feeling for the work, but one that was emotionally convincing, he said, "That isn't how I would play it, but perhaps your version is better." For him it was essential that his pupils should put "the whole of their souls" into their playing, and he made this significant remark, "Music that has no underlying meaning is false."

Only his most talented pupils were capable of absorbing his teaching, which was the expression of the artist in him rather than of the schoolmaster.

But if one tries to reconstruct the principles of his technical teachings from his scattered sayings, one finds them devoid of any particular originality and, except on certain points of de-tail, quite inadequate to support the view put forward by his contemporaries that they had "the secret of Chopin's piano playing."

In the first place, they concentrate on scales which produce that position of the fingers on the keyboard most likely to sup-
of this contention are those in B major and E major.
port their theories on the subject. The scales chosen in support
It is usual to begin one's efforts at playing the piano with the scale of C. Chopin thought, not without reason, that this scale is the most difficult of all. Its study, therefore, was left until the student was more advanced.

Mikuli, who has more to say on this subject than Chopin's other pupils, notes that in passing the thumb under the fingers the slight movement of the hand accompanying this action must not—paradoxically—affect the perfect evenness of tone demanded by all these exercises, and this applies equally to the fingers and the wrist. Frequent changes from legato to staccato are also recommended to develop a complete independence of touch.

Supple lateral movement of the fingers must be acquired if the student is to attain the perfect quality essential to the playing of the fast legato scales and arpeggios.

It is true that there is nothing very different in any of these suggestions from what is to be found in the normal methods of the period. Indeed, although it is not openly recommended, the shadow of the awful handguiding apparatus designed to act as an equalizer, then much in favor with certain professors of the pianoforte, lurks in the background—a specter ready to support any professorial hypotheses devoted to pedantry.

He allowed the possibility—and this aroused considerable indignation on the part of the purist, Kalkbrenner—of the player choosing either the thumb or the little finger when striking the black notes. This completely contradicted the sacrosanct tradition, observed by all pianists until that time.

It was a revolutionary suggestion, and one with which Liszt himself disagreed for some time. But, when based on the logical use of each finger in accordance with its striking power and not on a slavish regard for traditional dogma, it is fully justified.

A technical device already used by Clementi and Czerny as a form of muscular exercise, the crossing over of the fingers without using the thumb, was also developed by Chopin to the point of becoming a sensitive, melodious means of expression.

Considered from the point of view of interpretation aimed at the more effective production of tone, these two innovations are the only contributions of any consequence to be found in

Chopin's "system" that are likely to add to the development of piano playing.

For a precedent of equivalent technical value, one is tempted to compare them with Couperin's daring proposal for making use of the thumb in special circumstances—which until the eighteenth century had played practically no part at all—and to allow it to take its place with the other fingers of the hand, now that harpsichord technique was less a matter of arbitrary rules and regulations.

In Chopin's case, as with Couperin, it is not a question of technique or ease of fingering that is considered. It is aimed solely at developing equality of fingering. This is confirmed by Chopin's suggestions as to the amount of time that should be devoted to practice each day, which he fixed at a maximum of three hours. He made this rule in order to avoid the formation of any automatic or mechanical reflex likely to destroy the spontaneous flow of the music.

It is interesting to be able to compare Chopin's view, that practice should be adjusted to the demands of expressive interpretation, with that of Liszt. During the years which the latter devoted to the development of his virtuosity to the point of becoming a rival to Paganini, he formed the opinion that three hours, irrespective of any other time spent on musical matters, should be devoted to the development of technique.

It is not without interest to notice that the time spent in practice is the same for both of these geniuses of the piano.

No one would attempt to decide which is the better of these two methods. All the same, it is plain that the one sets out to be of service to music, while the other attacks the problem from the standpoint of the virtuoso.

Perhaps this is the place, while we are still considering

the views expressed by Chopin's pupils, to draw up a short list of those works he specially recommended for study.

In the first place, and in conjunction with the practice of scales and arpeggios, to which he attached the greatest importance, he advocated the study of Clementi's Preludes and Exercises. These had formed the basis for his own early efforts toward mastering the piano, and in his eyes were an indispensable adjunct to elementary exercises. For him, Clementi's works were the royal road to perfection, and because of the exceptional virtues he attributes to them, the majority of his pupils were required to make a thorough study of them.

According to Mme. Zaleska, Klesszynski told her of the affection Chopin had for the first Etude of the second group. His pupils were required to practice this study in every possible way: fast, slow, loud, soft, staccato, legato, until their touch was perfectly even and delicate, light but not weak.

The course of study was seldom varied. Following the Preludes and Exercises came the Etudes of Cramer, next the *Gradus ad Parnassum* of Clementi, and finally what were then known as *Studies in Style* by Moscheles. On rare occasions, but still with the object of acquiring a melodic technique, he added either Field's Nocturnes or his own.

The place of honor in the repertoire of his more advanced pupils was given to the *Well-tempered Clavichord*. He could play some twenty of these Preludes and Fugues from memory, and would say, "It is impossble to forget them."

In a letter to his pupil, Frédérique Müller, it is quite clear that in selecting works for study he did not limit himself, as has sometimes been suggested, to his favorite composers, Bach and Mozart. On the contrary, although for him Mozart was the apotheosis of music, he does not recommend the study of his works. Instead, he insists that the pupil study Beethoven's

Sonatas up to and including the Appassionata Op. 57.

It is obvious that in selecting Hummel's Concerti and Field's Nocturnes for study, he had no fear of a possible comparison with these composers. He seems to have taken considerable pleasure in recommending their work. The list is completed by the addition of works by Handel, Scarlatti, Weber, Dussek, and Ries, and from his immediate contemporaries the names of Hiller, Liszt, and sometimes Thalberg appear.

But it is difficult to explain why he systematically ignored Schumann, and why he would tolerate only a few of Schu' bert's Marches and Polonaises, which he occasionally played as duets with his pupils.

It has been suggested that he only recommended the first of Mendelssohn's Songs without Words for study. I am able to contradict this. Mme. Camille Dubois told me that she studied the Concerto in G minor with Chopin, and that he coached her in this on the legendary Pleyel upright piano. This piano was placed at the side of the grand reserved for the pupil of the moment, and played a great part in the lesson. Indeed, Chopin used it whenever he wanted to illustrate a point, a thing he did frequently. These personal illustrations were often so num' erous that the pupil, for whose benefit it was done, was some' times able to play only a few bars during a lesson, which often exceeded the hour to which he was entitled.

Few of his pupils could boast that they had studied the Preludes and Etudes under his supervision. The interpretation of his own works caused him considerable pain, and led him to complain that people never played them correctly without him having to show them how.

Although this speaks well for his modesty, it leaves one somewhat skeptical as to the so-called tradition of "nonvari' ability" to which so many of his pupils have claimed the magic key. And perhaps one should mention that while he displayed an exemplary courtesy, and, as one of them has said, "treated them with patience, perserverance, and enthusiasm," so far as his feminine followers were concerned, his lessons could often become stormy.

Mathias recalls that he saw him break a chair when an inattentive pupil bungled a passage. Hair would be torn out, pencils reduced to fragments and strewn over the floor as a result of bad playing or wrong notes. There was nothing for the wretched pupil to do but escape from the room. His exit would be followed by a thunderous decree forbidding him to show his face there again.

As George Sand has put it, "When roused Chopin was terrifying." These outbursts of fury were, of course, common symptoms of a lurking disease, the disease which had for many years past been undermining the musician's frail constitution. There is no need to offer excuses for him, since they were entirely independent of the victim's will. In fact they were a typical example of the wholly uncontrollable reaction of the personality to some slight physical cause.

One can only pity the unfortunate victim of these violent attacks. No doubt they had their origin in Chopin's urgent endless material cares of his daily existence. Confirming this, Frédérique Müller quotes his pitiful remark, "I am furious, I have no time to be ill."

Before finishing this brief discussion of Chopin's activities as a professor of music, mention must be made of his intention of producing a new treatise on music. If George Sand is to be believed, this was not only to cover the art of piano playing, but also the theory of music. It is a vast subject. He conceived the idea as the result of a chance discussion with Eugène Delacroix on the problems of aesthetics. He discussed his intention with several of his more intimate friends. In the work he dedicated to his glorious rival, Liszt mentions it as follows, "He had conceived the idea of writing a treatise on music. In this he was going to gather together his ideas on the theory and practice of his art together with his knowledge derived from his experience and the fruits of his long study. Even for so determined a worker as Chopin, a task of this magnitude demanded redoubled efforts. Perhaps he felt the need to escape from the emotional strain of his art, to see it in the different light of serenity and solitude. What he sought was an absorbing and equable task, of which he asked what Manfred had demanded in vain of the forces of Magic. oblivion . . . oblivion.

"But Chopin's strength was not equal to his aspirations," Liszt continues, "the work was too abstract, too absorbing. He formed an outline of his subject matter, but, though he mentioned it on several occasions, he could never complete it; only a few pages were sketched in and they were burned with the rest."

Liszt's last words refer to an earlier passage in his book, in which he says that before his death, Chopin had expressed the wish that his uncompleted manuscript should be burned, "showing a care and respect for his posthumous fame."

A whole generation of pianists and students of music needs no more than the words of the most famous of Chopin's biographers to regret that a work of such significance and importance was never completed.

It is a sad reflection that, owing to the faithful execution of the master's last wishes, we have been robbed of evidence which would have thrown so much light on Chopin's theories concerning the practice of his art. Proceeding entirely by guesswork, some people, as if to express their regrets, have dared to attempt a reconstruction of the basic principles that formed the foundation of this work.

In about 1883, Mme. Natalie Janotha, a Polish pupil of Clara Schumann, published as an appendix to the English and German translations of some discussions with Jean Kleczynski called "Great Works of Chopin," "Notice pour la Méthode des Mèthodes" from a manuscript of Chopin.

As a matter of fact, people are likely to be misled by this document. Instead of the great work which we know Chopin to have had in mind, the importance of which is amply confirmed both by George Sand and Liszt, we find nothing more than some oddly disconnected phrases about the elementary teaching of music, strung together in the most haphazard fashion. One feels a trifle skeptical.

The manuscript bears no sign of any personal touch and is of such surprising vacuity that one can only regret that it escaped the bonfire that consumed the master's unfinished works.

All this has been foisted on him by the fertile imagination of Mme. Janotha. Quite by chance I am able to prove that Chopin was not responsible for this "Notice," at least not in the form in which it was presented to the public.

During 1936, in London, where Mme. Janotha spent her declining years, I was able to acquire this Chopin manuscript, the text of which Mme. Janotha said she had published.

It consists of nothing more than a dozen sheets varying in size and quality, from cheap note paper to music paper ruled *a l'italienne,* that Chopin always used, written in very bad French. The pages are not numbered, and there is no logical sequence of ideas. It is little more than a puzzle made up of the most commonplace clichés on the teaching of the elements of music.

Why such an elementary work should contain so many crossings-out, alterations, and words written one on top of the other to the point of illegibility is hard to understand. So far as one is able to judge from these notes carelessly strung to-gether, Chopin's intentions fall far short of the high ambitions Liszt attributed to him.

It seems clear, after reading these elementary instructions, that, far from being the declaration of artistic faith Mme. Janotha would have us believe, they are no more than the hint of a proposal to make money by the publication of an elemen-ary piano tutor. A publication such as his contemporaries, Moscheles, Herz, and Kalkbrenner, had already produced to their considerable profit, without in any way damaging their reputations as virtuosi—indeed rather the contrary.

If the reader will forgive the pun, it was not a "collection of notes" about his art that he was considering, but a very different sort of "note"—a "collection of thousand franc notes," and it was with this in mind that he jotted down his rough ideas.

One cannot accuse Mme. Janotha of deliberate fraud, since her paraphrase is based on a perfectly authentic text, but can only express surprise that she should have gone so far as to publish it as one of Chopin's works after having given it some semblance of order, an order not to be found in the original and one that is likely to mislead the reader.

Again, she should never have given these loosely formulated scraps of theory a title implying a definite theme.

The two sheets I have chosen contain the more unusual suggestions about the use of the thumb and little finger on the black keys, which I have discussed earlier in this book. The reader will find an exact translation, with the pages in the order in which I found them, in the next section.

Following the usual practice in dealing with manuscripts of this kind, I have given the kind and format of the different papers used in the holograph.

I do not recommend a study of this document to those of Chopin's admirers for whom music is a language of the spirit and not a cold theoretical science. It will certainly not bring them into closer contact with the genius who produced those "joys so full of sorrow" that Heine speaks of.

However, those whose curiosity still remains undamped by my preliminary warning will at least find one attempt to define the expressive power of sound that is worthy of preservation.

On the eleventh sheet of this text, so strangely remote from Chopin's music, with its strange emotional force, groping with an almost naïve simplicity after the deeper meaning of an art that is always probing into the hidden depths of the human mind, Chopin writes: "The unfettered language of man (that is to say the language by which he gives expression to his innermost soul) is sound."

With this saying we can see Chopin's ideas on teaching, especially those dealing with the limitations of instrumental technique, in a clearer light than that given to them by those who have attempted to identify "his system." For one can deduce from it that, for Chopin, playing an instrument well was not an end in itself, but rather a means to an end, a means to be kept as flexible and sensitive as possible to permit of the transmission of those qualities in which music plays the part of a mysterious messenger.

Full Transcription of Chopin's Manuscript
SHEET 1.—*Seven stave, Italian style, music paper.*
FRONT.—Second stave, scale of B major with

fingering for the right hand, two octaves from

to ; thumb positions indicated by figures below

the notes; 1, 2, 3—1, 2, 3, 4, etc.

Note (half in Polish, half in French): The elbow on a level with the white keys; the hand neither too far in nor too far out.

BACK.—Written in pencil: scale of E minor minus the leading note.

SHEET 2.—*Plain note paper, written on the front only, heavily corrected.*

TEXT.—The notes and their corresponding keys on the piano. Every sound is, in relation to another sound, low or high, flat or sharp. Therefore, in writing down sounds, it is natural to make use of steps, similar to those on a ladder, placed one above the

other on stave like this. Let us form an

imaginary picture of a ladder with sufficient steps to give every sound, from the lowest to the highest. It would obviously be impossible to read music written on so many lines, since the eye would be incapable of taking it in.

The sounds that all voices sing, that all instruments make in imitation of the voice, are marked in the middle of this vast ladder. Consequently, in a range of sound, neither too high nor too low, the note do, ut, or C, as the Italians or Germans call it, occurs. A note which it is agreed shall not be sung low or high or . . .

SHEET 3.—*Plain note paper written on both sides.*

TEXT: FRONT.—The notes and their keys on the piano.

Their sound, relatively speaking, is high or low, flat or sharp. To represent the sounds, use is made, therefore, of lines superimposed one on another.

To make reading possible, the sounds that all voices sing and all the chief instruments play are written on the rungs. In a range of sound, neither high nor low, a note occurs which we have agreed to call do or ut.

With this note as our starting point we shall find high notes as we go up and low notes as we go down.

BACK.—Omitting the other rungs for the convenience of the eye we divide the range of sound into treble and bass. In writing those in the treble part we shall find that the voice seldom calls for a note to be written higher than the first rung or lower than the fifth rung. Thus it will be of great assistance to the eye to omit the lines beyond the fifth in the treble or those that go below the fifth in the bass, except to add them when required.

SHEET 4.—*Plain notepaper written on one side only.*

TEXT.—To learn the notes and the piano keys. This sound, relatively, is high or low, flat or sharp.

To denote the different sounds we, therefore, make use of a certain number of lines superimposed one on another.

Since the distance between the lowest and the highest sounds that the ear can detect would be too great for the ladder, on which we propose to write this series of sounds, and since very high or very low, notes are seldom used, the note that any man, woman, or child can sing that all string and wind instruments can play, is placed in the middle of a ladder, like the middle of . . .

SHEET 5.—*Plain note paper, written on half the front page. Pencilled initials F.M.*

TEXT.—Its pitch being the business of the tuner, the piano is free from the chief difficulties we meet with in the study of an instrument. Therefore we have only to study a certain arrangement of the hand in relation to the keyboard in order to obtain the best quaility of touch, to be able to play long and short notes, and to acquire infinite dexterity.

SHEET 6.—*A double sheet of plain note paper, written on both sides. The writing running crosswise over the width of the page, marked II in pencil.*

TEXT.—No admiration can be too great for the genius who was responsible for so cleverly adapting the construction of the keyboard to the shape of the hand. The black notes, intended for the long fingers, make admirable points of purchase. Could anything be more ingenious?

Thoughtless people, knowing nothing of piano playing, have frequently suggested leveling the keyboard. This would do away with all the ease of movement and the support which the black keys give to the hand: it would, as a result, make the passage of the thumb extremely difficult in those keys involving sharps and flats. If the keyboard were leveled, it would be necessary to remove a joint from each of the long fingers in order to play a staccato passage. Legato thirds and sixths, indeed all legato passages, would be enormously difficult, and, since the tone is set by the tuner, the mechanical difficulty presented by a piano with a keyboard which assists the hand is less difficult than one would suppose. Of course, no question of musical feeling or style arises, it is purely a matter of technique— which I refer to as the mechanics of piano playing. I divide the mechanical aspect of piano playing into three parts:

1. The training of both hands to play chromatic and diatonic scales, that is to say to play notes a half tone and a tone's distance from one another.

2. Notes at a distance of more than a half tone or tone from one another, that is to say from an interval of a minor third onward.

The octave divided into minor thirds so that each finger rests on one key.

3. Double notes, in two-part harmony—thirds, sixths, and octaves. When we know thirds, sixths, and octaves we can play in three-part harmony, and, knowing the distance between the notes, be able to play arpeggios.

Having played the same chords with the left hand, there is nothing further to study so far as the mechanics of the piano is concerned.

Sheet 7.—*A large double sheet.*

Text.—To those who are studying the art of touch, I submit some very simple practical considerations which, in my experience, have proved to be of real value.

Many futile methods have been tried to teach pupils to play the piano, methods which have no bearing on the study of the instrument. They are analogous to teaching someone to walk on his hands in order that he may go for a stroll.

As a result of this, people have forgotten how to walk properly and know very little about walking on their hands either. They are unable to play music in the real sense, and the difficulties they practice have nothing to do with the works of the great masters. These difficulties are theoretical— a new kind of acrobatics. I am not dealing with ingenious theories, however valuable these may be, but go straight to the root of the matter.

Sheet 8.—*Two large sheets of glossy paper,*

touched up in pencil, only the front of the first page being used.

TEXT.—Having some idea of notation, key signatures, and the mechanism of the piano, the next step is to sit down in front of the keyboard, so as to be able to reach either end, without leaning sideways. Placing our right foot on the pedal, without bringing the dampers into play, we find the position of the hand by placing our fingers on the notes E, F sharp, G sharp, A sharp, B.

The long fingers will be found to be on the black keys with the short fingers on the white. In order to obtain equality of leverage, the fingers on the black keys must be kept in line. The same applies to the fingers on the white keys. The resultant move will be found to follow the natural formation of the hand.

The hand should remain supple and the wrist and forearm round themselves into a curve making for ease of movement that would be unobtainable if the fingers were outstretched. The pianist has nothing to do with the tuning of the instrument, this is the province of the tuner. It is useless to begin to learn scales with that in C major. While it is the easiest to read, it is the most difficult for the hands, since it contains no purchase points. We shall begin with one that places the long fingers comfortably over the black keys—B major for example. (Two blank sheets follow, continuing on the back of the fourth.)

TEXT.—Dear child—you have had excellent music lessons. You have been taught to love Mozart, Haydn, and B. (Beethoven or Bach?). You can read the great masters at sight with ease. You have a feeling for them and understand them to the full.

All that you need is a fluent technique in order

to express in your playing that feeling for the great masters, whom you have grown to love.

SHEET 9.—*Four pages of music paper, Italian style, the front of the first page.*

TEXT.—Music progresses by sounds. As soon as there are two sounds, one is higher than the other. Therefore we naturally use lines placed one above the other in order to denote these sounds. We can imagine sounds rising and falling to infinity. In this infinity of sound there is one region where the vibrations are more perceptible to us than at any other.

Let us take one of these sounds, one that can be sung with ease by man, woman, or child and call it ut, do, or C. This note is found almost in the middle of the keyboard, a white note next to a group of two black keys. To the right of this note sounds going higher and higher will be found, and to the left of it sounds going lower and lower. To write these sounds we simply use the lines above the point named ut or do for the notes ascending and the lines below it for the notes descending.

SHEET 10.—*Four pages of music paper, Italian style, the front of the first page.*

TEXT.—Provided that it is played in time, no one will notice inequality of sound in a rapid scale. Flying in the face of nature it has become customary to attempt to acquire equality of strength in the fingers. It is more desirable that the student acquire the ability to produce finely graded qualities of sound, or so it seems to me. The ability to be able to play everything at a level tone is not our object.

Since each finger is formed differently it is far better to develop their special characteristics rather than attempt to destroy their individuality. The strength of each finger is relative to its shape. The extremities of the hand are formed by the thumb, which is its strongest member, and by the little finger. While the third finger has a greater freedom as a point of support, the second finger . . . , the fourth finger is bound to the third by the same tendon like a Siamese twin and is the weakest. One can try with all one's might to separate them, but this is impossible and, thank heavens, useless. There are as many different sounds as there are fingers. Everything hangs on knowing how to finger correctly. Hummel is the most knowledgable person on this subject. It is important to make use of the shape of the fingers and no less so to employ the rest of the hand, wrist, forearm, and arm. To attempt to play entirely from the wrist, as Kalkbrenner advocates, is incorrect.

SHEET 11.—*Single page of music paper, Italian style, only the front written on.*

TEXT.—The expression of thought by means of sound.

The indefinite (imprecise?) speech of man is sound.

The manifestation of our feelings by means of sound.

The indefinite language of music.

Art that manifests itself in sound is called music.

The art of expressing thought by sound.

The art of controlling sounds.

Thought expressed by sounds.

The interpretation of our perceptions by sound.

1. An abstract sound does not make music just as a word does not make speech.

2. To produce music several voices are necessary.

3. As soon as there are two sounds one is higher and the other lower.

4. To write music it is logical to make use of lines graded in accordance with their height.

5. The relationship between two sounds indicates which is high and which is low. One can imagine sounds stretching up or down to infinity.

6. Within this vast range of sound we find a part in which the vibrations are most preceptible to us.

7. In the middle of this range of sound we find one that can be sung with ease by anybody, men, women, young or old, called ut, do, or C. This note is found in the middle of the piano keyboard, a white key next to two black ones.

8. Starting from this note on the keyboard, toward the right we shall find sounds rising higher and higher and toward the left sounds getting lower and lower.

9. To write down these sounds the lines above that on which we placed our ut will be used for the high notes and those below for the low notes.

SHEET 12.—*One page of music paper, Italian style, only the front page written on.*

TEXT.—The value of modern notes and rests, synoptic table of note value, rests and bars.

4

CHOPIN'S WORKS IN THE LIGHT
OF HIS CORRESPONDENCE

IF THE READER EXPECTS to find any opinions or statements which throw light on the composer's aesthetic outlook or on the interpretation of his work in the collection of Chopin's letters made by the industrious Opienski,* he will be disap-pointed.

In spite of their number (there are 337 in the collection) addressed to a small group of friends, relatives, and compatriots, not a single significant spark appears that can compare with the depth of feeling to be found in the music of the Polish master.

For the most part they are written in an intimate, half-joking style. Many are concerned with commercial details regarding his publications, details that are dealt with most meticulously.

Except as a means of identifying dates, which are of more concern to the musicologist than to the artist, the rare allus-ions to his music, scattered through this collection of letters, are, for the most part, hardly worth preserving.

A typical example of the evasive tone he adopts when re-ferring to his works, about which so many theses concerning

*These letters are translated from the Polish by Stéphane Danysz, not without some unfortunate mistakes, particularly as regards musical matters.

their ideal interpretation have been written, may be found in the comments he makes on his immortal *Sonata Funèbre.*

Writing to Fontana, from Nohant (August, 1839) he says: "I am in the middle of writing a Sonata in B flat minor in which the funeral march you know comes. There's an Al-legro, then a Scherzo in E flat minor and a short Finale, not very long—three pages of my writing, in which the left hand prattles (Stéphane Danysz uses the word "plays") away in unison with the right after the march." Nothing could be more laconic or further from his "torture of writ-ing," as he is pleased to describe the labor involved in the correction of his scores. We can only be astonished at the detachment shown in his letters: the excessive modesty; the overwhelming bashfulness; the inability to express in writ-ing the superhuman quality of his work; the flash of posses-ive genius. When we find him belittling the importance of this "poem of death," a work which after a century of con-stant repetition still preserves in accents of terror and dismay all the innermost feeling of human sorrow, it is difficult to know which of all the various interpretations is the true one.

Considering them in chronological order and ignoring ref-erences other than those to do with his work, we come across the following.

Writing to his most intimate friend and confidant of his childhood, Titus Woyciechowski, on December 27, 1828, he refers to the Krakow Rondo Op. 14 for piano and orchestra, the work which, together with one or other of the Concerti, was to occupy an important place in the programs he per-formed at Vienna or Warsaw and would, he hoped, make his name known as a composer:

"I have finished the scoring of the Krakow Rondo. The Introduction is original—even more than I am myself, got up in my glad-rags! But the Trio is not quite right yet."

Brief as it is, it is worth noticing that, in spite of the jocular comparison he makes, this boy of eighteen shows a respect for the idea of originality.

It is the first allusion to his efforts to free music from the tyranny of formalism and base it on the solid foundation of nationalism. Efforts by which so many of his melodies were to achieve immortality.

A few lines further on he mentions the Rondo for two pianos which he had just written, the work that was published posthumously as Op. 73. He records his impressions on hearing it for the first time. Discounting the almost excessive modesty with which he refers to his own work, it shows at once how essential it was for him that music should contain a "something" which a strict rendering of the score is powerless to give. He says: "My orphan child the Rondo for two *pantaléons** has found a godfather in the person of Fontana . . . he has put in more than a month studying it, but he has at last mastered it and that just recently . . . we have experienced the effect it *will be* capable of producing.

Will be because the *pantaléons* were not perfectly in tune with one another, the delicacy of feeling was not always present nor were all those other trifles which, as you know, tinge everything with their light and shade.

It was these same *trifles* that gave to Chopin's playing an inexpressible note of inspired improvisation. Those who heard it gave up all hope of ever hearing anyone else attain to it.

Is it not this same sensitivity that gives rise to the deeply

---

**Until his arrival in France he always called the rectangular pianos,* *shaped something like a flat, upright bureau, forerunners of the concert* *grand and then familiarly nicknamed "giraffes," by the name of their* *designer, Pantaléon.*

felt emotion so eloquently expressed in the Larghettos of the two Concerti?

In a letter to the same correspondent, dated October 3, 1829, the first of these (here called the Adagio of the Concerto in F minor) calls forth the following confidence: "For the past six months, for my sins, I have devoted myself to an Ideal without daring to mention it. The Adagio of my Concerto is dedicated to it. I dream of it ceaselessly. I tell my piano," he adds further on, "what I can confide to no one but yourself."*

To repeat a phrase I have already drawn attention to and one on which it is right to be insistent, it is impossible for Chopin to conceive of music "without an undertow of meaning." In spite of the extreme reserve with which he speaks of his works, this is confirmed for us by the slow movement of the Concerto in E minor—that inexpressibly beautiful Nocturne which seems detached from all material things, that commentary which grasps the inner mysteries of sound so closely.

Again, in a letter to Titus, written from Warsaw on May 15, 1830, we find this fragment, the only passage in the whole of his correspondence giving us the undisputed right to consider it as a true indication of interpretive values: "The Adagio of the new Concerto is in E major. I have not sought

---

This letter also mentions that the Waltz in D flat, published posthumously as Op. 70 No. 3, is due to the same inspiration. "Notice," writes Chopin, "the passage marked with a x. No one will know its meaning except yourself. How lovely it will be to play it to you. . . . In the trio the bass should dominate as far as the E flat in the fifth bar. But there is no need for me to tell you, you understand these things." "These things," which he modestly refers to as "trifles," contain all the most intimate yearnings of his inspiration.

for power in it—it is more of a Romance—calm and melancholy. It should give the impression of a gentle lingering
glance toward places that evoke a thousand charming memories. It is a reverie in fine spring weather—but lit by the
moon. It is for this reason that the accompaniment is muted."

Characteristically these last words suggest Chopin's feeling
for the half lights to which, in preference to all else, he un-
hesitatingly devoted his genius.

Doubtless mistrusting the extent of his friend's musical
knowledge, Chopin is at pains to explain the exact nature
of the process employed for this effect. "The violins," he tells
him, "are muted by means of a kind of comb, which, fitted
over the strings, gives them a nasal, silvery quality." Although
the Mazovian violinists must have often used it at their rustic
concerts, Chopin seems surprised at his own audacity in mark-
ing the bowing *col legno* in the Finale of the Concerto in F.
He writes, "Perhaps it is bad, but why be ashamed to write
without conforming to the rules? Results alone can show
whether one is right or wrong."

We find Beethoven saying almost the same thing: "Nothing
should be forbidden when its purpose is *schöner,*" meaning
when it seeks a greater poetical effect or a more eloquent expression.

One can only regret that, in the rest of his correspondence,
reticence or cautious reserve should have stayed Chopin's pen
from taking us into his confidence. Colorful suggestions of
this sort would have enabled many of his interpreters to leave
the problems of technique where they belong—in a place of
secondary importance—and allowed them to place their imagination rather than their fingers at the service of the inner
significance of his music.

This incursion into the realm of aesthetics should be sufficient for us to admit that, while abstaining from comment likely to give us any real insight into the hidden mysteries of his art, Chopin definitely implies its power to convey emotion.

We come very close to the latent expressionism reflected in his work, when we define it as the translation of an intimate dream, or secret asperation, and do not remain satisfied with the approach made to it by certain dull executants who are occupied solely with the pleasure it gives to the ear.

Hereafter, alas, we find only a few meager references to his other compositions: allusions buried in the six hundred pages of the volume to which we refer. But for the fact that persistent research has thrown some light on the part played by certain adjectives describing both the performance and publication of his works, it would seem idle to mention them.

Resuming our reading, and turning back to a few months before his mention of the Adagio in the E minor Concerto, we find this in another letter to Titus dated November 14, 1829: "While I was staying with him (Radziwill) I composed an *Alla Polacca* for cello. Just one of those brilliant little drawing-room pieces for the ladies. You see, I wanted Princess Wanda to be able to learn it." This refers to the *Introduction and Polonaise Brillante Op.* 3 for piano and cello, composed during a visit to Prince Radziwill at his princely seat at Antonin. Since he had every reason to be satisfied with the slightest thing he produced himself, it is surprising to find Chopin, a youth of nineteen, judging his work from a purely objective standpoint.

The Adagio, which serves as an introduction to this brilliant but superficial composition, was added in April, 1830. After trying it over with Kakzynski, Chopin, in a letter dated the 10th, declares himself satisfied with it and makes no further comment on the superficiality he attributed to the rest of the piece.

If one is to judge from the rest of this letter, taking care to preserve a sense of proportion, it seems as though this *pièce d'occasion,* which Chopin tries to excuse for its lack of musical significance, was inspired by just such another mood as gave rise to the Adagio of the F minor Concerto. Again speaking of the Princess Wanda, one of his host's daughters, he adds: "During the length of my stay I gave her lessons— so-called. She is young—seventeen—pretty and, by Jove, it is extremely pleasant to teach her how to place her fingers on the keys. But pleasantries apart (and the impressionable adol- escent was certainly capable of taking this "pleasantry" far more seriously than he admits) she really has a great deal of musical sense. So much so that there is no need to tell her, crescendo here, piano there, or play another bit faster or slower, etc." From this confidence alone we can see that, for Chopin, a piano lesson was more a lesson in interpretation than in technique and a preoccupation with the clock played very little part in it.

This same period saw the birth of the E minor Concerto. Apart from mentioning that, in a friend's opinion, the Al- legro is superior to that in the F minor Concerto, Chopin goes no further, in a letter dated May 18, than to hope that he will be *en veine* to complete the composition of the Rondo. To "avoid disorder" at the rehearsal that is to precede its public performance, he mentions, in August, trying over the work with the orchestra's string quartet, to ensure that the instrumentalists were familiar not only with the notes but also with his authoritative interpretation.

We also find him indulging in one of the rare expressions

of satisfaction he allowed himself. In this same letter to Titus of August 31, 1830, he says: *"Last Saturday I tried the Trio again. I don't know if it is because I had put it on one side for some time, but I was tolerably pleased with myself. Happy—not to say presumptuous man—you will not fail to tell me!"

Composed in 1828, this Trio Op. 8, for piano, violin, and cello is a work which in my opinion at any rate does not, unfortunately, seem to jusitfy his high opinion of it. He goes on: "However, it has occurred to me that since the violin, whose first string has the predominant overtones, is hardly used at all in my trio, it might be preferable to use the viola instead and thereby obtain a better balance with the cello." This intention was to remain unfulfilled, but bears witness to the doubts that assail him when any instrument other than the piano is used as a vehicle for his musical thought.

A few days later, in the middle of September, Chopin announces that the proposed run through of the Concerto with the quartet has taken place and that he was "fairly well satisfied with it but not particularly so." Mentioning the compliments he had received on the Finale, which some regarded as being "prettier" than that of the F minor Concerto, he thinks that this is due to the fact that it is more easily understood by the uninitiated. He reserves his personal opinion until it has been rehearsed with full orchestra, when it will be necessary for him, he says, "to judge the Concerto on its merits," for he mistrusts the opinion of the audience of connoisseurs and dilettantes invited to the performance.

Omitted, for no apparent reason, from Karazowski's version

*I have used Karowski's German version of this letter. Stéphane Danysz's knowledge of music is so slight that the meaning in this case becomes obscure.

of this letter of September 22nd, is the following significant passage:* "It is now a question of playing my second Concerto. I feel exactly as I did when I was ignorant of the very existence of such a thing as a piano. It calls for very careful playing and I am afraid of finishing up by making a mess of things."

These are fears which have, in truth, been experienced by all performers of this work. It presents, to a far greater extent than the F minor Concerto, an abundance of thorny problems in virtuosity that sometimes overlay the essential magnificence of the material employed.

Further on, Chopin returns to his expression of half satisfaction with the first orchestral rehearsal, and in so doing throws an interesting sidelight on the amateurishness with which concerts were presented in Warsaw at this time: "I must run and make sure of the music stands and the mutes, which I forgot all about yesterday; without them the Adagio will be a fiasco. In any case it won't be much of a success so far as I can tell." He has obviously taken heed of the opinions passed by those who heard the trial run through. However, by way of special pleading on his own behalf, he adds, "the Rondo is quite striking and the Allegro is strong," an appreciation he excuses himself of further on by saying: "Oh horrible vanity!"

Although he was unaware of it, the concert of October 11, was to be his farewell to his native land. His account of it tells of the success of the Concerto, which had been the subject of so much detailed preparation. "Deafening cheers," he announces to Titus and, what tells us a great deal about the mentality of the Warsaw public at that date, "not a single whistle." His success was still more marked after the

---

Stéphane Danysz's version is obviously faulty.

playing of the Fantasia on Polish airs, during the performance of which Chopin ingenuously declared that he understood himself and the orchestra as well, and that "the gallery recognized what it was all about."

The Fantasia was, in fact, a paraphrase of popular Polish airs, which made no demands on the average listener other than the slight effort involved in recognizing familiar tunes clothed in brilliant virtuosity, exaggerating their popular appeal.

This condescending criticism of an uncultured public was a meager reward for the young composer whose work already gave promise of miraculous genius.

As yet unaware of the value of his message, one cannot but feel that the time was ripe for the composer to seek surroundings where he would be better able to find understanding and appreciation. He was able to carry away an idealized memory of those years of adolescence during which the slightest glimmer of understanding seemed to him a reward far in excess of his deserts. Out of his sorrowful longings as an exile he created a Polish atmosphere, a Polish sky, which became stronger in proportion to the sufferings endured by his oppressed country. With an incomparable eloquence, the masterpieces that are Poland's glory were to burst forth in a flowering of his heart, from beneath his fingers.

We can only bless the sufferings Chopin endured as a result of his separation from his native land, since they were the means of freeing his musical soul for us, cutting it off from all the ties of period and style which his surroundings unavoidably imposed on it. In spite of his innate genius, he would certainly not have flourished to the same extent had he maintained contact with the tune-mad music fans of Poland.

Our attention must now be turned to the letters from Vienna. These contain a few scattered references to his works, and one written to his family on the Wednesday before Christmas, 1830, contains some sentences worth quoting. In it he speaks of a plan to write a duet for violin and piano in collaboration with Slavik, who is lauded as a genius: "Except for Paganini I have never heard the like; he takes ninety-six staccato notes with a single stroke of his bow, it is unbelievable." Chopin's respect for virtuosity as such, to which he never failed to respond, is well in evidence here. It seems that the idea for the duet had occured to him while he was in Warsaw. It was to have taken the form of Variations on a theme of Beethoven's. To use Chopin's own words, an Adagio for it seems to have been "wept on to his piano." For reasons that are not clear from the rest of this correspondence, the composition was abandoned. It was the same with the Concerto for two pianos which was to have been played by Chopin with a pianist named Nidecki.

This was not completed in its orginal form, but it is possible that the material was incorporated in the Allegro de Concert Op. 46, which appeared in 1842. At any rate it was in a sufficiently advanced stage of completion for Nicodé eventually to make a passable version for piano and orchestra.

Bearing in mind the significance he attached to his para-phrases of popular Polish airs, both as musician and patriot, it will not be out of place to give the following quotation which incidentally reveals his awareness of the stupid outlook which then possessed Warsaw's circle of musical dilettantes. Writing to his family he says: "I am not sending you my Mazurkas because I have to make a fair copy of them. Besides they are not written for dancing."*

Concerned with the effect that these fifty national master-

---

*He undoubtedly refers to the Mazurkas that Fontana published posthumously as Op. 68.

pieces would have on the spirit of a patriotic people, the Czar, then the master of this martyred country, thought of proscribing them. Schumann was later to describe them as "guns buried in flowers."

Writing to Matusynski in the same week, he alludes to the victorious struggles of Sobieski's troops against the Tartars beneath the walls of Vienna in 1683: "The tears that should have fallen on my piano have bedewed your letter. If I could I would call upon all the sounds which a blind, unbridled fury of emotion arouse in me to evoke the songs of the army of King John—songs, the scattered echoes of which still haunt the banks of the Danube." Here again he returns, almost in spite of himself, to those emotions which were to become prophetic echoes in his music.

Already the spirit of the impassioned revolutionary begins to show, which, when the fall of Warsaw was announced a few months later, was to be imprinted on the irrepressible outbursts of the two studies now known as the Revolutionary Etudes. In a celebrated passage in his diary, written in Stuttgart on September 8, 1831, Chopin, haunted by the threat over-hanging his family, gives free rein to his indignation with all the fire of his imagination, showing himself to us as being "overwhelmed with grief and crying out my despair on my piano."

Destined for immorality, these agonizing passions were confided to the piano through his fingers. An emotional patriotism, which was never to lose its throbbing eloquence. One would have expected a more personal reaction to these moments of ineffable tenderness rather than one deriving from his blood and country. The music of his country! He has already shown what that could mean to him in a passage in a letter to his family, written some months before the one I have just quoted. He pours scorn on the profanation to which it was subjected by hack musicians, for whom the public's passing fancy for any particular style was sufficient pretext for making profit at the expense of genuine inspiration. "Herz," he writes, "had to play some variations of his own on Polish airs! You have no idea what ingredients they were seasoned with and then, to draw the public, called Polish music."

For the remainder of the quotations, which finish the slender documentary basis for this essay, we turn to the letters written from Paris, Nohant, and London.

A reference to the Variations on *ci darem* is the first allusion Chopin makes in these to his works. During a visit to the Imperial Library of Vienna he had been childishly surprised and proud to find a copy "beautifully bound and inscribed with his name."

He takes the opportunity of mentioning this again in a long lettter to Titus, dated December 12, 1831, in the course of which he describes a ten-page critism by a certain German "whom they had aroused to enthusiasm."

One cannot help feeling slightly irritated when one finds that the "certain German" in question was none other than Robert Schumann, acclaiming his brother artist, on the threshold of immorality. His famous article: "Gentlemen, hats off to a genius . . ." had just appeared in the *Allgemeine Musik Zeitung* and was in fact the first sign that the *Davidsbündler* had shown in favor of his new musical style. The terms of the criticism, in exact agreement with the opinions expressed by the enthusiastic pen of Florestan, are gratuitously satirized by Chopin in the résumé he makes of it for his childhood friend.

After lengthy preliminaries, he—the 'he' is the 'certain German'—makes an analysis of the piece, phrase by phrase, explaining that these are not like other variations, but a sort of fantastically evocative picture. Speaking of the second variation, he says that in this Don Juan gathers Zerline in his arms, while the left hand describes Mazetto's anger, and finally in the fifth bar of the Adagio Zerline allows Don Juan to embrace her on a D flat!

"Plater asked me yesterday the precise spot in her anatomy where this D flat is to be found!"

This virtuoso paraphrase was intended to do no more than arouse the dilettantes of Warsaw to applause. And, if one is to judge from the sarcastic references the composer makes to the romantic figures with which Schumann had peopled it, it was the work of his unconscious genius. From this theme of Mozart's he had evoked, almost unknown to himself, vivid, sentimental improvisations in a decorative instrumental setting.

Chopin, perhaps from a retiring modesty, only attributes the value of sound to them. Schumann adds that of the imagination. I am well aware that here I am siding with the executant against the composer. The latter has everything to gain from such romantic outpourings, since any speculative appreciation must enhance his appeal. But it is only fair to say, conjecture having led me beyond the limitations modestly attributed to the work by its composer, that, although without any great initial significance, this composition holds its place in Chopin's work since it shows quite clearly the workings of his original mind.

In spite of Chopin's bantering attitude (and he was, no doubt, secretly flattered by such an expressive dithyramb) it is possible that the echoes of this appreciation aroused the attention of the publishers in Paris. For Chopin, at the end of the same letter, remarks that Schlesinger had asked him to write some variations on *Robert le Diable,* the first performance of which had just taken place and been a "prodigious success."

This project was not immediately pursued and was only destined to see the light of day in 1833, as a grand Concert Duet for cello and piano, written in collaboration with Franchomme. A second invitation of the same nature followed shortly afterward and resulted during 1833 in the publication of the Variations on the air *Je vends des scapulaires,* taken from Harold's unfinished posthumous opera, *Ludovic.* It is a composition of secondary importance and was subsequently discarded. The composer shows himself to be wholly subservient to the demands of the kind of virtuoso who suited the taste and style current in Warsaw at that date.

In his letter of Christmas, 1831, to his faithful confidant Titus, he finds a further occasion for returning to the misdeeds and lack of understanding shown by certain musicians when dealing with the music of his native land. He fiercely criticizes the musical behavior of his demoniac compatriot, Sowinski, who, when paying him an occasional visit in his two-room apartment in the Boulevard Poissonière, sits down at his piano "and pounds the keyboard in a most disorderly fashion," or "he makes my ears burn" with picking out the motif of one of his Mazurkas, "the whole value of which," Chopin adds, "is, as often as not, to be found in the accompaniment." Again, "he sets about playing it with the taste of a village organist or that of a musician of the lowest kind of booth or eating house. And this when, as you know (and here he calls his friend as witness to a sincerity which one cannot fail to appreciate), I was so very anxious to explore and interpret the deepest emotions of our national music."

Except in a long letter to his family, written about Easter 1847, this feeling, amounting to an uncompromising devotion, is never mentioned again. Here a chance phrase informs us that, tired and melancholy, he stayed at home, dinnerless, to play and hum the folk-songs of the Vistula. He has no further need to put it into words. From the moment he left Poland, all his work bears witness to it with an incomparable eloquence. And to this a touch of sadness, occassioned by the melancholy outcome of a platonic love affair, was to be added, the echo of a soul wounded past healing. During the same year, 1834, in sending a copy of his recently published Waltz Op. 18 by her brother, Felix Wodzinski, to his esteemed colleague, Mlle. Marie," he tells her how happy he was to receive her composition and the recent news of her from Dresden; how, that same evening, he had improvised on her gracious theme, the theme of her with whom he had played "catch" at the Pszennys' house, in one of the salons he frequented.

This improvision was the genesis of the flying Etude in F minor, now Op. 25 No. 2.

Although the manuscript, which remained unpublished until Chopin's death, had been sent to her and antedated "September, 1835," the time when he had made the improvisation, there is naturally no mention in the rest of the correspondence of the *Valse des Adieux,* the waltz which with such signs of tenderness was to serve as a musical epilogue to this unfulfilled but beautiful dream.

There is not much to be gathered from the letters from Majorca and Chartreuse de Valdemosa concerning the compositions which were either on the stocks or completed during his stay of four months which, in spite of his distressing physical and moral condition, was undoubtedly one of Chopin's most productive periods, and one which saw the birth of some of his authentic masterpieces. It was there, in fact, that he finished the Preludes, of which only half had been roughly sketched out since 1837. The final version of the *Sonata Funèbre* was written there, and in a letter dated

January 12, 1839, he was able to announce to Fontana that he would soon be sending him the second Ballade, the two Polonaises Op. 40 (those commonly known as the "triumphal" and the "dramatic") and the third Scherzo—to which should also be added the two Nocturnes Op. 37.

His correspondence is confined to a series of instructions concerning the publication of his works and the conditions he requires from the publishers. For the first time, questions of money interfere in Chopins' preoccupation with his music, and, until his return from Marseilles at the end of May, it is matters such as these and his contacts with "these music dealers" that give rise to the only mention of his compositions.

It is to *Histoire de ma Vie* and to *Hiver á Majorpue*, from the pen of George Sand, that we must turn to catch a glimpse of the conditions under which the frail musician worked; books obviously dramatized by her fertile imagination, though having a basis in fact. "The little one," as she calls him— with his naturally exaggerated sensibility—was the victim of his disease, of uncomfortable surroundings, of the sullen hostility of the native inhabitants, all of them things well suited, by their thousandfold daily aggravations, to overwhelm him. These books are too well known to Chopin's admirers, and one might almost say are too much a part of the legendary accounts of this period in his life for one to wish to make use of them in pages devoted solely to musical matters.

A few brief sentences, scattered through his letters to Fontana, are all that we can learn of his reactions to a country, the initial enchantment of which was not long in giving place to a feeling of discouragement and isolation.

"The sun shines all day long . . . I feel better" (November 15, 1838). "My piano has not arrived yet. I dream music but do not write any" (November 21). "I still have no piano . . ."

(December 2), to which in a letter to Grysmala, written the same day, George Sand adds: "The lack of a piano makes me feel very sorry for the little one. He has hired a local one, which annoys him rather than calms him." Let us remember that this still refers to their stay at *Son Vent*, that little laborer's cottage, lost amid the olive groves, that had been their shelter since their arrival from Barcelona, far from any center and devoid of all creature comforts.

It is only the battles with his publishers over royalties, contained in his letters from Valdemosa, which gives us the names of the works in course of composition. But the surround-ings in which they were born give us a better clue to the spiritual atmosphere which inspired them than any allusions to their musical character.

There is the famous letter to Fontana describing the move to la Chartreuse de Valdemosa: "My cell is the shape of a huge coffin; there is an enormous arch covered in dust; a little bay window looking out over orange trees, palms and cypresses . . . there is silence . . . one can cry out . . . and there is still silence. In a word, I am telling you about a most extraordinary place." These last words are characteristic, coming from the superstitious Chopin .What he omits to say, however, is that the cell which served as his room was so resonant that the vibrations of his piano were amplified to such a jangle of sound that the chromatic sequences in some of the Preludes, among other pieces, could certainly not have been conceived there.

From personal experience on this point, it is possible for me to suggest that only the slow-moving Preludes could have been composed there. No suggestions as to interpretation occur in the subsequent references he makes to his works, which are concerned solely with conditions regarding the sale of publication rights. No doubt, his peculiar frame of mind was in some way connected with George Sand's efforts to extract those indispensable royalties, with which to deal with their day-to-day expenses, from Buloz.

Toward the end of their stay in Marseilles, a prelude to the travelers' reinstatement in the house at Nohant, which they had idealized until, in their eyes, it appeared as a veritable haven of bliss, just one passage, contained in a letter to Fontana, written on April 25, 1839, seems worth recording, It refers to a performance of the G flat major Etude, Op. 10, given at a performance in Paris by Clara Wieck. "How could she have chosen the most uninteresting of all the Etudes, at least for those who do not know that it is written for the black keys alone, in place of something more important?"

Only at rare intervals in his correspondence, from now on, are we to find a word or two about the work he has in progress. I have already mentioned the extraordinarily laconic way in which he speaks, in a letter dated August, 1839, of the Sonata in B flat minor. In this same letter he refers to the Nocturne in G major, Op. 37, No 2, which was published under the same opus number, as an addition to the Nocturne in G minor which, consequently, since he askes Fontana if he remembers it, must have been written before his departure for Palma. He also announces the birth of four new Mazurkas: "One in C minor, written at Palma, and three composed here (at Nohant) in B major, A flat major, and C sharp minor.*

"They are very welcome, as is always the case with the

In spite of differences of key, no doubt errors on the part of Stéphane Danysz, the compositions mentioned here must be the four Mazurkas Op. 41, published in 1840, which Chopin played at a concert in Paris on April 26, 1842.

youngest children of parents who are getting on in years, or so it seems to me."

In conclusion, he asks Fontana to return the manuscript of the second Ballade, as he wishes to make some revisions. He refers, no doubt, to the Coda, which Schumann, to whom it was dedicated, asserts was ended originally by a resolution in F major; a somewhat surprising opinion in view of the basic key of the composition. Writing from Nohant on October 10, he tells Fontana that, in order to alter the second part of the Polonaise in A major, Op. 40, which he had dedicated to him, "he dried up his brain for at least eighty seconds." But in spite of this great effort, he fears that the new version will not be to his liking. In speaking of the second Impromptu, he declares himself unable to guarantee its quality. He thinks that its birth is too recent to justify his attempting a true assessment of its value.

The rough draft of a letter to Mme. Oury-Belleville (1840) mentions a little waltz that he has had the pleasure of writing for her alone, and tells her that he does not want her to let it become public property. It is an Album piece such as he was in the habit of writing or having copied by Fontana or Franchomme for his feminine admirers.

The "little waltz" in question is that in F minor, published for no particular reason under the Opus No. 70, No. 2. All trace of it would have been lost if a posthumous edition had not brought it to light, to the great satisfaction of pianists of moderate ability.

In an undated letter (probably written from Nohant in the middle of 1841) to Fontana, the tireless intermediary whom Chopin badgered persistently on all questions of a practical nature, although the affectionate tone of his letters sets this off to a great extent, a curious technical question comes to light. No opinion is passed regarding its character—the piece in question was the Tarantelle—but the passage is worth quoting almost in its entirety:

"I am sending you a Tarantelle. Please be so kind as to recopy it, but first of all go and see Schlesinger or Troupenas, look up the collection of songs by Rossini and find the Tarantelle (in A). I can't remember whether it is written in 6/8 or 12/8. One can write it either way, but I would sooner it was written like Rossini's. If it is in 12/8 or, as is possible, in triplets, make one bar out of two when you are making the fair copy. That will give . . ." and here Chopin inserts in his letter, by way of example, the first two bars hypothetic' ally reduced to one.

This lack of decision is astonishing in a musician such as Chopin. The division of the rhythm of a Tarantelle into four is an absurdity almost impossible to understand. And he goes on: "If the bar shown in my manuscript is incorrect, don't use it but recopy it in the way I tell you."

Maintaining his usual attitude of contemptuous indifference toward everything coming from his pen, he adds further on: "Recopying all these stupidities will be a bore for you, but I really hope I shan't write anything as bad for a long time."

He returns again to this dissatisfaction with himself some weeks later, when he tells Fontana that the weather at Châtre has been beautiful for the last few days, but that his "music is bad." But this "bad music," this inspiration of his restless genius, came to life in the immortal accents of the Fantaisie, of the third Ballade, of the Polonaise in F sharp minor, of the sublime Nocturne in C minor, and of the Polonaise-Fantaisie, the themes of which took shape unconsciously in Chopin's mind during this same summer of 1841.

On September 15 he writes, instructing Fontana to send

a large *pâté* to Nohant, adding: "Toward the end of the month I will send you my own *pâtés,* confections of my own smoky kitchen. It will be necessary to whitewash the kitchen, but the whitewash has disappeared into the country. For any other cook a white kitchen would be essential, but for me it can remain smoky."

Reading between the lines of these cryptic phrases, we can see that he is referring to his own works. Conceived during the early stages of his personal clash with George Sand, they were elaborated in an atmosphere already hostile, which made their price a heavy one. This clash was the prelude to a part-ing, and one cannot help asking oneself if it was not the best thing that could have happened to him.

However, two weeks later when telling Fontana of the birth of the C sharp minor Prelude, which was to find a place in the Album published in Vienna by Mechetti in honor of Beethoven, he allows himself a self-congratulatory "satis-fecit." "Yesterday, Thursday, I stopped here (at Nohant). I have written a Prelude in C sharp minor. . . . It is well modulated and I can send it without fear." In truth, the atmosphere of dreamy homesickness permeating this page, fading into the subtle chromatics of a dying cadence, shows us, with a magic more telling than any modulation, that the confidence with which Chopin so modestly made his claims for the technical value of this work, was well placed.

The same period brings a letter to the ever faithful Fontana, giving him a detailed list of the works he has ready for the publishers and their suggested selling prices (500 francs for the Fantaisie, 300 francs for the two Nocturnes Op. 48, the same for the Ballade in A flat, and the Polonaise in F sharp minor). He also asks him to take the greatest care of the manuscripts he is sending for recopying, since they represent so many "torture writings" for him. This phrase, deriving, as I have already pointed out, from a play on the similarity of two Polish words, has become legendary and, nonetheless, states a profound truth. A cursory glance at the first draft of a Chopin manuscript, covered with innumerable erasures and alterations, is sufficient to show the emotional suffering inherent in his work.

A little while later, on October 10, a discussion as to the price to be paid for the Tarantelle causes him to protest vehemently at the "stupid titles" with which Wessel, his London publisher, "that idiot, that swindler," tricks out his compositions. His indignation was more than justified since, for example, the three Nocturnes, Op. 9, were announced under the title, *Les Murmures de la Seine;* Op. 19, had the title *Les Zephirs,* the first Scherzo was put out as *Banquet Infernal,* and the Nocturnes of Op. 37 became, in the ridiculous jargon of the British tradesman, *Les Plaintives and Les Soupirs.*

Allusions to his works from here on become more and more scarce. Apart from his family, the tone of his correspondence to Franchomme, who had succeeded Fontana in the role of friendly secretary and honorary copyist, does not suggest any particular intimacy.

The fact is that, after 1846, following the publication of the *Polonaise-Fantaisie* and the *Barcarolle,* Chopin wrote only the two Nocturnes, Op. 62, the three Mazurkas, Op. 63, and the three Waltzes, Op. 64. For the rest, silence.

He had been telling his family of his disinclination for work since 1845. Writing from Nohant on July 18: "I am not made for life in the country, but the fresh air does me good. I don't play much, because the piano is out of tune, and I write even less." This is a phrase which recurs constantly in his letters. On October 11, 1846, he writes: "I play a little, I write a little. Sometimes I am satisfied with my Sonata for cello and piano and sometimes dissatisfied. I throw it in a corner and then I pick it up again. I have three new Mazurkas (those of Op. 63) and I don't know whether they have the old (a word follows which is unreadable—"faults" or "qualities"?) but it needs time to form a judgment. When one is actually writing, one supposes that what one is writing is good or one would not write at all. It is only afterward, and on reflection, that one can decide what to preserve and what to discard. Time is always the best critic and patience the best master."

Already, a year earlier (in a letter to his family written October 1, 1845) he had shown a similar attitude toward the publication of his Sonata, Op. 4. "I am told that the Sonata dedicated to Elsner has been published by Haslinger in Vienna. As a matter of fact he did send me a printed proof some years ago in Paris. But as I did not correct and return it to him and told him besides that I would like to make a number of alterations in it he perhaps held up the printing. I was very glad as it is too late for this sort of thing now. There was some excuse for publishing it fourteen years ago."

This was a youthful work, written in Warsaw in 1828. Showing a "Hummelliene" influence in style, it was, in fact, no more than a student exercise, relieved in parts by a personal originality, already curiously significant.

His using time as arbiter is all the more justified, since in the same letter he announces the completion of the Sonata in B minor, Op. 58. One can well understand that in comparing the imaginative transports which fire this magnificent poem for the piano with his earlier work, he was forced

to show a certain severity toward a childhood relic, bearing, as it does, so little relation to the musical outlook which
constant self-criticism had finally freed from the formalism
of bygone years.

Yet the completed work of the moment, stamped with his
genius though it was, failed to satisfy him, for he adds: "I
don't know what is happening to me, but I can't write anything good. And yet it isn't idleness, I don't wander from
one place too another like you do (his sister had just been
staying with him at Nohant); I stay whole days and nights
in my room. I must, however, finish certain manuscripts,
as I cannot work in winter." A phrase to be remembered,
because, though one may take into consideration the beginning of his teaching and other mundane affairs which
the material necessities of existence forced on him, to
justify the interruption of his creative work during the winter
season, one cannot prevent oneself, on the other hand, from
giving this statement a meaning less strictly confined to its
literal sense.

Everything in Chopin points to the existence of a secret
link between the radiance of nature and the internal blos-
soming of his musical ideas; the unconscious reaction of the
creative mind to the seasons, coinciding wth the period of
the year when his cough eased and his fits of suffocation
became less frequent. We can see how, with a symbolism
completely in tune with Chopin's genius, his inspiration adjusted itself to the rebirth of the year, the harvesting of the
earth's abundance, to the time when the flowers open and
nightingales sob out their songs into the night. One pays
even closer attention to that natural instinct which bound
the frail musician to physical phenomena which seem to
bear no relation to his art, but which he suffered to enter into

him in the way that a still pool holds the heat of the sun's rays. "A reflection of reflections"—his conversation with Delacroix comes to mind.

In the last letter he was to write from Nohant, to which he was destined never to return, he refers yet again to the state of his work at the moment. Either he was too critical of himself or sadly disillusioned, for he says to Franchomme: "I work a little. I scratch out much." He is to come back to this problem of musical sterility on July 8, 1846. It indicates the gradual failing of his health. He writes: "My friend, I do everything I can to work, but nothing happens," adding in an attempt to make a joke of it: "If it goes on, my new compositions will remind you more of the noise of breaking crockery than of warblers' twitterings!"

A few passing remarks concerning the Sonata for cello and piano, which he decided to publish in June, 1847, after playing it at the Countess Potocka's house with Franchomme, are all that one finds in his letters that follow. From Franchomme we learn that he submitted an orchestral version of the *Sonata Funèbere* to Chopin, who gave it a chilly reception. He also showed Chopin an arrangement for voice and piano of an O *Salutaris* to the music of a Nocturne.

"That sings well," Chopin conceded, but he certainly could not have foreseen the result of authorizing the use of his music for religious purposes. When we realize that the only theme which lends itself to Latin words is the C sharp minor Nocturne, we tremble to think of what might have happened. Nonetheless, the very piece that reminded Chopin of his native land so strongly that it moved him to tears whenever he heard it, that moving Cantilena from the third Etude of Op. 10, has now become a menace. With a lyric of an unbelievably mawkish sentimentality, it is inflicted on us under the name of "Tristesse."

From now until the time of his arrival in England, his final break with George Sand, the organization of the last concert he was to give in Paris, the echoes of the revolution of 1848, form the subject matter of his letters. There is no reference to his work other than this cry of despair: "I must work in order to live, so I must tear some Mazurkas from my embittered heart."

Here and there we find a few sorrowful notes about his music, all similar to those sad expressions we have already quoted: "I am here (in Edinburgh) like a violin E string on a double bass . . . not a single real musical idea. . . . I have a piano by Broadwood in my room and Miss Stirling's Pleyel in the drawing-room . . . I am not short of pens or paper . . . I wish I could write a little, if only to give pleas- ure to these charming ladies" (his hostesses)—and the sad phrase trails off unfinished.

Again from Edinburgh, August 19: "I wish I could write a little, but it is impossible . . ." From Keir, October 1: "I feel weaker and I can't write anything . . ." From London, in November—words that resound with unspeakable suffer- ing: "What has become of my art? I can scarcely remember how they sing in the countryside!"

In spite of the long desired return to Paris and the ap- proach of beautiful weather that did him so much good, there is the same incapacity for work. In a letter to Gryzmala he confesses: "I have not begun to play again yet; I can't write." Two months later, in July—and so far as his music is con- cerned, these were to be his last words: "I play less and less; I can't write anything!"

And so on this tragic note, the few sentences relating to

Chopin's music come to an end. If we were unable to find valu-able suggestions concerning the interpretation of his works or the sentiments which inspired them, it is because he did not feel the necessity for giving any great wealth of explana-tion to a music which, as Beethoven had previously said of his own, "coming from the heart should in turn be able to find its way to the hearts of others."

With the greater number of his admirers he was not mistaken. The disappointment one may feel at not having had the benefit of some revealing hint as to the source of his inspiration or the correct interpretation of his work should not spur us on in a search for the ideology of an art so obviously full to overflowing with the language of the spirit, but rather serve to remind us of the words with which Chopin rejected a title that illustrated the idea contained in one of the Nocturnes.

"No, it is better to let them find that out for themselves." "Themselves"—performers as well as listeners.

5

CHOPIN'S DEBT TO FRANCE

WE KNOW WELL ENOUGH the debt France owes to him. From the moment when this delicate young man—touched by displays of sympathy, sensitive to spiritual affinities, uncertain of his future, if not his genius, decided to prolong his stay in Paris (which at the beginning he had only regarded as a steppingstone) the musical taste of our country was changed.

The musical style of our contemporary composers still reflects the subtleties and quivering aspirations that fill the many masterpieces he produced during the following twenty years which he spent with us. In no other music but his could Fauré, Debussy, and Ravel have discovered a harmonic language so bewitching, so light, so flexible and penetrating, whose emotional poetry he revealed to us over a century ago.

French thought and feeling have never been expressed with such a wealth of understanding, completely in accord with racial characteristics, as they were in the subtle musical vocabulary of this frail Pole.

In return, was he not in some way beholden to France, was not his musical personality influenced by his long stay among us? Would he have been the same person, would he have expressed himself as he did, had he lived beneath other skies?

These are questions that can be answered only hypothetically, questions on which I fear I can throw little light. I have often tried to picture Chopin as he really was, not from a study of the literature about him or from the documentary evidence, but by living with his music.

I have tried to call him into being, both spiritually and physically, consumed by his fever, by chaste but passionate torments, by that noble melancholy which runs throughout his music. Perhaps I am not entirely mistaken in claiming a semblance of reality for my assumptions.

What does Chopin owe to France? In the first place, his father, a native of Lorraine with all the inevitable characteristics that were his birthright.

We know that, in 1787, the sixteen-year-old Nicholas Chopin fled alone from the village of Marainville, near Nancy, where for generations his ancestors had followed the rural crafts of wheelwright or wine-grower (vine dresser) and how, after many adventures, he arrived in Poland, which became his second home. Why he left Lorraine we do not know. The most likely explanation is that he was obsessed by the idea that he was the bastard son of a gentleman in the court of King Stanislas, with whom his mother had had an affair while the exiled King was residing in the capital of Lorraine. His impulsive flight to Poland may have been due to the belief that there he would find the evidence of his birth.

With no basis in fact, the story is pure supposition. Chopin himself was never quite sure of the motives for his father's escapade. Until his death he remained ignorant of the existence of his two aunts who were still living at Marainville in 1845.

No matter how completely Nicholas assimilated Polish ways and customs, however complete the rupture with his family—who referred to him as "the fugitive"—no matter how complete a silence he preserved as to his origins and youthful background, the essential Frenchman remained, if only through his language. By teaching the rudiments of French to the children of some of Warsaw's great families, he preserved the habits and thoughts of his youth, which were assimilated by children quick to react to foreign influence. In this secret alliance between ancestry and education lies a factor destined to influence Chopin's rapid assimilation of French ways and customs, which was evident from the moment of his arrival in Paris.

If I stress his French ancestry, it is because it justifies in some degree the French citizenship so generously conferred on him by other countries, by virtue of his father's birth and his long residence on the banks of the Seine, a citizenship finally made legal by the issue of a passport in 1837. But what France still held in store for him was the much talked of love affair that linked his name with that of George Sand. The love story of this famous pair has become legendary, and the actors are enshrined in the Panthéon.

It was an adventure of prime importance and, if not dearest to his heart of the three *affaires de coeur* to which he admits, it was the one that by virtue of its duration and the alternating rhythms of exaltation and despair to which, in the feverish flow of his disordered existence, it gave birth, the one that exerted a decisive influence on his physical and moral faculties. His patriotic fervor and love for all things French, the development of his musical genius, can only be understood in the light of this affair.

Meeting with a widespread sympathy for Poland's cause, he was naturally incited to give vent to his patriotism, which perhaps might not have found expression with such violence and pathos had he felt himself to be isolated amid hostile surroundings, indifferent to the fate of his country. France, then, is mysteriously involved in the three primary factors of his destiny—his birth, his love, his patriotism. As if to set a seal on this strange hold France had on him, Chopin, ill, en-feebled, already nearing his end, returned from England just in time for his adopted country to become the repository of his frail body and that tiny handful of Polish soil which was to become for those who love the music of this man of destiny a shrine to be venerated for all time.

While his musical thought was undoubtedly Polish, the means whereby he gave expression to it could not escape being influenced by the constant flow of new ideas and sensa-tions derived from his association with all that Parisian society stood for in the way of intellectual and social refine-ment.

I am not thinking solely of the semi-intimate associations Chopin formed with the habitués of the drawing rooms who idolized him, but rather of his instinctive liking for elegance —elegance of dress, of wit, that could be satisfied in lux-urious surroundings, by graceful feminine society and dis-tinguished company, in a manner best suited to the expression of his genius.

Unconsciously a bond of sympathy grew up between the romantic composer and his aristocratic audience. His music takes on a perfection of detail, a high surface polish, which conceals the fiery passion inspiring him, that irresistible na-tional feeling which runs through the least of the Mazurkas of this period, prompting Schumann to say: "The music of Chopin is that of cannon buried in flowers."

Where else but in Paris would he have met such a ready response to this spirit of patriotism. The fashionable salons of the exiled Polish nobility, smarting from their country's defeat, supplied the luxurious background against which Chopin paid homage to nostalgic memories of the gaiety that was once Warsaw.

All the pent-up hopes of his youth found an outlet among these aristocrats who received him with a fervent, admiring enthusiasm.

Chopin's love of his country was inflamed still further by the ovations which greeted Poland's national bard, Mick-iewicz, whenever he appeared at the Collège de France to declaim in fiery verse the magnificent epic of a martyred country. Every time Chopin evoked the legendary, sorrowful picture of his native land in a Ballade or Polonaise, he could rest assured that his audience would be with him heart and soul in an equal state of fervor and emotional enthusiasm —circumstances well suited to the development of his genius.

In another country, deprived of this encouraging atmos-phere, who knows but that he might have been content with developing as a musician of talent instead of becoming the liv-ing embodiment of the shriven soul of an oppressed people—a nation's symbol of revolt?

Yet there were other influences, less apparent perhaps, but nonetheless powerful, which were to point the way to a more lofty conception of his work. George Sand, whose insatiable curiosity ranged haphazardly over the problems of sociology, moral philosophy, religion ethics, and some-times literature, could not have failed to stir Chopin's inborn laziness and to have goaded him to work. During the whole of his time at Nohant these influences must have been at work, leading this born improviser to see the problems of artistic expression in a clearer light, engrossing him with the methods whereby he was to translate this into fact with an ever increasing precision. Although we know he carefully avoided anything that might have sprung from an association of ideas—as George Sand says: "He only wants to understand what he can identify with himself"—we have to admit that his work was bound to have been affected by his discussions on aesthetics with Eugène Delacroix. To take but one example, Chopin saw at once that the theory of reflection suggested by the great painter had its relationship to music, and, in a nature so subtly impressionable as his, this must have been a lasting influence.

The relationship between these two great artists must have been close for Chopin, who was not a talkative person by nature, to have let himself go on the subject of music, the gist of his conversation being noted down by Delacroix on his return home after a long walk which they had taken.

There can be no doubt that this close association between the most instinctive of musicians and the most analytical of painters must have been to the great intellectual advantage of the former, leading as it did, in the final years of his life to an enrichment of his work, a more critical approach to harmony, a growing refinement of style, and the deliberate simplification of his technique.

If I am accused of overemphasizing his relationship with Delacroix, it is because, of all Chopin's contemporaries, it was he who saw most clearly Chopin's innate idealism and, having an affectionate regard for him, was able, because of their mutual friendship, to exercise the most beneficial influence on him. By the word "influence" I do not intend to imply that Chopin would have allowed himself to be influenced by theories at variance with his artistic integrity. On the contrary, the mystery of summer nights is the only source from which the nightingale learns the miracle of its voluptuous song.

On the other hand, Chopin the man was undoubtedly the richer for his contact with the exceptional people who crossed his path in such numbers.

Every new creation of his sublime imagination evinced a livelier feeling for beauty of form. The fourth Ballade, the last Scherzo, the Barcarolle, the Polonaise-Fantaisie, all give convincing evidence of this. He has become more confident of himself, his work has taken on a richer sound, and yet, in some way becomes more impersonal. This "Sarmatian soul"—as Schumann says—has become international.

We may wonder to what extent his contacts with Pierre Leroux, Lamennais, Balzac, Victor de Laprade, Edgar Quinet, Legouvé, the brothers Arago, Louis Blanc—to mention only a few of those whom he was to meet almost daily—affected the character of his thought and artistic striving. While it would be foolish to ignore these influences, at the same time it would be rash to pass final judgment on them.

His letters to his family during 1845 contain references to scientific, historical, and even architectural questions, from which we can infer that he took a lively interest in a wide range of contemporary subjects.

It would, however, be too much to suppose that he took any great part in contemporary intellectual or philosophic speculations that were the staple diet of the regular guests at Nohant. These were matters with which he did not concern himself.

In an earlier essay on the influence that French thought exercised over Chopin, I concluded that it was to him and not to an obscure namesake—a teacher of French with the Christian name of Auguste, who happened to live in the neighborhood of La Châtre at about that time—that we owe the copy of Maurice de Guerin's letters, the original of which had been given to George Sand by the sister of the author of *Le Centaure.*

Ambiguous statements by the first publisher of this famous correspondence supported my contention and led me to conclude, not without emotion, that the musician of genius had devoted the greater part of his leisure to transcribing a homesick longing very similiar to his own, the long arm of coincidence wedding the destinies of these two young contemporaries—suffering from the same disease and exhibiting a marked similarity in their passionate idealism.

When Maurice de Guerin says "I did not know that I possessed so sensitive an imagination or one that could stir my heart so deeply," do we not hear the echo of Chopin's own *cri de coeur?* If we wished to attempt the description of the Nocturnes in words, passage after passage from this corre' spondence provides the only possible prose equivalent.

In the face of incontrovertible evidence, I have been obliged to abandon the thesis by which I associated Chopin with the discovery of this correspondence. Nevertheless, one cannot help but observe the strange spiritual and physical affiinity between these two young men, both of whom had been endowed by an inexorable fate with so slender a hold on life. I often imagine the music of the Polish composer in the terms of the French writer.

The development of Chopin's music after his arrival in Paris is best summed up in the penetrating remark made by the Marquis de Custine in a letter written to Chopin after one of his last public performances: "You have attained through suffering to poetry. The melancholy of your music penetrates the heart more deeply."

There is no better description of the debt Chopin owed to the friendly appreciative atmosphere in which he passed the days of his exile.

The same correspondent marvels at "the maturity revealed in your latest works by their emotional significance."

Reading between the lines, we can without exaggeration see in this search for a more tense melodic line, a more precise phrasing, a greater unity between the idea and its expression, a reflection of our own artistic tradition.

Unfortunately, there is no justification for attributing to any French musician the honor of having contributed to the development of Chopin's genius. The only two avowedly romantic composers of the period, Berlioz and Felician David, were both alien to Chopin's sensitive nature. Indeed, he feared the one and ignored the other. Nevertheless, French "taste"—that irresistible, mysterious influence, emanating from modes of thought and behavior, the fruit of centuries of culture, certainly played a part in the evolution of his art. It is little enough—nothing more than a fine patina on that imperishable work of art whose value time alone can show. But it is sufficient to warm those of us who can detect its subtle influence with a glow of pride that grows in intensity when, in speaking of the French, Chopin says: "I have become as attached to them as if they were my own people."

6

CHOPIN'S CONCERTS

THE LIGHT OF FAME illumines the name of no other pianist with greater brilliance than that of Chopin—an almost legendary brilliance that even to this day is associated with the exceptional nature of his playing, and this quite independ- dently of his genius as a composer.

Paradoxically, it is almost impossible to mention a virtuoso who had less contact with the public during the course of a professional career destined for immortality. Thirty concerts, the greater number of which were given without any sort of monetary reward and which in no way enhanced his reputation as an artist (indeed, they were often no more than a casual appearance at a charity show)—these make up the sum total of his career as a soloist before the general public.

This random career was spread over three decades of his short life, commencing with his debut in Warsaw on February 24, 1818, where he was far more concerned with the impression likely to be caused by an embroidered collar than with the reception accorded to his youthful performance, and closing with that final humiliating adventure in London on November 16, 1848. Here, at a charity show in aid of Polish refugees, his miraculously ethereal playing was rudely interrupted by the clamor from an adjacent ballroom which soon robbed him of an already distressingly small audience.

Of necessity, we shall have to examine Chopin's motives for his aversion to seeking the verdict of the public on his consummate artistry. There can be no doubt, however, that by embarking on the career of a virtuoso in this way he could not hope for success—certainly not if we judge it by contemporary experience. Several hundred performances, supported by an intensive publicity campaign, are necessary to build up a reputation for the most talented artist, which may, even then, not reach much further than the confines of his native country.

As we have seen, the number of concerts Chopin gave was surprisingly few, and for the most part they met with little success. If we keep this in view, and take into account the fact that his reputation was rivaled only by the spectacular fame of Liszt and Thalberg, who were both familiar platform heroes inured to the ovations of the multitude and to the praise of the critics, then we must ask what was the secret of Chopin's success?

I think I am not wide of the mark in attributing Chopin's brilliant reputation and widespread fame to what at first glance may appear to be a paradox. I refer to that atmosphere of jealous exclusiveness that enveloped Chopin to the point of becoming a cult. Admittance to this aristocratic circle was reserved for the happy few whose monopoly it was. When he appeared on the artistic horizon of the French capital, he was debarred from acquiring an immediate popularity. He was nevertheless able to secure those social amenities most pleasing to him as a lover of elegance and essential to the development of his art.

Without the aid of high pressure publicity, a tacit understanding was gradually established, a kind of "confidential" fame which circulated only among the chosen few. What Chopin lost, or appeared to lose, by it in immediate gains, was repaid by a wealth of understanding. He was reimbursed by a kind of spiritual mortgage secured by the devotion of a wordly élite, which was the more inclined to extol his virtues when it could regard him as a discovery to be kept for its own private delectation.

"One does not merely love him; one loves oneself in him," remarked one of the regular visitors to the happy musical gatherings that resulted from this mutual understanding.

This uncompromising attitude was all that was needed to excite the curiosity of that larger circle which is always interested in the smallest tidbits of gossip likely to indicate the current opinions of the aristocracy.

It was not long before conversation turned on the person-ality of this curious young artist who, contrary to all the accepted practices of his profession, reserved the favors of his allegedly miraculous talent for an audience of his own choosing, denying them to a public on which he might have had to depend.

Relying, then, on the good faith of a number of com-mentators who have voiced their astonishment, if only to lead us to infer that they were better informed than other people, we can observe the gradual multiplication of rumor, as voice was added to voice, until these anonymous creators of reputations had surpassed that acclamation more usually awarded on the basis of merit alone. If we transpose the theme of calumny to one of extravagant eulogy, it is all very like a story by Beaumarchais.

Chopin's reputation was not limited solely to his qualities as a virtuoso, but was enhanced by the sympathy aroused by his charm of manner and by admiration for his elegant appearance.

I hope it is obvious that I am not suggesting that Chopin's fame—which is all I am concerned with here—can be attributed to nothing more than an excess of society snobbishness. One had to admit, however, that it had a strong influence on the attitude of subsequent generations. In imitation of the Paris drawing rooms of the 1830's they accepted blindly as an article of absolute faith Princess Belgiojoso's *pronunciatio ex cathedra*: "Perhaps Chopin is not the greatest of pianists; he is more: he is the only one."

In trying to understand the origin of this worship of Chopin as above all rivals and master of every secret of the keyboard, which amounted to a cult, still to some extent alive today, we must attempt to follow the chain of reasoning that led him to reserve his art for the select few. We must also take two factors of a physiological nature into account—both closely bound up with his slender reserves of bodily endurance.

The first of these is a kind of pathological inhibition similar to that which present-day virtuosi refer to as *le trac*. It is sometimes incurable and has caused the stultification of many brilliant careers. Chopin makes no attempt to excuse himself for it. Although his debut in Warsaw took place before an audience consisting, if not wholly of friends, certainly entirely of everyday acquaintances, he does not conceal from his friend and confidant, Titus Woyciechowski, that, in spite of his success, he would prefer to abandon the extra concert he had been asked for. "You can't believe," he writes, "what a martyrdom it is for me during the three days before I play in public." Even after he had gained experience and was protected by his growing reputation from any effect on his standing as an artist that criticism might have had, he again admits, this time to Liszt, the apprehension he feels at the mere idea of having to appear on a platform. "I am not the right person to give concerts. The public intimidates me. I feel asphyxiated by the breath of the people in the audience, paralyzed by their curious stares and dumb before that sea of unknown faces."

He completes the picture with a half-joking, half-bitter remark on the subject of his famous rival's exceptional physical prowess: "But as for you, you are made for it. When you don't hold your audience, you are quite able to overpower it."

Here he touches on the second reason for the reluctance he felt at parading a method of playing before a public not yet able to appreciate its special qualities.

"Chopin," we read in the collection of impressions and recollections which Liszt devoted to the memory of his friend, "knew that he could make no impression on the masses. Like a sea of leaden waves, although they become malleable in response to every flame, they are nonetheless heavy, and need the strong arm of an athletic workman to move them." "He knew," Liszt continues, "that he was never fully appreciated except at those gatherings where everyone was willing to follow his lead."

With these inhibiting physical factors in mind, the search through his correspondence and contemporary writings for some reference to a concert career, weighed down as it was with the formidable burden of mental apprehension and constitutional incompatability, becomes a moving experience.

In order to make our account of Chopin's few appearances before the public as complete as possible, it will be sufficient to record the dates of his early concerts which were little more than exhibitions of an exceptional and precocious amateur talent.

February 24, 1818: Chopin was then eight years old.* He gave a necessarily immature performance of an insignificant Concerto by Gyrowetz in keeping with the anecdote regarding his embroidered collar, which is too well known for me to quote it again here.

May 27 and June 10, 1825: Chopin took part in two charity concerts in Warsaw, at which he played an Allegro by Moscheles and improvised on a hybrid instrument rejoicing in the unlikely name of Aelomelodicon, which embodied the dissimilar characteristics of harmonium and piano.

This demonstration found favor with the publicitymongers, and was repeated that same year in the presence of the Czar Alexander, who was graciously pleased to reward Chopin with a diamond ring.

August, 1826: Chopin appeared at another charity concert in aid of some young children who had been left destitute as a result of their mother's sudden death. It took place at Reinertz, a small watering place in Silesia, where his sister, already dangerously ill with the pulmonary disease which was to prove fatal the following April, had been sent by the doctors. Chopin himself also underwent a preventive regime of "fresh air and curdled milk."

What the program consisted of is not clear, but it probably included the Rondo in C minor, which had just been published. In any case, the performance was handicapped from the start by the deplorable instrument he had to use,

*He may have been nine, if one agrees with the findings of recent research which, since Chopin's baptism was apparently deferred owing to administrative difficulties resulting from the military occupation of Mazovia between 1809 and 1810, fixes the date of his birth a year earlier.

and the financial results were in no way commensurate with the generous impulse that had prompted the concert.

During the three years which followed his return to Poland, Chopin played exclusively to private gatherings of the aristocracy in and around Warsaw. However flattering these may have been to the young boy who was the star of the Conservatoire, they excited no notice in the local press, which might have told us something about them.

Chopin embarked on his professional career quite unexpectedly during the course of two music festivals at Vienna in 1829, the first taking place on August 11 and the second on August 18. Had it not been for the fact that the publisher Heslinger, who had just undertaken the printing of the *Variations sur la ci darem la mano* and the *Rondo à la Krakowiak*, thought it good business to profit by the presence of the young composer to secure a public presentation of the two works he was about to publish, there would have been no question of his making an appearance in the Austrian capital on his first visit.

The first concert was to have included Beethoven's *Overture de Prométhée*, the *Variations sur la ci darem,* a group of Rossini's songs by a singer of the name of Welthen, and to have concluded with the *Rondo á la Krakowiak*.

However, at rehearsal the orchestral parts of the Rondo were found to be so badly copied and full of mistakes, that there was an uproar from the orchestra. Chopin, to avoid disaster, withdrew it at the last minute and substituted a solo improvisation on themes from *La Dame Blanche*. In great favor at the time, it was a display of pyrotechnics calling for great virtuosity and inventive power on the part of the composer, depending as it did on the spontaneous inspiration of the moment. A performance for which, incidentally, a fortnight's traveling without the opportunity of touching a piano was not the best of preparations. It seems, however, to have been the success of the evening, but, though not without merit on purely spectacular grounds, it was devoid of any aesthetic significance.

The Polish musician, Nidecki, happening to be in Vienna, and meeting Chopin by chance, undertook the revision and correction of the offending orchestral parts in time for the Rondo to be included in the program of the second concert, which also included an Overture by Lindpaitner and a Polonaise, played by the violinist Joseph Khayl, by Mayseder. It is possible that, at the request of the audience, Chopin had to repeat his former success by extemporizing on popular Polish songs and dances.

In writing of these concerts, Chopin gives a completely honest account, neither deprecating the criticism of his playing nor attempting to disguise his youthful satisfaction at receiving compliments on the score of his personal appearance. Criticism was chiefly aimed at the extreme tenuity of his playing: "Too feeble, or rather too delicate, for those who are accustomed not only to hear, but also to see the artists who play here, almost bang their pianos to bits."

Continuing his account, Chopin mentions the pianist Blahetka, whose gifts, incidentally, he was to praise a few weeks later when he had formed a passing infatuation for her, saying: "I forsee that I shall be accused of the same fault in the press—especially as the daughter of one of the leading critics herself hammers away furiously at her instrument."

"But," he adds, already fully conscious of the fact that his intensely personal style put him in a class apart, and perhaps, too, by the way of consolation, "it is impossible to please everyone and I prefer them to say that, rather than be blamed for playing too loud."

He also tells his family of a remark passed by a lady in the audience and repeated to him by his friend Hube: "Schade um den Jungen, dass er so wenig Tournure hat!" which may be translated: "What a pity the boy does not show himself off to better advantage!"

This purely chance remark, overheard by an amused listener, emphasizes the contrast between the unassuming behavior of the frail Pole and the theatrical posing of the fashionable virtuosi, who claimed that they impressed their audiences as much by the arrogance of their bearing as by the bravura of their playing.

However, these were but passing shadows that did nothing to dim the joy he felt at his very warm welcome. The only real annoyance—the orchestra's displeasure at the first rehearsal of the Rondo—was more than counterbalanced by the particularly flattering reception which the piece received at the second concert. Chopin tells his family that it gained for him the esteem of all of the professional musicians, and that "from the conductor down to the piano-tuner, they all said how struck they were with the beauty of the piece."

"I have had a triumph with the connoisseur as well as with the music lover," he continues, "and the press will have something to talk about." As though to emphasize the exceptional warmth of his reception, he adds the following: "When I had finished, there was so much applause that I had to appear a second time to make my bow"—a sentence that should give present-day virtuosi, accustomed to being recalled dozens of times and to receive ovations as though by right, food for thought.

As he points out, Chopin only agreed to take part in

the second concert (for which, like the first, he received no fees) in order to anticipate those people at home who might have said: "What's wrong? He's only given one concert and now he's off!"

To the end of his days, he was to be obsessed with anxiety about "What they would say in Warsaw." This childish dread often led him to make sudden changes in his plans and social life, which would be difficult to understand if no allowance were made for this strange fixation. In part, also it explains the reluctance he felt in dedicating himself to a career demanding complete subservience—a career which had already become a martyrdom to him. It is hard to say whether he appeared at these concerts to enhance his reputation as a composer or as a performer.

He was invited to appear at concerts in Prague and Dresden during visits he intended making to these cities. His excuses to his parents for his refusal to play are rather feeble: "It would be a mistake to spoil what I have been able to achieve in Vienna." Reading between the lines, we can see that his anxiety about "What they would say in Warsaw" accounts for the subterfuges he indulged in to avoid the invitations offered him.

The long letter to Titus, written on September 12, after his return to Warsaw, contains the following: "The sight of the Viennese public did not frighten me at all," and apart from a few details connected with the two concerts at Vienna, adds little to our knowledge of Chopin and his audience, an audience, which, incidentally, was not very numerous. However, toward the end of this same letter a sentence occurs which gives the lie to the slightly juvenile boast of imperturbability: "For," he writes, "I was quite pale when I sat down in front of a marvelous piano by Graff, with a rosy-cheeked assistant to turn over for me (it was not customary at this period for an artist to play from memory, even when he was a composer playing his own work) and then, believe me, I played like one possessed." In order to forestall criticism of his light touch, he adds that Beethoven's friend and patron, Count Lichnowski, had offered him the use of a very resonant piano he had had constructed for Beethoven as he became more deaf. "But," he writes, "it would have made no difference, for this characteristic is an essential feature of my playing, and, moreover, is much liked by the ladies." This slightly conceited excuse prophesies quite clearly the place that his art, by virtue of a mysterious affinity, was destined to hold in the feminine heart.

To end his letter, he quotes a passage from a criticism of his second concert; "We are concerned here with a young musician who will go his own way, who instinctively holds our sympathies, and who exhibits a talent of a sort quite different from the conventional type offered at most concerts." A judgement which sums up and anticipates the opinions to be passed on the characteristics of his work both as a pianist and as a composer at all his future appearances in public.

To form an estimate of the atmosphere surrounding the three concerts he gave in Warsaw, some six months after his debut in Vienna and a few days before he left his beloved Poland forever, we have to rely on Chopin's personal evidence.

The comments he makes in a letter to Titus on the reactions of the local press to the first and only concerts submitted to the judgment of his compatriots have an objectivity which adds a particular significance to this document.

The first concert, given on March 17, 1830, at the Théâtre, had a curiously arranged program which I give below, as originally printed:

FIRST PART

1. *Ouverture de l'opéra Las ek Biaty,* par Elsner.
2. *Allegro du Concerto en fa mineur,* composé et joué par F. Chopin.
3. *Divertissement pour cor,* composé et joué par Gorner.
4. *Adagio et Rondo du Concerto en fa mineur,* composé et joué par F. Chopin.

SECOND PART

1. *Ouverture de l'opéra Cerylja Piaceczyuska* par Kurpinski.
2. *Variations de Poer,* chantées par Mme. Meier.
3. *Pot-pourri sur des airs nationaux,* composé et joué par F. Chopin.

Chopin organized this concert himself, and preparations for it were made much farther in advance than for the impromptu appearances he made in Vienna. It is difficult to imagine him in the role of impresario. One would have thought that it would have repelled him even more violently than the public career of virtuoso on which he was embarking.

Financially, the concert was a great success, for, as Chopin tells us, it was impossible to get a box or a stall three days before the event. He was not, however, particularly satisfied with its success from the artistic point of view. Writing to Titus, he says: "And so my first Concerto . . . did not have the effect on the audience I had reckoned on. The opening Allegro, which is only likely to be understood by the few, received some applause, but only, I imagine, because it seemed the thing to do to feign astonishment and follow the lead of the cognoscenti. The Adagio and Finale had a greater success and warmer reception. But the Pot-Pourri on Polish songs (afterward published under the title of *Grand Fantasia on Polish airs,* Op. 13) did not, in my opinon, get anything like the reception I had hoped for. They applauded, but only half-heartedly. No doubt they wanted to give me the impression, before leaving the auditorium, that they had not been too bored."

His delicate touch came in for criticism, as it had done in Vienna, since he says: "Elsner found it deplorable that my pantaléon should be so dead that the bass passages could not be heard. It was the same in the pit, where they said it was a pity my playing was so faint."

Further on, in the same letter, he mentions a notice in the *Courrier Polonais* referring to the same point, which "after extolling me to the skies for my interpretation of the adagio," nevertheless calls for "more energy."

It is interesting to notice that in Chopin's eyes appreciation of his playing was of as great an importance as that dealing with his compositions. To the end of his days he never made a clear distinction between the praises showered on the pianist and those reserved for the composer.

The observations made by the Polish editor did not fall on stony ground after all, as was the case in Vienna, and at his second concert Chopin used a larger instrument, a change welcomed by his friends, since it would allow him "to do better justice" to his qualities as a virtuoso by adding volume to his playing. This piano was lent for the occasion by a Russian general who was visiting Warsaw at the time. Elsner, to whose opinion Chopin could not remain indifferent, hastened to declare that it was only with the aid of such an instrument that his ex-pupil could show off his talents to the full.

Chopin, nevertheless, was far from sharing this opinion; he deplored the fact that he would not be using the instrument to which he was accustomed. The question of volume of tone seemed to him to be of secondary importance compared to the subtle expressiveness of his rendering. However, the audience shared the view expressed by Elsner, for the success of the second concert was certainly more conclusive than that of the previous one.

The program of March 22, noticeably similar in its general design to that of March 17, was arranged as follows:

FIRST PART

1. *Symphonie* de Nowakowski.
2. *Allegro du Concerto* en fa mineur par Chopin.
3. *Air varié* de Bériot, joué par le violiniste Bielawski.
4. *Adgio et Rondo du Concerto en fa mineur,* par Chopin.

SECOND PART

1. *Rondo à la Krakowiak,* par Chopin.
2. *Air d'Elenae Malvina de Soliva,* chanté par Mme. Meier.
3. *Improvisation sur des avis nationaux,* par Chopin.

The concert was given, as was its predecessor, at the Théâtre. The improvisation reserved for the last item, Chopin tells us, was well received by the smart set in the boxes and dress circle. All the same, he maintains that he was not able to improvise as he would have wished since: "What I wanted would not have been suitable for this particular audience."

It so happened that the theme he chose, more by accident than design, bore the ironically appropriate title, *Habits of the Town,* hardly the theme to inspire the young composer, although with touching modesty he admits its appositeness.

Chopin expressed astonishment that the Adagio du Concerto should have produced such a favorable impression. "Where-ever I go people talk to me about it," he says with obvious satisfaction. He goes on to mention that Orlawski was churning out Mazurkas and Galopades on themes taken from his work, but since the small change of his local fame had been added to by this flattery, he was not as furious as he might have been.

But, in spite of the appreciable material gain—the two concerts had brought in five thousand Gulden—in spite of the complimentary notices in the *Gazette de Varsovie,* the *Courrier Polonais,* and even the *Journal Officiel,* in spite of the laurel wreath presented to him on the platform by a young admirer, a French girl; in spite of the poem proclaiming his genius in the most emphatic terms, he refused to entertain the idea of giving the next concert he had been asked for.

It is here, in a letter to his friend, that he makes the confession I quoted earlier in this essay: "You could not believe what a martyrdom it is for me to play in public."

This desire to run away, this instinctive refusal to take advantage of opportunities so many others would have jumped at, seems for some reason to have been encouraged by his chosen confident, or so it would seem if we are to judge from Chopin's final sentence, which replies to what appears to have been advice: "You are right about the concerts. It so happens that I have already refused several, as if I knew beforehand what your feelings were on the matter."

It is difficult to see what value this policy of folded arms, or idle fingers, could have had in the eyes of the two friends. What possible advantage could it have for a career that depended on a growing reputation fostered by public approval? It would be rash to attempt an answer.

It is a fact, however, that another invitation to take part in a concert given by Grumberg, a blind flutist, found Chopin just as adamant. He excused himself by pointing out that having already refused numerous similar proposals, it would not for him to appear to show preference. But, wishing to soften his refusal by some sympathetic gesture toward his "comrade in instrumental art," he offered to sell some tickets for him.

Nevertheless—as he neared the completion of his E minor Concerto, the composer won the battle over the apprehensions of the performer—from May onward the idea of a third concert began to take root.

Perhaps the hope that Constance Gladowska, the Constance who had inspired the Larghetto of the F minor Concerto which had proved the most successful item at both previous concerts, might consent to appear on the same platform and share the applause with her impassioned lover, who had yet to confess his infatuation, was another, more potent reason for him to summon up his courage and face anew "those curious stares and that asphyxiating breathing."

And so, on October 5, he was able to tell Titus that "She" was going to sing at a concert, which had been definitely fixed for October 11, and that the program was as follows:

First Part

1. *Symphonie* de Görner.
2. *Premier Allegro du Concerto en mi mineur,* Chopin.
3. *Air avec choeurs de Soliva,* chanté par Mlle. Volkow.
4. *Adagio et Rondo du Concerto,* Chopin.

Second Part

1. *Ouverture de Guillaume Tell,* Rossini.
2. *Cavatine de la Donna del Lago,* Rossini, chanté par Mlle. Gladkowska.
3. *Fantaisie sur des airs polonais,* Chopin.

The week was devoted to careful preparations, which, as

for the two previous concerts, fell entirely on Chopin's shoulders. There was a piano to be chosen, orchestra and chorus parts to be checked, music stands to be collected, preliminary rehearsals to be held with some of the players, and the selling of tickets. On top of this accumulation of worries, for one whose public appearances were so few, there were new clothes to be bought, which had to be ready, with the rest of the young traveler's luggage, for his imminent journey, from which he was never to return.

Having surmounted all these obstacles, Chopin was able to tell Titus, on October 12, of an artistic triumph. It would be a pity not to quote this in full, since it shows his intense personal satisfaction, to which the realization of a lover's dream adds an especial poignancy.

"My concert yesterday was a great success. . . . I wasn't a bit nervous. I played as I do when I am alone and I know that I was quite good. The house was full. The concert started with the Görner Symphony. Then 'His Majesty' played the *Allegro in E Minor,* which went all by itself on a Streycher piano. Deafening applause. Soliva was very pleased. He was conducting because of his *Choral Aria* which Mlle. Walkow sang very prettily, dressed in blue and looking like an angel. The Adagio and the Rondo followed; then the interval.

"When everyone had come back from the buffet and left the stage, where they had come to tell me how much they liked the first part of the concert, the second half began with the Overture to William Tell. Soliva conducted well and it had a good reception. . . . He also conducted for Mlle. Gladkowska's song. She was dressed all in white, with roses in her hair, which suited her divinely.

"She sang the Cavatina from *Donna del Lago* and

the recitative as she had never sung before, unless it was in the Agnès aria.

"You know: O *quante lacrime per te versai,* she gave the *tutto detesto* in such a way that Zielinski declared that it was worth a thousand ducats for itself alone.

"After having led Mlle. Gladkowska from the stage, we set about the Pot-pourri on the theme of *La tune se lève.* This time the orchestra, the audience in the pit, and I, myself, all felt at home. Applause came thick and fast after the last Mazurka—there was not a single whistle—and I had to come back to take a bow—Brandt having taught me how, I did it this time more like a human being. If Soliva had not taken my score home to study it and if he had not conducted in such a way as to make it impossible for me to get in a tangle, I don't know what would have happened yesterday evening."

And so, on this note of professional modesty and lover's enthusiasm the correspondence from Warsaw comes to an end. This third concert which his fellow countrymen were privileged to hear was, though he did not know it, his farewell performance.

About November 1, on the eve of his departure, he was the guest of honor at a reception. Here he was presented with that silver goblet filled with Polish earth, which was to be the symbol of his dearest memories during the loneliness that was to come. "May you, no matter where destiny may call you, never forget your country nor cease to love it dearly. Think of Poland. Think of those who are proud to be your compatriots. They expect great things of you, and their good wishes and prayers go with you."

This oration, made by the speaker entrusted with conveying

the good wishes of his friends, foreshadows with an extraordinary insight the love for his country that was to be expressed in a miraculous outpouring of masterpieces. With this prophesy ringing in his ears, Chopin set out on the career of virtuoso—a career for which he felt himself to be sadly inadequate in spite of the fact that his musical baggage contained the two Concertos, and although he had in his possession a ribbon given him by Constance and carried with him always that inestimable treasure—his genius—which was to increase in value beneath the spur of suffering.

The opportunities for studying the reactions of an audience as yet unaccustomed to his personality and genius are so rare that mention must be made of the improvised performance he gave at Breslau, the first stop in that haphazard journey which ultimately ended in his exile. This took place on November 8, 1830 and provided him with yet another reason for avoiding contact with foreigners, although in this instance it bore all the outward signs of sincere flattery.

Schnabel, who was an old friend of Elsner's and conductor of an amateur orchestral society which was in the habit of meeting three times a week in the hall of the "Resource," asked Chopin to be present at the rehearsal of their concert that same evening. Chopin accepted the invitation, and on arrival found "a sort of amateur pianist," as he puts it in a letter written on the same day to his parents, "who was getting ready to play a Concerto by Moscheles."

The worthy Schnabel, who had not heard Chopin play since his last stay in Warsaw, asked him to try the piano, which was already in place for the evening performance. But let Chopin tell the rest of the story.

"It was difficult for me to refuse. I sat down and played some variations. Schnabel was overcome with joy. Monsieur Hellwiz (the amateur pianist) took fright and the others begged me to play in his place that evening. Schnabel insisted with such enthusiasm that I could not say no. However, I told him that I was only doing it at his special request and because of his friendship with Elsner, for I had never intended to appear in Breslau. The old man replied that he understood perfectly, but he never' theless persisted. He told me that when he had seen me in church yesterday he had wanted to ask me to help them, but his courage had failed him. So I went with his son to fetch my music, and I played them the Romance and the Rondo from the second Concerto. At the performance my playing astonished the Germans, who said: 'Was für ein leichtes spiel hat er!'* but they said nothing about the composition. Titus even heard one of them say 'He can play, but he ought not to compose.' . . . Apart from the Rondo, I improvised for the connoisseurs on a theme from 'La Muette de Portici.' They played an Overture to finish up with, and after that there was dancing. Schnabel wanted to give me supper, but I only accepted some soup. I must say that with the exception of Schnabel, whose pleasure was obvious, and who cajoled me and kept pinching my chin, none of the Germans knew quite how to take me. They were surprised, but since I do not as yet possess an established reputation, they were at pains to conceal their astonishment. They were obviously afraid of committing themselves regarding

---

* *"How lightly he plays!"*

the value of my compositions, or of risking a judgment likely to compromise their reputation as expert
critics. However, one of the local cognoscenti came
up to me and ventured to praise the originality of the
form of my music. I don't know who he was, but
he was the one who understood best."

Then the letter ends on a note of disillusionment: "These
Germans are terrible people."

In spite of the unwarranted assertion which he made to
his family on his arrival that "Dresden will certainly not
bring me fame or fortune," during his week's stay in the
middle of November he was offered an opportunity for
making a better managed appearance than in Breslau.

Klengel, the learned organist, author of the *Canons and
Fugues in all Keys,* which Chopin does not hesitate to place
on a par with the *Well-tempered Clavichord,* extended a
warm welcome to his young admirer, and at once made
inquiries in order that Chopin might appear at a concert in
the Theater. These attempts to organize a concert came to
nothing, since Chopin demurred, excusing himself on the
grounds that he could not possibly prolong his stay in Dresden.
He did, however, play in private, and was able to obtain
letters of introduction likely to be of use on his uncertain
itinerary to the Queen of the Two Sicilies at Naples, and to
the Princess Vlasino in Rome, thus profiting from the
satisfaction his playing gave to the two princesses of Saxony
before whom he appeared.

Continuing from Dresden to Vienna, after breaking his
journey for a few hours in Prague, he stayed there, in company
with his friend Titus, for nearly eight months, apparently
uncertain of how he was going to manage to give concerts

there. He does not appear to have made tentative inquiries about a concert, since he mentions in a letter written on December 1 that he had been advised to refuse to play for nothing, as he had done on the previous occasion on which he had played in the Austrian capital. Writing on the same day, he refers to a certain M. Geymuller, who told him all in one breath: "That he was glad to make his acquaintance, but that he would not advise him to give a performance since there were so many good pianists in Vienna that it was necessary to have a great reputation before it was possible to make any money," adding that personally he was not able to be of any assistance to an artist newly arrived in the capital, "because times are hard." A statement which, since his opinion on the matter had not been sought, was, to say the least, untimely, and one which left Chopin, to use his own words, "staring at him in blank amazement."

At the end of this letter we find the following: "I don't know how this week has gone by. I haven't had time to turn round, and still nothing certain is arranged about my concert. And now the question arises: shall I play the Concerto in F or the one in E? . . . Graff advises me to play in the Lands Landischen Saal, where the 'intellectual' concerts are held, that is to say in the best and most beautiful spot in Vienna. For that I shall need an authorization, which will no doubt be quite easy for me to get."

Except for some "preliminary negotiations" with Dupont, the once-famous French dancer, who had become Director of the Karthner Theater, about the possibility of giving a concert there, the date and conditions under which Chopin would appear remained completely vague. "If he offers me too little," says Chopin, "I shall give a concert in the great hall of the 'Redoute,'" but nothing definite had been arranged by the end of December.

He found the lack of any definite aim and his state of indecision, in a city where he had hoped to benefit by the favorable impression he had made with his two previous concerts, most disconcerting, and began to wonder whether he should not risk a journey to Italy.

The publisher, Haslinger, who had previously encouraged him to appear in public, would no longer even consider publishing the works Chopin offered him. His musical activities were confined to taking part in a few intimate gatherings, mostly in Polish circles. He played a little, he danced a little and, in short, was very bored.

"I can do nothing in the way I want," he confides to Jean Matuzynski. "I have to dress up, do my hair, put on shoes and have a detached and satisfied look on my face in their drawing rooms—it is only when I get home that I can let myself go on the piano just as I please. I am the intimate friend of nobody, but I have to be cordial with everyone. . . . But how am I to get away? Go to Paris? Here they advise me to wait a little longer."

Then he adds a sentence which again shows his lack of fighting spirit: "I think no more about my concert."

He found justification in his own eyes for this self-imposed silence by the anxiety he felt over events in Poland.

Writing to his old master, Elsner, at the end of January, 1831, he says: "You will not take it amiss, sir, if feelings for my home are at present uppermost in my mind and I have still not thought of busying myself with my concert. Every day greater difficulties seem to arise. Not only has there been an uninterrupted flow of concerts given by pianists, resulting in a surfeited public on whose interest it would be impossible to rely, but more particularly the events in Warsaw have been as unfavorable for me here as they would have been favorable had I been in Paris. I hope, however, when the Carnival takes place to play my first Concerto, which has remained Wurfel's* favorite."

He was still obliged to beg his family's indulgence in May for not having found it possible to give a single concert, despite his desire to obey their wishes. In fact, he had actually taken part in one of the concerts at the Redoute—concerts that were almost variety shows—on April 4. The tendency of these concerts to play to the box office had already aroused Beethoven to a fierce attack, in which he likened their tickets to pieces of paper fit only for the material usage.

Two violinists, one cellist, a couple of horn players, the Levy brothers, and several singers took part in this very doubtful artistic enterprise, Chopin himself being cast in the role of "incidental piano-player" amid a tutti-frutti of mediocrity. Writing in his diary a few days beforehand, Chopin was obviously under no illusion: "The posters and newspapers have announced my concert, which is due to take place in two days time. And it is as much a matter of indifference to me as if it were never to be given."

The concert attracted only a thin audience, and the receipts did not cover expenses. From a notice in the *Allegemeine Musik Zeitung*, the following September, it is clear that on this occasion Chopin played the Concerto in E minor. Although the opinion given was somewhat more reserved than that accorded by the same paper to the Concerto in F

An old friend of Elsner's to whom the latter had given him the warmest recommendation.

minor when Chopin played it the previous year, he never-theless expressed himself as satisfied with it.

After waiting for eight months, a notice that reads: "This is a serious composition which can only confirm our previous judgment. A musician who shows such sincerity in the exercise of his art is in return worthy of our highest esteem," can only be considered, taking it as a whole, to be a pitiful result. So far as composition is concerned, he did nothing but edit a few Waltzes and Mazurkas and make a rough draft of a Concerto for two pianos, which was abandoned almost as soon as begun. The basic material was eventually to be incorporated in the Allegro de Concert. A draft of a series of Variations for piano and violin on a theme by Beethoven was also to remain nothing more than a sketch.

Each day brought more alarming news of threats to the liberty of his country and to his family's safety; a tragic reality, which an artificial social gaiety, as empty of artistic meaning as it was bereft of material benefit, did nothing to hide. In truth, it was a time of confusion and loneliness for Chopin. Vienna had offered nothing but a useless and disheartening experience, which had lasted only too long. He awoke to the fact that it was high time to shake off this stultification of his musical faculties.

The making of any decision was always extremely burden-some to him, but, though it meant a great effort, he made up his mind to venture into the unknown and resume his travels.

After obtaining the necessary passport, though not with-out difficulty, to take him to London "by way of Paris"—a journey destined to last eighteen years—Chopin left Vienna on July 20, 1831. He proceeded by stages via Linz and Salzburg to Munich. According to Karazowski, it was here, on August 28, that he played the E minor Concerto at the

Philharmonic Concert, "rousing his audience to enthusiasm by the beauty of the work as well as by the poetic quality of his playing."

A single sentence in a letter to Titus, written from Paris on December 16, is the only confirmation Chopin gives of this performance: "I played the Concerto in E minor, that the people in the Bavarian capital liked so much, to Kalkbrenner."

Karazowski's opinion is fully confirmed, however, by an extract from the newspaper *Flora* of August 30: "M. Chopin played a Concerto in E minor of his own composition and gave evidence of a remarkable virtuosity. In addition to a highly developed technique, great appreciation was felt for his enchanting delicacy of touch and an equal admiration for the expressive rendering of the main themes of his work.

"As for the work itself, it is on the whole brilliant and correctly written, though it does not pretend to exceptional originality or depth, with the exception of the Rondo, of which the main themes, as well as the way in which the central episode is treated, have a singular charm, which springs from a curious mixture of melancholy and fancifulness."

The Concerto was conducted by the Swiss composer, Stuntz; as for the rest, it was another of those concerts made up of miscellaneous items, several artists, four singers, and a clarinetist among them.

The anonymous editor of the periodical intended, judging by its title, for the ladies, was one of the first of Chopin's critics to make pertinent comments on the individuality of his musical style. He was able to discount the highly ornamental writing for the piano demanded by the period and appreciate the exceptional quality and value of this blending of a dreamy sensitivity and a lively fancy with which the young Polish composer invested the popular rhythms of his country.

Apart from this notice, the concert received no publicity whatever, and brought Chopin's career as a concert pianist in Austria and Germany to an end. If we include the incidental adventure in Breslau, he had made a total of five appearances.

He gave no concerts on his flying visits to Aix-la-Chapelle, Dresden, Leipzig, Carlsbad, and Heidelberg and played only to a circle of his intimate friends. Before reaching France he made a short visit to Stuttgart, and while he gave no performances, it was there he received news of the Polish disaster, which stirred him to give vent to his outraged feelings in the Revolutionary Etude.

After his arrival in Paris, toward the middle of September, he came into contact with a better informed and more enterprising musical milieu. Here the hesitation, even fear, he had exhibited for almost a whole year at the possibility of appearing before the public, suddenly gave place to the making of plans for the future.

Lighthearted, self-confident, he informs Titus that his first concert has been arranged for December 25. In his eyes the fixing of his first appearance for Christmas Day must have been a most favorable omen. "Baillot, Paganini's famous rival, and Brod, the celebrated oboist, will be taking part in it and I shall play my F minor and the Variations in B flat major. With Kalkbrenner I shall also play his March for two pianos, accompanied by four other pianos, followed by a Polonaise. It is quite mad. One of the two pianos is an enormous Pantaléon (last trace of the Warsaw vocabulary!) which goes by right to Kalkbrenner; the other is a little single-string piano, which carries quite a long way all the same, like a lot of little bells on the neck of a giraffe—and that one is mine. As for the four others, they are large and act as an orchestra. They will be played by Hiller, Osborne, Stamaty, and Sawinski.

"Mosblin, Vidal, and the celebrated Uhran—who is a cellist such as I have never heard before—are also helping me. The tickets are selling, but the most difficult thing is to get singers. Rossini would have done what he could for me at the Opera, if he had not feared a refusal from the Deputy Director and so on."

The names of these celebrated artists—who were regarded in Warsaw as demigods hidden in clouds of glory—are men' tioned with an air of innocent pride, with the familiarity of one who already belongs to a select circle. Circumstances have changed for him. He has at last reached that spiritual climate best suited to his most ardent aspirations. A new life is beginning full of hope and rich in opportunity. We can share his pleasure.

During these first weeks in Paris, everything is a matter for wonderment: "Herz, Liszt, and Hiller are mere no' bodies compared with Kalkbrenner."

La Malibran is the "wonder of wonders," *Robert le Diable,* the "masterpiece of a new school," and he finds the singing of its interpreter, Mme. Centi Damoreau, "even better than La Malibran's." At the Opéra Comique, Chollet, known as Dome-Chollet, "showed himself to be a genius." Pleyel's pianos are *ne plus ultra.* Everything comes in for a share of his ecstatic eulogy.

In the midst of this happiness he confides to his old teacher, Elsner—who advised him to persevere with his composition above all else—that he longs to be able to add the recognition of his talent as a pianist to his reputation as a composer. He feels that there is a wide field open for one who could be simultaneously "author and actor."

Chopin's essential disposition has, for the moment at least, certainly undergone a change. His courage, that so cruelly deserted him in Vienna, has returned in full force. He exults in it. Without a trace of modesty he declares his ambition to be nothing less than to be "among the best known virtuosi of the piano," nor does he hesitate to add: "I met no one in Germany who could teach me anything as an instrumentalist."

Unexpected though this is, in view of the fact that only a short time before he appeared to reject the obligations involved, it is clear that he intended to stick to the career of concert artist.

However, the "Soirée Musicale" announced for Christmas Day had to be put off till January 15, 1832. A well known singer, whose assistance appeared to him to be essential for the success of his first concert, could not be obtained for the earlier date. Kalkbrenner became indisposed, and in its turn January 15 was given up. It was not until February 26 that Chopin at last made his appearance in Pleyel's concert rooms. Three celebrities from the Opéra, Mlles. Isambert, and Toméoni and M. Boulanger, and not the well known singer, as had originally been planned, came to add their talents as vocalists to the list of artists already mentioned.

In spite of this imposing programme, the expenses were in excess of the receipts. The audience was largely Polish. For the most part the French came by invitation. At that date the concert hall was capable of accommodating only about three hundred and left no effective margin for profit. But the impression made by Chopin's playing on a number of important musical celebrities, Mendelssohn and Liszt among them, who had been invited for the occasion, appears to have been in the nature of a revelation.

In the *Revue Musicale* of March 3, 1832, in a particularly comprehensive article, Fétis underlines the exceptional character of this concert. It gave an opportunity to a young artist, for whom we can find no model from whom he might have derived his inspiration, of "exhibiting, if not an entirely original method of piano playing, one which shows, at least, a wholly new manner of personal expression. It makes use of a number of ideas that are completely original, to which it is impossible to find anything similar in other works."

He follows this up by drawing an ingenious parallel between the music Beethoven wrote "for the piano" and that written by Chopin "for pianists," concluding by saying: "Form is renewed in the inspiration of M. Chopin. It will without doubt exercise a profound influence on all future works written for this instrument." A prophecy confirmed by the future.

Fétis describes his playing as being elegant, full of charm and grace. His sparkling precision comes in for equal praise. But—and this is a remark that could have come as no surprise to Chopin—"the volume of tone he extracts from the piano is very small."

Hiller affirms that there was no one in the hall who did not go into ecstasies over such an absolutely perfect technique. Liszt, recalling his glorious rival's debut in Paris, was to record: "I remember his first appearance in the Pleyel rooms. The most resounding applause seemed inadequate to express our enchantment with this talent that revealed a new phase of poetic sentiment and such charming innovations in the form of his art."

On May 20 in the same year he took part in a concert organized by the Prince de la Moskowa in aid of the poor, and thus had an opportunity of consolidating his success in the eyes of the public. On this occasion he played the first movement of the Concerto he had played in February, a choice prompted, no doubt, by a "special request." This time, however, Fétis, a stickler for the facts, mentions that his success was less striking. He attributes this to the fact that the instrument Chopin used had a rather heavy touch and restates his former opinion, all too familiar to us from other reviews of Chopin's concerts, that "the volume of tone he extracts from the piano is very small." "However," he continues, on a cautionary note that was absent from his previous article, "there can be no doubt that this artist's music is sure to gain ground in public opinion as it become better known."

The hero of the evening appears to have been Brod, the oboist, who received an ovation. The public, less critical than at Pleyel's, seem to have regarded music as an incidental item in this philanthropic effort.

During the preparations for his debut, all Chopin's inhibitions and anxieties had been cast into the background. But with the doubtful reception accorded his second appearance in Paris they returned unabated. Once more he became disheartened and considered leaving for America or returning to Warsaw.

By accident, by a chance meeting on a street corner with Prince Valentin Radziwill, his plans were changed. The necessity for courting an uncertain public, which he found abhorrent, and against which the very nature of his genius seemed to raise an almost insuperable barrier, was removed. Chopin's musical activities were turned toward the realms of high finance and the aristocracy.

An evening party at the house of Baron de Rothschild determined the direction which Chopin's career as a pianist was to take. He became their especial favorite, assured of all the attendant privileges.

Once more Chopin's life in Paris followed, so far at least as appearances went, the habits he had formed in Vienna: a domestic life by day with social visits of an evening. A love of idleness, formed by overwhelmingly boring months of inaction in Austria, was to some extent defeated by his new and remunerative activities as a teacher and by the society in which he moved.

He was still subject to periodic attacks of melancholia, and the letters to Titus are full of descriptions of his distressing symptoms. But, on the whole, his outlook was brighter than in Vienna, material cares receded into the background and his growing fame became assured within a circle which had completely succumbed to him.

His first two concerts had been an almost inescapable necessity, but now instead of having to enlist the support of patrons, he was in the position of being able to lend his patronage to others and to take a more appreciative view of the opportunities to appear in public that came his way, which formerly had aroused in him an instinctive hostility.

In company with Liszt, he took part in a concert given by Hiller on December 15, 1832. The three artists played an Allegro from Bach's Concerto for three pianos with, to quote a contemporary critic, "a rare appreciation of its character and a perfect delicacy in the treatment of its subleties."

Performing during the intervals in a play given for the benefit of Miss Smithson, the English actress, shortly to become the wife of Berlioz and immortalized by him in the *Symphonie Fantastique,* Chopin again appeared with Liszt. In April, 1833, still in association with Liszt, we find him lending his support to the brothers Jacques and Henri Herz by taking part in a performance of a *pièce d'occasion* for eight hands on two pianos.

His fellow pianists had come to regard him as a public draw, and the importance they attached to being able to announce his name as a performer at concerts, given under their auspicies or for their benefit led to other invitations coming his way.

Amédé de Méreaux, the erudite composer of works for the French clavecinists, asked him on two successive occasions during the same year to join him in a duet based on themes from Pré-aux-Clercs.

His name alone was sufficient to guarantee the success of a great reception given at about the same date in the house of Maréchal Lannes.

In short, now that he was known far beyond the confines of drawing rooms, he took his place, during the winter of 1832-33, among those artists in the pubic eye who, to quote the Paris correspondent of the *Allegemeine Musik Zeitung*, "hold the ear of the public and often charm it."

It was during the course of the next two seasons that Chopin really found himself as a pianist-virtuoso. His public appearances reached a climax with a memorable performance with the Société des Concerts du Conservatoire on April 26, 1835, which set the seal of public approval on his art for all time.

He played the Andante from his F minor Concerto at the last of the concerts to be organized by Berlioz on December, 7, 1834. Appearing among such extrovert works as the overtures to *King Lear* and the *Francs-Juges,* it is hardly surprising that the introspective melancholy of the Andante met with a chilly reception. On the 28th of the same month he appeared once more with Liszt in a Matinée Musicale at Pleyel's, organized by a Dr. Stoepel.

The two young masters played a *grande duo* for four hands by Moscheles and a similar piece by Liszt on a theme of Mendelssohn's. Their playing received the unanimous applause of critics and public. In an article devoted to the concert by the *Gazette Musicale* we find the following: "It is superfluous to add that these pieces were executed with unusual perfection and most polished artistry by the two great virtuosi of our time. The effectiveness of their playing combines the utmost delicacy with an extraordinary spirituality. The contrast between vivacity and absolute calm, between ethereal lightness and affecting gravity, the true value of every shade of meaning, all were given with a perfection only to be expected from two perfectly matched artists fired with the same deep feeling for their art."

It is not without interest to compare his panegyric with an impression of Chopin's playing given by Mendelssohn, at about this time, in a letter to his mother. "The foremost pianist today," he writes, "is Chopin. His playing provides us with as many surprises as we find under the bow of Paganini. Hiller is also a virtuoso full of power and grace. Unfortunately they both have a mania, so common in Paris, of posing as though they were in a state of utter despair. They exaggerate the emotional content, so time and rhythm suffer accordingly. But, as I for my part, tend to go to the opposite extreme, the result is that we are complementary to one another. While they play the top and dandy, I wear the guise of pedantry."

Of all the criticism devoted to Chopin's playing during his lifetime, that dealing with his personal mannerisms is the least apposite, failing as it does to take into consideration Chopin's highly personal style. Although Mendelssohn puts

Chopin among the greatest artists of the day, his commentary is hardly what one would have expected. On the other hand, we should consider this in the light of Chopin's opinion of Mendelssohn's countrymen: "These Germans are terrible people; they know nothing at all about music." Both points of view are exaggerated, which is so often the case with those who approach aesthetic problems from opposite directions.

On February 25, 1835, we find Chopin appearing at Erard's with Hiller, playing the latter's latest composition, a duet for two pianos.

Again on March 25, at Pleyel's his name is associated with those of Herz, Hiller, Osborne, Reicha, and Mmes. Camille Lambert and Leroy in a performance which, though little more than a display of pyrotechnics rather than of any artistic value, gave a certain cachet to the first performance of a Concerto Op. 2 by the young composer, Stamaty.

A concert in aid of some Polish refugees at the Théâtre Italien on April 5 was made the occasion for the first performance of his E minor Concerto under the direction of Habeneck and at this same concert he joined Liszt in a performance of Hiller's duet for two pianos.

Mlle. Falcon, the famous singer Nourrit, and the well known flutist Dorus, were also associated with this effort to raise funds for a cause that was very dear to Chopin's heart, the press referring to it as "this brilliant occasion arranged for the purpose of mitigating the misfortunes of his fellow countrymen."

Reporting the performance of the Concerto, the *Gazette Musicale* expressed itself in the following terms: "The Concerto by Chopin, so original in its conception, so full of unusual detail and soaring themes, had a great success. It is,

in truth, very difficult to avoid monotony in a piano concerto. While amateurs should be thankful to Chopin for
the pleasure he gave them, artists can only admire the skill
with which he avoided pitfalls and put new life into a
form which has fallen into disuse."

For the first time there is no adverse comment on Chopin's
playing. It should not be supposed, however, that he was
satisfied with this result, obtained in a larger hall and before
a bigger audience than he had hitherto been accustomed to
in Paris. Another member of the audience had not been afraid
to refer to it as a "half-success," and added that the more
general attitude of coolness, almost hostility, on the part of
the audience had been counteracted only by the applause
of the *avant garde* and of the composer's friends.

This fresh disappointment did nothing to lessen Chopin's
distaste for public concerts, particularly those involving an
orchestra, which he had evidenced ever since his debut in
Vienna.

Once again his personal style of expression, so much in
favor with the intelligent few, had failed to make an impression on a public with preconceived ideas as to what
constituted piano playing. It was incapable of seeing this subtle
and delicate art, which has never been surpassed, in its proper
perspective.

The memory of this unfortunate event was to some extent
dispelled by the reception he received on his last appearance
that year.

On Sunday, April 26, he took part in an afternoon concert
given by the Société des Concerts du Conservatoire under
the direction of Habeneck, whose benefit it was. Aided by
the incomparable acoustics of that famous hall he played the

Polonaise Brilliante, preceded by an Andante Spianato, which was to be published the following year as Op. 22.*'

MM. *les Membres du Comité de
la Société des Concerts.*

Sirs,
    I am anxious to have the honor of appearing at one of your excellent concerts. In default of any other title to the granting of my request, I rely on your generous attitude toward soloists. I dare to hope that perhaps you will regard my petition favorably.
    I have the honour to be, Sirs, your most humble and obedient servant,

Signed: FREDERIC CHOPIN.
Cité Bergére, No. 4.

Instead of a collection of virtuosi got together for publicity purposes and devoid of any real artistic value, this program, following the tradition of the famous body sponsoring it, was aimed at purely musical ends.

The concert was devoted to works by Beethoven, Schubert, and Chopin. The orchestral items included Beethoven's Pastoral Symphony, the Scherzo from the Ninth, and the Finale from the C minor. Mlle. Falcon sang Beethoven's *Ah ! perfide,* and Adolphe Nourrit, her famous partner at the Opéra and Schubert's most active propagandist in France, the Ballade from *Roi des Aulnes.* The place of honor, in the middle of the program, was Chopin's.

Although not called on to play a large scale work such as

It is not without interest to note that Chopin had tried since 1832 to get his name included in one of the programs given by the famous Société. This is borne out by a letter to be found in the brief, but well documented historical survey of the Society by M. Jean Cordey. Patronage by this august body was considered a high honor, especially for a newcomer to Paris.

a Concerto, on this occasion Chopin's playing left an indelible impression with his audience. The dreamy Andante
forming an introduction to the work, unaccompanied by the
orchestra, showed Chopin's unsurpassed delicacy of style to
full advantage, an intimate style never heard at its best when
competing with the full throated voice of the orchestra.

As a boy, Gustave Chouquet, subsequently director of the
Musée du Conservatoire, had the good fortune to hear Chopin
on this occasion and to compare him with Liszt, who appeared at the same hall and with the same orchestra a few
days later. A letter giving his impressions is published in
an important biographical study of Chopin by Professor
Niecks.

After praising Liszt's proud and soldierlike rendering of
Weber's *Koncertstük,* he compared it with the "ineffable
poetry" of Chopin's performance.

Following up this parallel, he writes: "In 1835 Liszt
was the perfect prototype of a virtuoso. He made the most
of every effect, as if he were a Paganini of the piano. Chopin,
on the other hand, communed with voices within himself
and never appeared to notice his audience. He was not always in form, but when in the mood he played as one inspired and made the piano sing in an ineffable style." The
word "ineffable," repeated by the writer of this letter, is,
perhaps, the most apt adjective to describe the impression
left in the listener's memory by Chopin's playing on that
day. My old teacher, Emile Decombes, a mine of information
on matters concerning the Polish master, often described for
me this characteristic of Chopin's playing, this passing beyond the bounds of music, in exactly the same terms and
with the same word, "ineffable."

The only audience in Paris at that time with sufficient

musical intelligence to appreciate him, had revenged Chopin for the indifferent reception accorded to him a month previously. One would have thought that this would have fired Chopin with the ambition to repeat his success. On the contrary, until 1841, that is to say for more than six years, with the exception of a single appearance in Rouen, and at a concert given by Ch. Valentin Alkan, he consistently refused to appear on the concert platform or before a paying audience. During his short stay in London, from July 11 to 22, 1837, he was so anxious to preserve his incognito that he consented to play at a private evening party given by Broadwood, the piano manufacturer, only under an assumed name.

Though, during these long years, he was lost to the world of music as a concert artist, it gained the more from his genius as a composer. Twenty masterpieces of incomparable quality, played solely to a small and select circle by the composer, set a seal on this period.

This divine gift, which an inattentive public was unable to assess at its true value, in due time, and in the way best suited to it, was to be bequeathed to coming generations of musicians and music lovers.

It is music of a kind that seeks no other contact than that of a delicate receptivity, it needs no other atmosphere than that of a refined sensitivity. One might, perhaps, describe the moment when Chopin definitely deserted the concert hall as being the "royal moment" in his life as an artist. No longer was there any necessity for him to meet, to surprise, or to vanquish an ignorant audience. From now on his fame as a composer was to shine with a glory far greater than that which he had gained as a pianist. For the future it will be for others, better equipped for the battle against the difficulties inherent in the career of a virtuoso and inspired by the ideals of which he has made them the guardians, to spread this glory among the hearts of mankind.

In his stead, a vast army of pianists has transmitted his message, a message inspired by an unceasing poetic invention, to the far corners of the globe.

The secrets of this musical revelation, which was a closed book to all but a few marveling initiates, have been re-created in the imagination of all those pianists who feel called upon to act as his interpreter.

This ideal, the result of so much research, may be larger than life. Perhaps our dreams of Chopin's playing are greater than the Chopin who lived.

But in the last resort it is of little consequence, since this fabulous idolatry has given birth to an idealized craving for perfection that can only help to make the playing of his work and the interpretation of his thought more sensitive and more convincing.

It has been suggested by certain of Chopin's biographers that his retirement from the concert hall, during the period of which we are speaking, was not as complete as is generally supposed. A note in the *Gazette Musicale* of October 18, 1835 would appear to confirm this: "One of the most famous pianists of the day, M. Chopin, has just returned to Paris after a trip to Germany, which took him in turn to Carlsbad, Dresden, Leipzig, and Heidleberg. He was continuously greeted with ovations. Everywhere his wonderful talent aroused the most flattering enthusiasm."

One must admit that the tone of this paragraph, inspired by Schlesinger, the editor of the paper, may have misled some commentators. But, in point of fact, the truth is quite otherwise. Toward the end of July, 1835, Chopin went to Carlsbad to meet his father, who had been sent, by his doctors in Warsaw, to take the cure at this celebrated spa. Since he had been an exile and deprived of all direct contact with his family for the past five years, Chopin, prompted by filial affection, visited him.

From there he journeyed to Marienbad as the guest of some old Polish friends, the Wodzinski family, and later tra' veled with them as far as Dresden, which became the scene of that innocent love affair, immortalized in the waltz *Les Adieux*. Then, at the beginning of October he went to Leipzig.

According to Schumann, he spent only a few hours there, but since he found time to play his most recent compositions to some fellow artists, Mendelssohn, Schumann, Clara Wieck, and her father, the learned teacher, among them, it was more probably two or three days.

Apart from the Concerto in E minor, Chopin played several unpublished works to his astonished listeners, the Bal' lades in F and G, a new Nocturne (probably Op. 27, No. 2 which had just been completed) and the Etudes from Op. 25.

There can be no question of anything other than some private performances, given in the homes of Hensel and the excellent pianist, Henriette Voigt, who put them at his disposal.

It was the memory of Chopin's playing of the Etudes, as well as the miraculous fashion in which the notes seemed to vanish into thin air from beneath his fingers, that fired Schumann to make his enthusiastic commentary.

The itinerary of Chopin's journey was solely determined by feelings of love and affection for his family and friends. One can only assume that the *Gazette Musicale* has mis' represented his intentions, turning them into "M. Chopin's concert tour" for publicity purposes.

The same applies to the report which also appeared in the

Gazette Musicale on February 25, 1838. It gives an account of a reception at the Court of St. Cloud, to which Chopin had been summoned, informing its readers that "this pianist, as remarkable as he is modest," had just made his appear' ance among an "intimate circle," and that his astounding improvisations were the most important item in the evening's entertainment, astonishing all those who heard them. The audience who had had the honor of being invited were per' sons of the most cultivated taste.

When we consider that Chopin, after playing some of his Preludes and Nocturnes, was asked to extemporize on themes from Grisar's, then popular romance *La Folle,* the "cultivated taste" of this august assembly becomes slightly suspect.

It did not fall to him alone to assure the success of the evening and to be honored with the praises of the royal family. The Andante of a Sonata for four hands by Moscheles, played by Chopin and the composer, was encored, thus giving the latter a share in this "spectacular success."

At the conclusion of the performance, Chopin was presented with an enamel bowl and Moscheles received a traveling bag. Chopin referred to this somewhat maliciously, as being symbolic of "the King's evident desire to be rid of Moscheles as quickly as possible."

A week later he took a minor part in a benefit concert given by Ch. Valentin Alkan by playing in a transcription of Beethoven's Symphony in D for two pianos, eight hands, the other painists being Zimmerman, Gutman, and the arranger, Alkan.

Writing on a concert given at Rouen a few days later, for the benefit of Chopin's fellow countryman, Orlowski, Legouvé gives us an article of such documentary interest as to deserve quoting in its entirety:

This event is not without significance in the world of music. Chopin, who has retired from playing in public for some years past, Chopin who confines his fascinating genius to an audience of five or six, Chopin who resembles those enchanted islands on which so few here set foot, who recount such marvels that they are accused of falsehood, Chopin whom one can never forget once having heard him, Chopin has just given a magnificent concert before an audience of five hundred, for the benefit of a Polish professor.

And indeed! his success was immense! immense! All those ravishing melodies, that ineffable delicacy of touch, that melancholy and passionate inspira-tion, the poetry of execution and composition, which grips both the imagination and the heart, penetrated, stirred, enraptured all five hundred listeners, as they do the five or six chosen ones who form his audience and religiously attend to him for hours on end. The atmosphere was electric, murmurs of ecstasy and wonder filled the hall, which are the applause of the soul.

On, Chopin, on! let this triumph persuade you; no longer be such an individualist, let all share your exquisite talent; settle for ever the great dispute between the artists; and when anyone asks who is the premier pianist in Europe, Liszt or Thalberg, let all the world be able to answer, as well as those who have heard you play; it is Chopin.

Once again it is the pianist and not the composer who causes this panegyric. It was a period in which the performer was held in as high esteem as the creator, indeed, if not higher. The works of the pianist-composer were regarded solely as vehicles for flights of virtuosity whereby he achieved a popular success.

Legouvé's reference to "the great debate that divides all artists" should be emphasized. Professionals were arguing whether the exquisite talent of Thalberg or the thunderous genius of Liszt was higher in the public's estimation. Liszt, sensing that his artistic throne was in danger, returned to Paris at once to defend it against the triumphs of his brilliant rival. Controversy raged back and forth in the press and in the musical world, so much so, that Legouvé's judgment of Solomon can only be regarded as the highest compliment.

But neither Legouvé's compliments nor his warm welcome at St. Cloud nor his triumph at the Conservatoire were sufficient to enable Chopin to overcome his instinctive loathing of the concert platform. It was not until three years later, about the spring of 1841, that Chopin decided to break his silence and appear once more before the public of Paris. In those three years his mode of life had changed. They marked the beginning of his affair with George Sand, the visit to Majorca, the long summers at Nohant, the home-making in Orléans Square, and the daily meetings with a whole group of writers and artists. Gradually this more informal way of life produced a change in the general atmosphere surrounding Chopin's work.

For those who subscribe to the theory of dividing Beethoven's career into three periods, this change may be said to mark the beginning of the second stage in the development of Chopin's style.

It was a period of intense creative activity producing many important works which were first performed to a circle of listeners less exclusively aristocratic than formerly.

The intimate, almost jealous atmosphere surrounding Chopin's first performances was still preserved, however, and we find George Sand, in a letter of 1840, admitting that there can be no further question of Chopin compromising his genius by submitting it to the judgment of an ignorant public.

It was some months after this, April 26, 1841, to be precise, that Chopin decided to break his silence and give a concert at Pleyel's. He would appear without an orchestra, not as one of a collection of well known pianists, but as a soloist, introducing an important group of his recent compositions, the Ballade Op. 38, the Polonaise Op. 40, the four Mazurkas from Op. 41, and the second Scherzo Op. 39, a group to which he added, so Liszt tells us, some Etudes, Preludes, and Nocturnes.

This performance, at which Mme. Damoreau-Cinti and the violinist, Einst, promised to appear, brought the cream of Parisian society to the Rue Rochechouart.

Having returned from a triumphal tour abroad, Liszt was staying in Paris before embarking on another, and suggested that he report this concert. Over his signature, the *Gazette Musicale,* on May 2, published the following article:

> On Monday last at eight o'clock M. Pleyel's rooms were brilliantly lit; the most elegant women, the most celebrated artists, the richest financiers, the most distinguished men, in fact the entire galaxy of birth, fortune, talent, and beauty arrived in a never-ending stream of carriages at the foot of a staircase which was covered with rugs and sweet-scented flowers.
>
> A grand piano stood open on the platform, everyone sought the nearest seats and settled down to

listen, telling themselves in advance that they must not miss a chord, a note, a suggestion, a thought that might fall from him who was to play. They were right to be so eager, attentive to the point of worship, for he whom they awaited, whom they were so desirous of hearing, admiring, applauding was not merely a skilled virtuoso, a pianist who was a master of the keyboard, not only an artist of renown, he was someone far beyond all this—they awaited Chopin!

Coming to France some ten years ago, Chopin, amid the crowd of pianists which at this period arrived from all over the world, did not struggle for first or second place. He performed very seldom in public, the poetic character of his talent did not show to great advantage in such surroundings. Like flowers which only open their sweet-smelling blossoms at nightfall, he needed an atmosphere of peace and retirement to express freely the wealth of melody he had within him. Music was his language: a divine language by means of which he expressed a whole range of feelings which could be appreciated only by the few. The music of his homeland sang to him the songs and sad lays of Poland, lending to his art some strange and mysterious poetry, which, for those who have taken it to their hearts, is incomparable.

If less fame attaches to his name, if an aureole less bright surrounds his brow, it is because his energy of thought or depth of feeling was less than that of his friend and fellow countryman, Mickiewicz, the famous author of *Konrad Wallenrod* and *Les Pélerins,* but because of the limitations of his mode of expression and the imperfections of his instrument; he could not with the aid of a mere piano unburden his soul to the full.

It was the origin, if we are not mistaken, of his reluctance to allow his innermost thoughts to become public property. As we have seen it was only rarely that Chopin performed in public. For any other artist that would almost certainly have resulted in obscurity and oblivion, but in his case it assured him of a reputation rising superior to the caprices of fashion, sheltering him from all injustice, jealousy, and rivalry.

For several years past artists from all parts of the globe have been following one another in the desperate scramble for public acclaim. Chopin, standing aloof from this hurly-burly, surrounded by faithful followers, enthusiastic pupils and warm-hearted friends, all of whom, while protecting him from irritating struggles and painful rebuffs, have never stopped circulating his works, their admiration of his genius, and respect for his name.

This refined and delicate artist has remained undisturbed by any attack. Criticism is silent, as though posterity had already delivered judgment; and among the audience which came to greet the poet who has remained silent for too long, there was no reticence, no restraint, praise was on every tongue.

We will not undertake a detailed analysis of Chopin's compositions here. Without an affected striving for orginality, he has expressed his personality both in his style and in his ideas.

For new ideas he has adopted a new style. The hint of a wild and fiery nature, which is a part of his inheritance, finds expression in strange harmonies and deliberate discords, while all his delicacy and grace is shown in a thousand touches, the thousand tiny details of an incomparable fantasy.

At Monday's concert, Chopin had specially selected those of his works most remote from classic forms. Instead of the Concerto, Sonata, Fantaisie, or Variations he played Preludes, Etudes, Nocturnes, and Mazurkas. He was playing to his own intimate circle rather than to the public and was able to show himself for what he really is, an elegiac poet and a dreamer. He had no need to startle or grip his audience; he was playing in an atmosphere of quiet understanding, not one of boisterous enthusiasm. From the striking of the first chords a bond of closest sympathy was established between the artist and his audience. Two Etudes and a Ballade were encored and, had it not been for the fear of adding to the fatigue already visible on his pale face, the audience would have encored every item on the program.

Chopin's Preludes are in a category by themselves. They are not solely, as their title would lead one to suppose, items intended to be played by way of introduction to other items, they are poetic preludes, similar to those of the great poet Lamartine, which bathe the soul in golden dreams and lift it to the realms of the ideal. Admirable in their variety, the work and skill that has gone into their composition is not obvious until after a careful examination. Every note seems to be utterly spontaneous and inspired. They have the great attractiveness which is to be found in all works of genius. And what is to be said of the Mazurkas, those little masterpieces so full of caprice and yet so polished?

Chopin used to say, when referring to this article which shows such a clear understanding of the composer's char-acter and such a generous artistic appreciation: "Oh yes, Liszt has thought fit to find me a place in his kingdom." His sarcasm does not seem to be justified.

In *La France Musicale*, also of May 2, an anonymous

critic, certainly of less authority than Liszt, nonetheless expresses himself in very similar terms.

After comparing Chopin to Schubert, he goes on to make the following illuminating statement: "I have referred to Schubert because there is no other composer with so complete an affinity with Chopin. What one has done for the voice the other has done for the piano." When we consider how highy Schubert valued the precious combination of spontaneity and emotion, we have to admit the strength of the argument. Having made the comparison, he goes on to add: "Chopin is a pianist of assurance. He composes for himself and plays for himself. Listen to him as he dreams, as he weeps, as he sings, with tenderness, gentleness, and melancholy; how perfectly he expresses every feeling, however delicate, however lofty! Chopin is the pianist of pianists.

"One can say that Chopin is the creator of a school of pianists and a school of composers. Nothing equals the lightness, the delicacy, with which this artist touches the keys. His compositions—so full of originality, of distinction, of grace—are unparalleled. Chopin is unmatched as a pianist and must not, indeed cannot, be compared to any other."

The tone of these articles, which for once had referred to his lightness of touch and delicate tone in order to praise them as being in character with his music, together with the enthusiastic reception he had met with, encouraged Chopin to repeat his concert during the following season.

Supported by Pauline Viardot and Auguste Franchomme, this project was realized on February 21, 1842, by a *soirée musical*, given once again at Pleyel's. Pauline Viardot, la Malibran's sister, was accompanied by Chopin, and received three encores for her singing of songs by Dessauer and Handel and piece called *Le Chêne et le Roseau* by an unknown composer. As for the cellist, Franchomme, no record has survived of the works he played. Chopin's program consisted of three Mazurkas, the Ballade in A flat, three Etudes from Op. 25, four Nocturnes, including No. 2 in F sharp minor from Op. 48, the Prelude in D flat major, and the Impromptu Op. 51.

The report in *La France Musicale* stresses the social character of the gathering rather than its artistic significance: "Chopin gave a charming evening, a party adorned with sweet smiles, with pink and delicate complextions, with tiny, prettily shaped white hands; a magnificent event at which simplicity was accompanied by grace and elegance—a lavish display in in perfect taste. The golden ribbons, the soft blue muslins, the chaplets of gleaming pearls, the freshest of roses and mignonettes in a thousand different shades, so beautiful, so gay, met and crossed one another as the perfumed heads and gleaming shoulders of lovely women, whose presence the drawing rooms of princes compete for, moved to and fro."

Whatever satisfaction Chopin may have derived from reading this flattering description of the decorations and the ladies' dresses, it is nevertheless probable that he would have perferred to read, even from Liszt's pen, some comments less strictly confined to the merits of the fashion designers and dressmakers.

These concerts merely caused Chopin to relapse into that state of *à quoibonisme* with which he was all too familiar. It was not until six years later, when the break with George Sand was complete and on the eve of his adventure in England, that he made an attempt to deal with his more pressing financial commitments and decided to seek the support of the Paris public.

For this, his last appearance in Paris, he decided on a more popular program, including the singer Antonia Molina di Mondi, the tenor Roger, who was to sing a new song from *Robert le Diable,* Allard the violinist, and his friend Franchomme, who was to join him in playing the three final movements from the Sonata for cello and piano—the first movement having been withdrawn by Chopin at the last moment with the excuse that some alterations were necessary. Chopin also reserved the first performance of a number of recent works for this occasion.

The program was performed in the following order on February 16, 1848, in "one of the concert rooms of MM. Pleyel et Cie, 20 rue Rochechouart at half past eight o'clock."

First Part

Trio de Mozart, executé par M.M. Chopin, Allard, et Franchomme.

Air, chanté par Mlle. Molina di Mondi.

Nocturne et Barcarolle, composés et executés par M. Chopin.

Air, chanté par Mlle. Molina di Mondi.

Etudes et Berceuse, composés et executés par M. Chopin.

Second Part

Scherzo, Adagio et Finale de la Sonate en sol mineur pour piano et violoncelle, composés par M. Chopin et executés par l'anteur et M. Franchomme.

Air nouveau de Robert le Diable, composé par M. Meyerbeer, chanté par M. Roger.

Preludes, Mazurkas, et Valses, composés et executés par M. Chopin.

His family had been told of the proposed concert in the following letter, which is still almost that of a child:

My thoughts are occupied with my concert, which is to take place on the sixteenth of this month. My friends came to me one morning and told me I ought to give a concert—that I had nothing to worry about execpt to sit down and play. There haven't been any tickets left on sale for a week past and they were all twenty francs apiece. The public is subscribing already for a second concert (which I have no thought of giving). The court has bought forty tickets, and in spite of the fact that the press has only announced that I "may" give a concert, letters have come in from Brest and Nantes to my publisher reserving seats.

Such excitement surprises me, and now comes the question of playing, which I only do to satisfy my conscience, for it seems to me that I play worse than ever.

I shall play a Mozart trio with Allard and Franchomme. There won't be any posters or any free tickets. The hall is well decorated and can hold three hundred. Pleyel teases me all the time about my stupidity and in order to encourage me to play he is going to decorate the staircase with flowers. It will be almost as if I were home, and I expect my eyes will encounter those of my friends everywhere. I have already got the piano I am going to play on at home.

The house of Pleyel has religiously preserved this piano to this very day, and many years ago, at a concert dedicated to the memory of the Polish master, I had the very great privilege of playing those very same works on that instrument which had known the revelation given by the imprint of his inspired fingers.

The delirious phrases used by the critic of the *Gazette Musicale* in his report of February 20 help us to imagine what Chopin's last concert in Paris was like.

A concert by the Ariel of pianists is too rare an event for the doors to be flung open to the world at large. Although the whole of society signed the subscription list, no one was certain of getting one of those precious tickets. Although the offering required was a louis, it was still necessary to have an introduction to obtain entry to this Holy of Holies, for when it is a case of listening to Chopin everyone has a spare louis in his pocket.

The natural result of all this was that on Wednesday Pleyel's rooms were filled with the flower of the aristocracy, with the most distinguished ladies in the land clad in their most elegant dresses.

Also there were leaders of the world of art and the connoisseurs, delighted to be able to catch this musical sylph on the wing. He had promised that they should be allowed to come near him to see and hear him for several hours on this exceptional occasion.

The sylph has kept his word and with what a success, what enthusiasm! It is easier to describe the reception accorded him, the wild enthusiasm he aroused, than enter into the mysteries of a performances which had no likeness in this world of ours.

If I possessed the pen that calls forth Queen Mab,

"In shape no bigger than the agate stone
On the forefinger of an alderman,"

it would be difficult to give any idea of a talent so completely ethereal that it transcends all earthly things.

To understand Chopin we need but to know Chopin himself. All those present at the concert on Wednesday were as convinced of this as we were ourselves.

The programme contained a trio by Mozart, which Chopin, Allard, and Franchomme played in such a way that we despair of ever hearing the like again. Chopin then played some Etudes, some Preludes, some Mazurkas, and some Valses. Afterward he gave us his beautiful Sonata with Franchomme. Do not ask me how all these masterpieces, both great and small, were played. I declared at the outset that I would make no attempt to describe the thousands of subleties of so exceptional a genius. I will only say that the audience was held spellbound by his charm, a spell that lasted until long after the concert was over.

Allowing for a journalistic rhetoric, these lines still retain a note of spontaneity which leaves no doubt that Chopin's performance had made an exceptional impression. His Paris audience were as yet unaware that they had listened to his swan song.

He had just recovered from a severe cold, and this, coupled with the fatigue, already remarked by Liszt, resulted in a distressing fainting attack on his return to the green room.

The emotion and physical effort demanded by the expression of his musical personality were not in themselves sufficient to account for this bodily collapse.

Other causes of an intimate nature, which weighed heavily on him, played their part: the domestic drama that kept him away from Nohant, the upheaval following the loss of the only experience of home life he had known since he had left his parents' roof, the futility of his daily life, the prospect of a solitary future and all the financial uncertainties such a future involved.

These factors must certainly have had some bearing on his decision to leave for England.

There for long months, at the cost of spiritual isolation as terrifying to him as his bodily illness, which was aggravated by a damp climate, he endeavored, as he tells us "to refashion a life for himself."

This resolution was contrary to all his normal habits, to all his instinctive reactions, which made him dread, as if it were an almost insuperable risk, any course of action which had the remotest resemblance to an adventure. And this adventure was to prove fatal. His correspondence throws rather more light than usual on the details of his various appearances in England.

His financial embarrassment was such that he was obliged to undertake three or four public engagements in addition to those private performances he gave before London society.

In a letter to his pupil Gutmann, written from London on May 6, 1848, a fortnight after his arrival, he gives vent to his old anxiety, his old terror at having to appear in public: "I must give a concert; it has been suggested that I should play at the Philharmonic Hall. I would rather not. In point of fact, after I have played before the Queen, I shall con-fine myself to playing at a matinée in some private house before a select audience. At least that is what I would like. But these are still only intentions."

Yet he could not fail to realize that it was impossible to escape indefinitely the curiosity aroused in musical circles by his presence in London. Erard, Pleyel, and Broadwood had each sent one of their pianos to his apartment in Dover Street. This he interpreted as a threat of imminent public engagements. He refused to consider these for the time being, insisting that he had no time to practice since his days were occupied in paying visits to those to whom he had letters of introduction and by the lessons he was giving.

At about the same date, writing to Gryzmala, he again refers to the offer that had been made to him to play at the Philharmonic Hall, but, he comments: "I am not interested in it because it would be with an orchestra." It is clear that he is anxious to avoid laying himself open, on his first appearance in London, to the reproach so often made against him, that his playing was too light and his tone too weak. He gives several other excuses for his refusal: "I have been there and seen what happens. Prudent gave a concert there and it was a fiasco. In this Hall one must play Mozart, Beethoven, or Mendelssohn and, though I am assured that my Concertos have been played there, I would prefer not to, for the effect would be nil."

The remark that follows is dictated by his loathing for any kind of music that relies for its appeal on meretricious effect: "Their orchestra, like their *rostbif* or their turtle soup is substantial, hearty, but it holds nothing more." For him, that "something more" was the only thing of real value.

He brings up yet another argument: "All that I have said would not of itself be a valid excuse, were it not for the fact that as 'Times is money' (*sic*) there will only be one public performance and they never have rehearsals, which makes it impossible."

When one thinks of the great care which Chopin took before appearing before an audience in Warsaw, calling the orchestra's quartet for several rehearsals that it might "understand his intentions," one has to admit that he was right to hesitate at taking part in a concert that was to be unrehearsed and to rely on an improvised, pedestrian accompaniment to sustain the flights of fancy demanded in any rendering of his music.

He was, however, able to inform an unknown correspondent, in a letter of June 1, that he had at last played
before the Queen, at Stafford House, the home of the Duchess
of Sutherland, and that Prince Albert, the Prince of Prussia,
and the Duke of Wellington were also present, together
with "all the most gartered society in London." "The Queen
was very gracious and spoke to me twice. Prince Albert
came over to the piano—a thing, I have been told, he rarely
does."

The fact that the celebrated singers, Mario, Lablache, and
Tamburini, were also engaged for this concert shows that
the first of Chopin's appearances in London was an event
of considerable social importance. But his hope of receiving
an official invitation to Court came to nothing, since the
royal family was in mourning. The question of his performing
at the Philharmonic Hall is again raised in this letter, and
he puts forward the same reasons to justify his refusal to
appear there: "I will not play at the Philharmonic Hall, in
spite of the kind offers made to me. I don't want to give
myself a lot of pain and grief for nothing but a single performance and that under bad conditions, besides taking the
place of those who are only too anxious to perform in these
surroundings."

He strikes the same note in a letter to Gryzmala on June 2:
"I do not want to play at the Philharmonic Hall, for that
would only cause me a lot of wearisomeness and not bring
in a halfpenny. There is only one kind of public performance
and at that one must play Mendelssohn to have any success."
He adds the most distressing details regarding his health and
his spiritual loneliness: "If I was not obliged to walk all
day with Anne of Caiphas, if I had not been spitting blood
for the past few days, if I were still young, if I were not

already swamped—that is the right word for it—by all the social obligations I cannot escape, perhaps I should be able to contemplate the idea of making a new life here. . . . My kind Scottish ladies (he refers to the Misses Stirling) would like me to pay a visit to their relations, when I am hardly alive . . . twenty years in Poland, seventeen in Paris—is it surprising that I am not at home in London?"

Is it apparent from a letter to his family, written from Edinburgh on August 19, that from the point of view of public recognition, he feels that he is making a mistake by refusing to play at the Philharmonic Hall. After referring to his disappointment at not having been able to play at Court, which would have given him the most valuable of all introductions to English society, he repeats his remarks about the orchestra in London: "This orchestra has asked me to play at one of its concerts, which is considered a great compliment here—one reserved for the few. For this reason neither Kalkbrenner nor Halle, in spite of all their persis-tence, have been able to arrange a concert. In fact, my re-fusal has made me unpopular in musical circles. But my re-fusal was made for medical reasons—at least that is the ex-cuse I gave. The truth is that I was not at all anxious to play one of my concertos with an orchestra, for these peo-ple have only one rehearsal—a rehearsal to which they ad-mit the public by invitation. How is one to rehearse under such conditions? Although they assure me that they know my concertos, Mme. Duklen, who passes for a famous pianist here, having, so it seems, played one of them last year, we should only have played badly."

Chopin's reasons for his refusal would seem, as usual, to derive as much from his terror of the concert platform as

from his musical conscience. Be this as it may, socially speaking he was by no means inactive.

He played in several private houses, among others those
of the Marquis of Douglas, Lady Gainsborough, and Mrs.
Grote. Of the last-named, he wrote: "She is a kind woman
and never asks me to sit down at the piano, if she sees that
I am not in the mood for playing." He remarks humorously
that it is a rare privilege "if people do not talk while I am
playing."

Referring to the pianists who were seeking to take London
by storm, he says: "As for my comrades in arms, they seem
to look upon me as some kind of an amateur, because my
shoes are clean and my visiting card does not have on it
the usual: "Lessons given at his own house. Takes engagements for the evening." He mentions that an old lady of the
Rothschild family asked him what his fees were: "When I
told her twenty guineas, she advised me not to charge so
much, for, so she said, this 'season' it was necessary to 'come
down in price'! I have come to the conclusion that they are
not very openhanded here. . . . As for the bourgeoisie they
are only interested in music in so far as it has extraordinary
or mechanical properties, which I do not pretend to offer.
In the world of high society there are so many forms of
entertainment in progress and it is so taken up with matters
of social precedence that whether the music it hears is good
or bad it couldn't be less interested. I am thinking of giving a concert in a private house; if that is successful I shall
get about a hundred and fifty guineas."

After only a short delay this project, prompted no doubt
by financial considerations, took place on June 30. He was
able to report to Solange Clesinger: "I have given an afternoon concert. Society was there. It was a great success and

I got a hundred and fifty guineas. There were a hundred and fifty seats and every one was taken on the previous evening."

Mrs. Sartoris had put her house at his disposal for this occasion, and the singer Mario was also on the program. He repeated this concert on July 7 at Lord Falmouth's house in St. James's Square this time supported by Pauline Viardot, "who sings my Polish songs. It went off very well, but I don't know whether I shall get a hundred guineas out of it." He adds: "For hours at a time I am quite well. But, coughing the way I do, I often wonder of a morning if I am going to cough up my soul. My spirit is sad, but I try to forget about it. I avoid being alone so that I do not get a chance to think, because one is not ill for long here. As I have very little money to carry on with I do not know what I am going to do. If this season had lasted for six months I could perhaps have succeeded, by degrees, in getting myself known."

Worried about what the summer held in store for him in a city where, by tradition, music sleeps once the "season" is over, Chopin resigned himself to accepting the hospitality offered him in Scotland at the home of Lord Tirpicher, a relative of his pupil, Jane Stirling. To have stayed in the capital would have been quite useless from every point of view. No concert of any artistic value would have taken place to justify it. Those London critics who, on the strength of the articles in the *Gazette Musicale* and other Paris papers, had written up his arrival in England as heralding a revelation in the field of piano playing, became disinterested in this famous virtuoso who so curiously absented himself from all the concert halls.

One of their number, F. W. Davidson, a disciple of the lately deceased Mendelssohn and music critic on *The Times,* seeing in Chopin a possible rival to his idol in London's drawing rooms, did not hesitate to condemn his works, in default of being able to criticize his playing, which was as yet virtually unknown. He went so far as to write the following: "Chopin presents nothing but the most ridiculous and extravagant themes in his music. . . . All his compositions have to offer the listener is a surface distorted by unintelligible overstatements and atrocious discords. And when he is not showing himself off in this guise, he is no more than a purveyor of the dullest waltzes."

These ungracious references were offset, however, by a very warm account of the concert given in the house of Mrs. Sartoris, which appeared in *The Daily News* over the signature of Hogarth.

Chopin's stay at Calder House, on the outskirts of Edinburgh, was both comfortable and luxurious, and he thought of remaining there until the end of August. Musically, however, it provided him with nothing more than an opportunity of playing Scottish airs during the long evenings for his host who stood beside him and hummed them. There was a rather vague plan for a concert in Edinburgh. His habitual repugnance seems to have been overcome by financial necessity, for he says: "It will bring in something and if I am strong enough I shall do it." He continues in this bitter vein: "If I were younger I would allow myself to be turned into a machine; I would give concerts everywhere and play my brain-wave, however devoid of taste, provided it brought in some money. But it is too late to make a machine of me now." It is distressing to read lines such as these coming from Chopin's pen. They tell us a great deal about his pre-occupations at this time.

It was during this period that he accepted an offer to appear at a concert *without orchestra* in Manchester, for a fee of sixty pounds. In a letter to his friend, Gryzmala, written from Glasgow on September 4, he makes a brief allusion to it: "Since I last wrote to you I have been to Manchester. I had a very good reception and was recalled three times. A fine hall; twelve hundred people." But an account given by the pianist, Osborne, who was the accompanist for the evening, gives us a more complete picture of the sort of concert it was.

Chopin shared the program with three well known singers, Alboni, Mme. Corbari, and Signor Salvi. The orchestra played three overtures: *The Barber of Seville* by Rossini, *Prometheus* by Beethoven, and *Rübezahl* by Weber.

Between these items, Chopin played an Andante, probably the Andante Spianato Op. 22, a Scherzo, some Etudes, a Nocturne, and the *Berceuse,* as well as the encores called for at the end of his performance.

According to Osborne, Chopin begged him not to listen: "You have so often heard me play in Paris, keep those impressions untarnished. My playing will be lost in so large a hall and my compositions will not make the slightest impression."

Osborne, however, did not obey his instructions, and, hiding in a corner of the hall, added his applause to that of the audience. Nevertheless, he had later to agree that Chopin had been right in his judgment. His touch was too delicate to arouse any marked enthusiasm.

The old and respected *Manchester Guardian,* reporting the concert, expressed itself in these terms:

Chopin appeared to be about thirty years of age. He has a very distinguished bearing, an almost sorrowful expression, and appears to be in delicate health. His melancholy and fragile appearance disappears when he takes his place at his instrument, which from then on seems to absorb his entire interest. Chopin's music and the manner of his interpretation of it have similar characteristics—refinement rather than strength—a subtle elaboration—a direct communication from the heart of the composition —a touch that is swift and delicate rather than firm and powerful.

Chopin knew that he no longer possessed the physical strength necessary to enable him to communicate all that was unique in his art to a large audience. It was no longer within his power to extend the range of his playing beyond that intimate circle which enjoyed his musical confidence. His advice to Osborne had been all too sound.

But for the need of providing himself with the necessary means of existence during the coming winter, it is unlikely that Chopin would have attempted any other concerts of the same kind. Nevertheless, while staying on the outskirts of Glasgow, where he was the guest of Mrs. Houston, a sister of Jane Stirling, we find him writing to Gryzmala on September 4, that, a concert is being arranged for him in the second city of Scotland, but that he does not know "what it will produce."

In point of fact this concert became a rather unimposing afternoon performance in the Merchants' Hall, before "a few dozen representatives of the nobility." Among these were the Prince and Princess Czartoriski, faithful friends of long standing, whose presence was a great encouragement to Chopin. He says: "I have come back to life again, thanks to the presence of the Polish element, which gave me the strength to play." The "few dozen" listeners naturally did not provide much in the way of takings—the price of seats was fixed at half a guinea—and the amount produced by the event was only some sixty pounds. Chopin had reckoned on double that amount. In his optimism he had overlooked the traditionally economical habits of the Scotch. The ordinary citizen of Glasgow considered that the price of the tickets was excessive. His concert in Edinburgh was, alas, to produce an even poorer result. The price of the tickets was the same as in Glasgow, and on the evening of October 3, the day before the concert had been arranged, the bookings were so small that Jane Stirling herself took a hundred tickets so that the hall should not be too empty.

One can well understand how discouraging this was to Chopin; indeed, in a further letter to Gryzmala, it is apparent that he looked on this concert with indifference: "I've got to play here tomorrow evening, but I haven't looked at the hall yet or settled on the program."

And elsewhere he confides to Mlle. de Rozières: "Lots of people here beg me to play and out of politeness I accept. But every time I play with a renewed reluctance, vowing that I will never do it again, for it reduces me to a state of nervous prostration."

The hall, which Chopin did not know, was the Hopetown Rooms in Queen Street, and the program, arranged at the last moment, consisted of the following:

1. *Andante et Impromptu* (The Andante was probably the introduction to the Polonaise Op. 22.)
2. *Sélection d'Etudes* (including Nos. 1 & 2 of Op. 25.)

3. *Nocturnes et Berceuse* (Nocturnes Op. 9 No. 2
   and Op. 55 No. 1)
4. *Grande Valse Brillante* (Op. 18)
5. *Andante précédé d'un largo* (These may have
   been two of the Préludes)
6. *Préludes, Ballade in F, Mazurkas, and Valses.*

As one can see, with the exception of the Ballade, the program contained nothing that would put too great a strain on Chopin's already very limited physical resources.

Writing to Gutmann on October 16, he says: "I played at Edinburgh. Everyone of any consequence in the neigh-borhood was there. I am told it went well. A small amount of success and a small amount of money."

Chopin was unaware of Jane Stirling's delicate subter-fuge that produced the "small amount."

We find the same old story in *The Edinburgh Courier* of October 7:

> Chopin's compositions may be counted among the best in the classical style (*sic*). His execution is the most delicate that one could possibly hear. He does not, however, possess the power or the brilliant technique of a Mendelssohn or a Liszt. In conse-quence his playing has less effect in a hall of con-siderable size. But as a performer of chamber music he has no equal.

This "hall of considerable size," as the critic has it, held two hundred and fifty to three hundred seats at the most, which could not have affected Chopin's range of tone. But some stories die hard, and journalists have convenient mem-ories.

After this last public ordeal, Chopin was, until the end of October, the guest at several houses in the vicinity of Edinburgh. He tells us that his "two kind hostesses" will end by killing him with their care and attention and their religious injunctions. But he was obliged to make the contribution expected of him—to seat himself at the piano after dinner.

In a letter to Gryzmala of October 21, he describes scenes bordering on the burlesque.

Discreetly omitting her name, but we may guess that he is speaking of Lady Belhaven, with whom he was spending a few days, he says: "Lady . . . brags that she is a first class musician. Well, once when I had been playing the piano, enduring her singing of all sorts of Scottish songs, she asked for a kind of accordion to be brought to her, on which she tried to play the most horrible tunes imaginable. . . . Another woman sang and at the same time accompanied herself on the piano standing up—which certainly produced an extraordinary pose. This time it was a French romance, the syllables of which she pronounced in the English fashion, *jaiie aiiemaiie,* by which is meant *j'ai aimé ! ! !*

"On another occasion the Princesse de Parme seriously confided in me that one of her maids whistled in a most remarkable fashion to the accompaniment of the guitar.

"The few of these charming people who have a slight knowledge of my work ask me: 'Oh ! please play me your second *Soupir !*' or else 'I do so adore your *Cloches !*' I have never played for an Englishwoman without her saying to me: 'Like water,' that is to say flows like water. When they play themselves they all look at their hands and wallow in sentimentality."

While he still retained his childhood love for comic situations, and was able to give his correspondents these vivid Hogarthian sketches, the behavior of these absurd society folk must have had a most depressing effect on an artist who for the past twenty years had been living at close quarters with a refined and cultured Parisian society, and could only have heightened his sense of spiritual isolation.

However, he prolonged his stay in Scotland, where at least he was assured of a roof and the means of livelihood, until the end of October when, in order to shake himself free from this numbing existence and these irritating exhibitions, he availed himself of a request from Lord Hamilton, who insisted that he appear at a charity concert, which was to be followed by a ball, to take place in London on November 16, in aid of the Poles.

He makes a casual reference to this concert—destined to be his last—in a letter to Mlle. de Rozières, announcing his imminent return to Paris. He asks her not to forget to put a bunch of violets by his bedside: "I have been at home since November 1 living in my dressing gown. I only went out on the 16th when I played for my fellow countrymen." It is only too certain, unhappily, that this, Chopin's last appearance in public, was, from an artistic point of view, of no consequence whatsoever. In this affair, given at the Guildhall, the ball took first place. No one paid any attention to the musical part of the program, to which it formed a sort of hors d'oeuvres, and the fact that Chopin took part in this odd mélange was completely ignored by the press.

He played only a few pieces, including, if the memories of some of the members of his scanty audience are to be trusted, the first two Etudes from Op. 25.

Dr. Francis Hueffer, who was present at this performance, wrote the following: "His presence and his collaboration on such an occasion were both equally out of place, the good intention does not excuse the mistake."

We can only agree with this ironic comment on the

lack of perception shown on the part of the organizers of the soirée in asking Chopin to appear on such an occasion.

What heroism this man showed in his last appearance before the public ! On the very day of the concert he was in bed, the victim of a cough which tore at his chest relentlessly. Further, he was tortured by severe neuralgia, and on top of all this he contracted an edema which alarmed his doctor. But this concert was in aid of his countrymen, "his own" as he used to call them, and nothing could stop him. When the evening arrived, the pianist, scarcely able to breathe and with very little strength left, was driven in a draughty carriage through London's November fog to the place where he could record his devotion to his beloved Poland.

Though considered as an artistic achievement, the result of this concert was negligible, it marks the apotheosis of the career of Chopin the patriot. This essential Chopin had no fonder dream than that his final effort as an artist should be addressed to the very soul of the people whose national spirit and heroic struggle were immortalized in his music. . . .

7

"HE WAS NOT LIKE OTHER MEN"

JANE STIRLING, A FRIEND WHO, during the last years of his life, was solicitous of his welfare to the point of contemplating marrying him, said this a few weeks after his death.

Simple though it may be, it is under this heading that I propose, by a brief consideration of Chopin's mental makeup and attitude toward other people, to supplement the study of his physical characteristics that already form a part of this book.

Though it is devoid of psychological subtlety, Jane Stirling's remark nevertheless indicates the approach that should be made if we are to obtain a clear picture of that manysided personality, whose unpredictable reactions may perhaps best be likened to April weather.

It is a somewhat hazardous enterprise to attempt to dissociate the human personality of the poet-musician from the manifestations of his genius, which alone express the essence of his being, viewing it apart from his work, only taking into account the effect on him of everyday affairs and the events in his private life.

Curiosity and research have added little to our knowledge of his artistic message, and the objection can justly be made that the important thing is what he created and not what he was. One can admit that the objective preoccupation with material detail, which is necessary to this study, might seem to discount the magic spell cast by the aspirations expressed in his letters and the widespread belief that every poetic licence should be granted him.

No doubt, the fact that my career as a pianist has been largely given over to the interpretation of his masterpieces will excuse me from emphasizing my unbounded admiration for the composer. On the other hand, many of the generally accepted legends concerning him will not stand careful examination. The facts indicate human weaknesses and a certain lack of mental balance, which most people at any rate will attribute to his poor state of health.

Without having recourse to the principles of psychoanalysis, which would probably excuse most of these anomalies on the grounds that they were complexes mysteriously implanted in the subconscious during infancy and not eliminated in the normal way, because his life was sheltered from any necessity for manly development, it is clear that his sudden transitions from a state of depression to one of excitability are the classic symptoms of tuberculosis from which he suffered more and more acutely during the unhappy years of unequal struggle between an enfeebled will to live and the growing threats of physical misery.

However, even if, as Stendhal maintained, a part of every great man's biography should be written by his doctor, it is nevertheless no part of my intention, nor indeed is it within my competence, to support my observations by venturing among the plausible hypotheses of pathological deduction or Freudian analysis.

I have been satisfied with what I could learn from the facts of a social behavior, which, as Jane Stirling said, was not the normal, and from written or verbal accounts by those of his contemporaries who came nearest to him, as well as from those rare passages in his letters, in which he reveals a little of himself. Also, I have been at pains to keep as close as possible to probability in interpreting both his reactions to the three or four important and authenticated events which mark, in a strangely similar fashion, the essential stages in his emotional life, and the nature of his relationship with those of his familiars who won his preference if not his affection.

I have attempted to use my imagination and not merely to rely on the methods of logical deduction. It is for the reader to decide whether the picture I have sketched in this way, with the aid of conjecture and an imaginative assessment of the possibilities, is plausible. I myself am conscious of the weakness of speculation as such.

I can, however, affirm that so far from having lessened the passion which Chopin's unique genius inspires in me, the sometimes surprising and disillusioning discoveries, which I have made when investigating the facts of his behavior in his contacts with life, which brought to light the limitations as well as the occasional extravagances of his personality, have merely heightened my consciousness of the unequalled emotional power which pervades the whole of his matchless work with such miraculous enchantment.

Apart from the artistic sublimation of "that passionate sob, which echoes from age to age," the moving eloquence of which has triumphed over a century of sometimes regrettable pianistic familiarity, it seems to me that the results of my study (which has nothing whatever in common with a musical exegesis) reveal certain shades of expression, which have a peculiarly penetrating significance. In my imagination they seem to intensify the bitterness of those conflicts which

ran their sad course in the depths of a melancholy conciousness
—those battles between the feverish seekings of an unsatisfied
imagination and the discouraged refusals of a hesitant will.

In Chopin as a child there was what one might call a
specifically innate characteristic, which was in marked contradiction to the leanings which governed his later behavior.

There was nothing to indicate that irresistible propensity
to anxious melancholy which was to possess him when he
was about twenty years old, at the time of his departure
from Warsaw and his separation from the people and places
he loved, which seems to have been an instinctive premonition, an irrepressible vision of the future solitary fate which
awaited him as an exile filled with regrets for the past.

On the contrary, his boyhood activities show him to have
been particularly prone to all kinds of playfulness and full
of roguish tricks, which were nearly always prompted by
a taste for banter and frivolity.

This is apparently something which, however harmless
in origin it may seem to be, is linked by certain students
of the infant mind to definite hypochondriac tendencies in
later life.

Leaving such considerations aside for the moment, one
cannot but remark on the humorous spirit of enterprise (in
which he was later to be so sadly lacking) which, when fed
by his fertile imagination and animated by the many resources of his contagious spirit of fantasy, resulted in the
usual entertainments which were the admiration of his school
and holiday companions.

It was the same Chopin who, so anxious for the approba-
tion of others in his youth, was later to rebel with such
determination against the demands made on him by the life
of a concert artist with all the showmanship necessary for

public performances—and this at just the time when these should have been the normal demands of his career as a virtuoso !

As a child we see him using all his ingenuity to invoke the applause of his playmates by means of what he describes as his "merry-andrew jests." These often took the form of burlesques improvised between arithmetic and grammar lessons, with Chopin as author and principal actor. In fact these were unconscious imitations of the Neapolitan pasquinade with the dialogue ornamented with many a pleasantry.

For several years he used the slightest pretext for indulging in buffoonery and adopting amusing disguises. In this he showed the early signs of an exceptional gift for mimicry, with which occasionally he was to astonish the salons of Vienna and Paris and to draw this somewhat surprising remark from the actor Bocage: "What a pity that the lad should have been misled into taking up music! He has the makings of a first-class comedian in him!"

He was always assured in advance of the amused indulgence of those friends, relations or teachers, whom he parodied, and it was to the great joy of his youthful companions that he ridiculed the eccentricities and phobias of the world he knew in a series of imitative caricatures.

Further amusement was derived from the test he set his young friends' imagination by having them guess whom or what it was that his fingers were portraying on the piano. However inexperienced, his fingers were already singularly obedient to his fantastic invention. In this he was, of course, still the leader of the game and was giving instinctive expression to that exceptional musical aptitude which made him say that, ever since he was eight years old, he expressed himself more easily in music than in words.

He kept this taste for shared enjoyment until the approach of adolescence, for he was nearly fourteen when he wrote a number of short sketches in verse celebrating family anniversaries, calling on the somewhat uncertain talents of his sisters and of some of his father's pupils to act in them. Presented for the judgment of a rather better informed audience, these miniature plays were, of course, more ambitious.

It is clear from the title (which is all that remains of it incidentally) of one of them, *The Misunderstanding or the Fate of the Suspected Pickpocket,* that such a childish conception of complicated intrigue was hardly likely to reveal any exceptional poetic gifts!

At about the same time, and with the same motives, he produced those carefully handwritten pages of the *Courrier de Szafornia* which have already been reproduced in so many biographies. The name is that of the country place where he spent his holidays. He wrote under the pseudonym of *Sieur Pichon*—a ridiculous anagram—beneath which cloak he pretended to shield himself from censure, which was occasionally supplied by facetious comments from his sister Emilie. It was in these pages that he told, in the sententious style of the serious Warsaw papers, of the trivial domestic events which helped to break the monotony of country life. A certain naïve sarcasm is also to be found in the caricatures with which he filled the margins of his school exercise books.

He founded a "Leisure-time Literary Society," ostensibly for the benefit of his friends at his father's school, in imitation of the then popular "Reading Circles" in the Polish capital, of which he himself, needless to say, was the President!

Perhaps this was the final fling of his childish initiative, a kind of full stop to what might, with a certain stretch of the imagination, be compared to intellectual preoccupations.

It was apparently only during these school years that he had any interest in the printed word. In this he was quite unlike his rivals of the romantic period—Schumann, Liszt, Mendelssohn, or Berlioz—who all felt a need for general culture. Once Chopin concentrated exclusively on music he deliberately turned his back on anything remotely resembling ideological speculation. Not only did he read very little, one is almost tempted to believe that he ceased to read at all. In any case, the fact that only two books were discovered among his belongings in the apartment at the Place Vendôme after his death at least gives credence to such a supposition. In the desolate seclusion in which he lived just before he died, it would have been only natural for him to turn to reading, particularly in view of the physical inaction imposed on him by his illness.

The two books in question were Voltaire's *Dictionnaire Philosophique,* still open at the article on *Taste,* and an anthology of popular Polish poetry. The later was obviously a simple school textbook, but it showed signs of fairly constant use, which gives a further and final proof of the haunting and deep-rooted feeling for his native land that even twenty years of exile had not succeeded in lessening.

However, to return to Chopin's childhood amusements, one cannot fail to notice that these were far removed from the wild gambols normal among boys of his age. In fact, in all his games, intelligence, and by this I mean certain intellectual leanings and not merely his malicious wit, held that first place which most children give to muscular development and purely physical playfulness.

This, perhaps, was the natural development of the vital faculties in a young being whose frail physique was, according to George Sand, "just as delicate as his sensitivity." Such a physique necessitated the taking of certain precautions right from the beginning, even though they amounted to nothing more that a diet of chicken broth and the prescription of one of the quack medicines fashionable at the time. On the whole, however, this frailness was more likely the result of the purely feminine atmosphere of his home, where he lived tied to the apron strings of his mother and sisters until he was about thirteen.

To quote George Sand, whose remark perhaps holds some trace of secret bitterness, "his mother was the only woman Chopin ever loved." She seems to have been gifted not only with all the domestic virtues, but also with a most attractive quality of affability, the gentle glow of which affected everyone around her.

She was the daughter of a country squire—a fact which Chopin was particularly proud of—although he only mentioned it occasionally. She was also a most devout Catholic, but by means of some poetic detour of the imagination, which for her held not the slightest hint of heresy, she also held a superstitious belief in the power of popular legends to enchant. This cannot have failed to leave an indelible mark on the sensitive mind of the future composer of the Ballades; it certainly played an important part in his spiritual growth. Although his religious beliefs did not at any time precipitate that mystical crisis which is familiar to many young people, one would have expected it from an impressionable nature such as his.

His mother's example gave him a lifelong respect for religious dogma, but even when the circumstances of his emotional life might have been expected to encourage it, he never felt sufficient confidence or eagerness to call this respect a convinced belief.

He was not an atheist; his attitude was rather one of indifference. For him, communication with the divine spirit was through his music and by virtue of aspirations quite independent of redemption by confession. This impression is confirmed by the purport of a confession which, two days before his death, Chopin made to a Polish priest, who left a highly questionable account of it.

Let us now turn to his three sisters. They were all about his own age, but his great favorite and inseparable companion in all his childish games was the youngest. She died before she was fifteen, victim of that disease of the lungs which Chopin probably contracted from her.

It is easy to imagine that they all adored their *Fritzel,* as they liked to call him. They were like so many little mothers to him. He was just like a living doll sent to them from Heaven, and to be cherished much more than any of their others. They marveled at his first steps as a baby, and later were filled with admiration at any independent expression of will on the part of the small boy whose slightest wish was their command.

The fact that he was continually spoiled in this way was to affect Chopin's whole existence; it undoubtedly emphasized the sensitivity of a nature already too much inclined to be affected by the slightest opposition, and made him particularly vulnerable to all kinds of disappointments.

Undoubtedly a firm hand on the part of the head of the family would have been necessary to counteract this over-whelmingly feminine atmosphere. But the pleasant personality of the father always remained somwhat outside the domestic picture.

This humble descendant of the wine-growers of Lorraine, whose lonely flight to Poland at the age of sixteen still remains unexplained, exhibited all the virtures of the tenacious and hardworking people from whom he sprang, in his efforts to assure the livelihood of his family. He was if anything inclined to be rather more indulgent than the rest of the family where his son was concerned. The Comtesse de Ségur has told us that Chopin, with his disarming charm, was a model child and had only to be reprimanded for the most insignificant peccadilloes.

It was within this warm family circle, where hearts and minds alike were in tune, toward which he so often turned his nostalgic thoughts during his later years of exile, that the childish Chopin developed some of those moral characteristics which left him so completely disarmed before most of the material demands of daily life.

This gentle, almost hothouse atmosphere was certainly unsuited to the development of any boldness of approach when dealing with the melancholy events which fate held in store for him. What he did derive from it, however, was a respect for femininity, which, while having nothing in common with a taste for women, lent a particular note of seriousness to his disappointing emotional adventures.

One is probably not far from the truth in imagining that his sisters' childish coquetry was responsible for Chopin's fastidious taste in dress, which was to become a kind of external expression of good manners for him when he was living in Paris.

All of his biographers have related the anecdote about his first contact with the public. He was eight years old at the time, and played an insignificant concerto by Gyrometz at a charity concert. Even though it did not reflect his already fastidious taste in music it was at least within his childish powers of execution. The whole point of this story is, however, that he assured his mother that his embroidered collar was the main cause of his success. Young Chopin was just like the infant Mozart in his anxiety to please, not only by his artistic gifts which seemed to him the most natural thing in the world, but by his appearance as well.

So we see in the child the germ of that elegant dandyism, "that serious consideration of the frivolous," as Baudelaire called it, which in Chopin's case should not be confused with the pretentious dressiness of the conceited fop. His elegance was one of the factors which determined his subsequent friendship with Eugène Delacroix; also it is more likely that it had something to do with the unusual sensation he caused when he appeared in the aristocratic circles of Parisian society, at a time when most of the young French virtuosi affected carelessness in dress as being the badge of genius.

But let us return from this digression into the still distant future to those years of his youth which were spent in the quiet calm of the family circle. We see him, from his seventh year onward, as a docile, intelligent child with a tendency to be rather easily distracted, making his first steps in learning under the guidance of his indulgent father. More advanced studies were deferred until he went to the lyceum at a later date, his parents having as yet no definite career in mind for him.

They regarded his surprising musical aptitude merely as an encouraging promise of amateur talent, which would be of value in the future as a means of securing social privileges.

The young scholar's time was thus sufficiently free to allow him to devote most of his leisure to a private and personal investigation of all the intoxicating secrets locked up in combinations of sound. It was during this solitary recreation that he developed those musical opinions. which he was to hold with such firmness. These opinions were quite amazing and have not been stressed sufficiently by his biographers. In fact, young Chopin was an unprecedented case in the annals of instrumental virtuosity, which was to be modified in all its aspects by his genius. He never took a piano lesson, either as a child or as a student at the Warsaw Conservatoire. We know that a single meeting with Kalkbrenner during the first few days of his arrival in Paris was sufficient for him to abandon his intention of asking Kalkbrenner's advice about perfecting his playing. He was so certain of the individual character of his talent that he preferred to keep what he called "my personal approach to piano playing."

This young man, of whom the Princess Belgiojoso was later to say: "Chopin is greater than the greatest of pianists. He is the only one," was entirely self-taught. He had no instruction in elementary technique, which would normally have simplified his first efforts on the instrument, which gave him so much childish pleasure, and the further novel refinements, which were later revealed in the poetic quality of his virtuosity which has never known a rival.

I feel that I should particularly emphasize this extraordinary artistic completeness and the exceptional tenacity of purpose that went with it, which was in such significant contrast with both his childish leanings toward carefree roguishness and to those states of chronic indecision which were to weigh so heavily on him later in life.

Before setting out on an analysis of this auto-didacticism to which I have referred, and the hints that may be gleaned from it concerning the potentialities of Chopin's character, it will not be out of place to recall his unusual reaction to his very first experience of musical sound. The fact is that until he was three or four years old, any and every musical phenomenon apparently disturbed him to so great an extent and in such a way as to make it seem that he had an incurable aversion to it.

From the cradle on he burst into sobs whenever his mother endeavored to sing him to sleep by humming one of the Mazovian songs, whose haunting melancholy was later to prevade the melodic substance of all his work. It was the same if his father attempted to recapture the country songs, which he remembered from his childhood days in far-off Lorraine, on the flute. Legend has it that Chopin gave way to uncontrollable childish rage and deliberately broke the fragile instrument, which had unwisely been given him to play with.

It took a little while for his parents to realize that far from being a sign of utter distaste, his abnormal reactions were in fact determined by a sense of hearing so acute that he was moved to tears where less receptive children would probably have been content to drift into sleep.

This initial hostility entirely contradicts the general opinion that it is necessary to be irresistibly attracted to music from the earliest days for there to be any guarantee of a true musical vocation. Chopin's attitude was transformed, as if by magic, once his small fingers began adventuring on the family piano, so that he himself produced the sounds which hitherto had aroused such unusual nervous tension in him.

In fact, within a very few years his instinctive reaction toward music, which had been, paradoxically, accepted as indicating physical abhorrence, was shown to be a love so passionate that his parents could do no less than satisfy it to the best of their ability. Even though they regarded it as a childish whim, which would probably not last very long, they searched for "the professional man" (as the fortunetellers always say) capable of teaching in odd moments, and within the limits of a restricted budget, those rudiments of musical knowledge so eagerly desired by the imaginative small boy of seven.

Without apparently having given the matter any very particular consideration beforehand, and largely because of a chance relationship, their choice fell on a Czech musician called Zwyny, who had been settled in Warsaw for a long time and was a member of Prince Casimir Sapieha's orchestra. The prince was a Polish aristocrat, who upheld the ancient custom of keeping a group of artists *da camera* attached to his household.

It happened that, so far as guiding young Frederic's aesthetic development was concerned, no happier choice could have been made. All his life Chopin retained grateful memories of the ideas he culled from his first teacher. The influence exerted by the excellent Zwyny considerably overran the limits of the task assigned to him. There is no doubt whatever that it was his fervent admiration for Mozart and Johann Sebastian Bach (his regard for the latter being quite exceptional for the time and place in which he lived) which gave Chopin, in the years which followed, that taste for classical discipline which resulted in the unequalled perfection of line to be found in all his work.

Zwyny, however, was primarily a violinist, both by education and profession. If he did happen to use the piano, it was only in the very simple way usual among musicians of his generation, to give, when occasion demanded, an interpretation of the figured bass which completed the harmony of some symphony by Wagenseil or Stamitz. Born in 1757, he was almost totally ignorant of the specific demands of piano keyboard technique and of the methods by which to encourage the progress of a fairly advanced virtuosity.

What a wonderful chapter of accidents, one is almost tempted to echo Phillippe Desportes: "Oh, happy mischance—harbinger of so many advantages."

Left to solve the enigma for himself, this paradoxical initiation to music, far from being a discouragement, incited him to the most stubborn search for a technique best suited to act as a vehicle for the aery flights of his enchanting melodies and impulsive rhythms. His perseverance was almost unbelieveable in a child of his age, and led him, without the benefits of qualified teaching, to the discovery of every subtlety of fingering. From the age of twelve, for five whole years, the young schoolboy used every moment left unoccupied by his father's very lenient timetable to work out for himself the mysterious rules governing that sublime artistry of the piano which destiny demanded of him, while his school friends disported themselves in the normal way with games of hide-and-seek or leapfrog.

One hesitates to conclude that this chance apprenticeship was the sole source of those original and individual qualities shown in both his composition and his playing. Other and more exacting factors than pure empiricism are needed to produce such a result, even if the practical experience is backed by an inspired genius, who instinctively overcomes the forbidding problems of pianistic theory.

It would be beyond the scope of these observations to attempt to assess the effect this lack of normal teaching had on Chopin's creative personality. It is true, however, that his later studies seem to have been written with an audacity amounting to defiance of the conventional methods used to develop technical skill. Zwyny's technique certainly favored the formation of a musical mentality completely free from any tendency to resort to meaningless scales and arpeggios, for it preserved, albeit quite involuntarily, the youthful sensitivity of his pupil from the constraint imposed by exercises repeated thousands of times in order to produce a mechanical dexterity quite regardless of any expressiveness of tone.

Shortly after Chopin had left Warsaw he received a letter from his father which confirms the existence of that inborn instrumental gift that enabled his son to dispense with the daily finger exercises which most virtuosi have found necessary. His father recalls the small amount of time that Chopin had spent on the technical study of the piano, and congratulates him on having preserved the individual character of his playing, while devoting his real efforts to the art of improvisation "occupying the mind rather than the fingers," as he puts it. We can readily admit the existence of that exraordinary aptitude which became evident immediately Chopin encountered the piano, which was to become the gentle confidant of his musical aspirations rather than a cold witness of his progress as a performer.

Returning to the main subject of this essay, which is Chopin's character as such, we find a quite astounding example of his childish determination in the fact that he persistently ignored every example and followed his own bent in the pursuit of technical knowledge which he knew to be the key to that magic door which opens on to the fabulous realms of the creative imagination.

Equally astonishing is the combination of this determination to master technique with his undeniable genius, this almost supernatural gift which permits an inspired child, without any previous relevant teaching, to penetrate immediately to the heart of the rarest of all musical privileges—the realization of the evocative power of sound "arranged in a certain order." On the other hand, we have the quite abnormal expenditure of energy represented by his solitary investigation of the problems presented by the instrument, without any competent advice to help him. On the one hand, the finger of God, and on the other the operation of the most surprising potentialities of character.

We are more than justified in drawing attention to this youthful battle against such heavy odds—this obstinate initiative in search for the basic factors governing an apparently insoluble problem. It calls to mind the unending task of Sisyphus and the example of the young Pascal, who rediscovered the principles of geometry. It proves that at that time Chopin possessed a combative energy he later exhibited only on the rarest occasions.

When he was about sixteen years old, Chopin's parents decided to enter him as a pupil at the recently founded Conservatoire, of which Joseph Elsner was the Director. They could not do otherwise than admit the futility of opposing the irresistible vocation which had left their son indifferent to any other form of intellectual curiosity during the course of his unspectacular career at the Warsaw Gymnasium.

Elsner was a prolific writer of no particular merit, and was, in fact, what is known as "a Sunday musician," having (or so it was maliciously said in the musical circles of the capital) "learned to compose while composing."

In common with Zwyny, he had no ability on any instrument other than the violin, which meant that the professional lessons Chopin might normally have expected in order to perfect an amateur education, which had relied for so long on methods of trial and error, were not forth-coming. Indeed, he seems to have been destined never to receive professional instruction in piano technique, and he continued on his lonely way in search of pianistic skill.

He did, however, gain in his study of harmony from the routine experience of his new master, and the mere fact that he was henceforth at liberty to devote himself exculsively to music was sufficient to maintain his eagerness and zeal.

He now broke free to a certain extent from the softening influence of the family circle. Now that he had a room of his own, he could spend whole days at the piano in his attempt to plumb the secrets of instrumental perfection.

He was to show himself eager to assimilate all the possibilities of an art, the way to which was now wide open for him. In a whirlpool of confused admiration he even included the concertos of Hummel with the fugues of *The Well-tempered Clavichord;* Mozart's Sonatas; the latest Paër opera; a concert given by Paganini; a roulade sung by *La Sontag;* and the Studies written by Cramer. Coming as they did within the domain which had for so long been denied him, everything of musical substance seemed good.

Perhaps it was in order to combat this indiscriminate enthusiasm that Elsner encouraged him not to imitate anyone, and, rather than be the pupil of others, either as a composer or as a performer, to discover the secrets of that new language which was to make him the chosen interpreter of the soul and feelings of Poland from within himself.

Elsner showed himself to be well aware of the exceptional gifts he had been called on to control, and he behaved with a kind of prophetic clairvoyance which is quite surprising in a musician governed so resolutely by the conventional discipline of his profession.

Relying solely on intuition, just as the good Zwyny had done, it is interesting to see the advice of Chopin's official mentor coinciding with his father's opinions. In point of fact, however, Elsner's exhortations were superfluous, for Chopin lost none of his originality because of his discursive youthful enthusiasms. He even made up the deficiency of qualified piano lessons by writing, first of all in the form of exercises for his own use, that collection of studies which remains to this day the outstanding work of its kind for virtuosi. Also, his imagination was sufficiently strong to pierce the obscurities of Simon's treatise on harmony, in which the rules are set out with a most discouraging lack of true musical significance, and to discover beyond them those refinements of style which foreshadow by nearly a century the enchanting impressionism of Debussy and Ravel.

His youthful fame, incidentally, was now beginning to go beyond a mere schoolboy's reputation, and he became naïvely but fully conscious of the fact that, just as Elsner had urged and encouraged him to be, he represented the musical hopes of his fellow citizens. In fact, the four years he was to spend in Poland before he left it finally—four years broken by occasional visits to Berlin, Prague, and Vienna—were a period of intense and stimulating social activity. It was during these years that he formed the taste for those social gatherings, where, in spite of his modest origins, he was welcomed as an equal, and never in any way treated as a paid performer. This intimate contact with society was particularly flattering to his budding self-esteem, and was destined to remain the most favorable field for the expression of his talent. Here, too, he acquired those habits of scrupulous politeness which seem to have been regarded at that time as essential to the maintenance of style in the social relationships of Polish high society. Liszt, who knew all about it, was probably not far wrong when he described his famous rival's bearing as being "princely."

This transition from childhood to adolescence meant not only the concentration of the whole of his attention on his art, but also the end of the *polchinades* and pseudoliterary amusements that Chopin had still indulged in during the time he was at college. He himself gravely affirmed that there could be no further question for him of such ridiculous frivolity now he was a man.

This did not prevent him, however, from employing his imagination in other directions, and the irresistible need for self-expression which had inspired such childish games was now to lead him to cultivate those exclusive friendships which were so full of passionate confidences.

Certain letters written at this time to the companions of his choice are those of a lover rather than a friend; but here, quite deliberately, I intend to ignore the insinuations of equivocal intimacies which have been made on account of them. All the evidence points to the fact that in these friendships, Chopin, in common with many adolescents whose minds boggle a little at the approaching revelation of the mystery of sex, was satisfied to pour out the overflow of an exaltation which had yet to find its object in a feminine ideal.

This is not to say, however, that there were not several ephemeral infatuations before the apparition of Constance Gladkowska caused an explosion of romantic delirium that robbed him of all idea of reality. Of this I shall have more to say later, but as far as the fleeting infatuations are concerned, even if they did offer his youthful vanity a sufficient pretext for those effusions which were intended to convince his intimate correspondents of the esteem in which his person and his talent were held, they left his heart completely un- touched.

He had begun to play with the idea of love, as with that of fame, in a completely ingenuous fashion. In other words, for the time being, youth itself was enough.

It is possible to identify some of the heroines of these infatuations which, in spite of the eternal love which is so readily envisaged in his enthusiastic accounts of them, never lasted for longer than a few days or even hours.

In accordance with the normal relationship between a young teacher and a pupil of the same age, we have, first of all, the ravishing Wanda, daughter of the enthusiastic amateur cellist, Count Radziwill. Chopin composed a Polacca for the Count, the accompaniment of which was intended to be played by "the pretty little fingers of the most divine of creatures," who was also gifted with the "most remark- able musical aptitude." He translated this opinion into slightly less exaggerated terms a little later on, when he said that "there is no need to telll her to play softly here and more loudly there, quicker at one point and slower at others." This surely implies an artistic ability which can hardly be called exceptional in character, and Chopin would certainly not have noticed it in the same way had there not been an extra-musical element in his appreciative admiration, which, for him, was supported by the most significant fact that the seductive young lady had insisted on sketching him in her private album.

Then there is Leopoldine Blahetka, whose acquaintance he made in Vienna where her father was music editor of the most important newspaper.

"She is not yet twenty," he wrote to his friend Titus, "and she is already the foremost pianist in the capital."

"She is witty as well as beautiful," he adds, "and I am very much in her favor, as you can imagine from reading the dedication which she insisted on writing in the copy of her compositions which she gave me."

Then again there was the sprightly Alexandrine de Mariolles whom he nicknamed "Diabolek" ("little devil"), the daughter of the Comte de Mariolles, a French refugee who had been forced by necessity to become tutor to the children of the Grand Duke Constantine. She displayed her feelings— much too openly for Chopin's taste, for he was already easily alarmed at the idea of "what people might think"—by sending him a crown of laurels after one of his concerts.

No doubt, there were many other momentary infatuations. Many years afterward, George Sand said that he remained as easily affected as ever he was in the days of his adolescence, and that he could become vaguely enamored of several women in the same evening, only to forget them competely once he had left their presence.

All these "little passions" were preliminaries to a search for happiness in an emotional state of which, for the moment, he had nothing but a vague premonition. They were the faint stirrings of love which for him had nothing whatever to do with flirtatiousness, and should be interpreted as the sign of an obscure need to find an anchor for his emotions which had so far evaded him. Feminine charm, no doubt, played its usual and natural part in these adventures, but nevertheless it was not the main cause of Chopin's interest. The accounts he heard of licentious associations aroused no curiosity in him concerning what he was to call, when the day arrived for him to be directly confronted by sensual temptation in the guise of George Sand's open advances, "the gross materialities of the flesh."

Writing to Kumelki, with whom he occasionally corres-
ponded, shortly after he arrived in Paris, Chopin makes a
solitary mention of the subject. He makes a veiled allusion
to the precautions he found it necessary to take after his
tiresome experience with a certain Thérèse, whose acquaintance he seems to have made in Vienna, deploring the fact
that these prevent him from profiting by the offers "of
the charitable ladies who wander the streets here."

Incidentally, this letter may explain to a certain extent
some of the significant mental inhibitions which we shall
have occasion to notice in connection with his later behavior.

But, to remain on the platonic level to which the idyllic
relationships we are at present discussing are confined, it
seems highly probable that they were caused by the unconscious transference of emotion, the elucidation of which is
the province of Freud. What Chopin expected of the as
yet unchosen being, who was still in the state of becoming,
as it were, was the equivalent of those delicate virtues, that
gentle cradling of the soul, the soothing sweetness of which
he had learned from his mother and sisters. He was, in fact,
quite unconsciously seeking not so much a lover as a loving
companion.

Such, then, would Chopin's emotional state appear to
have been during a particularly sensitive and vulnerable adolescence. Kept at a high pitch by the passionate exercise of
his art, his emotions were presently to become focused on
Constance Gladkowska.

Suddenly he was to be deprived of that feminine presence
which, in accordance with the time-honored lovers' formula,
was sufficient to bathe his days in glory or to plunge him
into the deepest gloom. He was to be parted from his family,
cut off from all contact with familiar social customs, and

from those intimate friendships into which he had poured the overflow of his dreams.

This was to result in a profound change in his reaction to life which became apparent as soon as he left Warsaw. He vaguely felt that he was never to return, and his whole being underwent a kind of psychic contraction.

From the very beginning of his stay in Vienna, dissatisified with himself and with others, he showed a taste for solitude and that habit of mental refusal which were soon to become his dominant characteristics.

He gave himself up to the unshakable conviction that henceforth he was nothing but a foreigner destined to live and die alone, surrounded by people indifferent to his fate who meant nothing to him. He made acquaintances, but not a single friend.

His state of mind at that moment—his tendency to withdraw into himself—is brought out in melancholy fashion by the following quotation from a letter to his friend Titus: "It is only the various dinners, evening parties, concerts, and balls that I am obliged to go to that sustain me a little. I feel so sad, lonely, and abandoned here. I have, of course, to dress for these receptions and to appear in the various drawing rooms with a reasonably contented countenance. But I hurry back to my room, where I can give rein to my suppressed emotions by sitting down at my piano, which now is only too well accustomed to the expression of all my sufferings."

It was while he was in this unhealthy frame of mind that the dramatic news from Warsaw, where his family faced what he called the menace of "the invading Russian hordes," reached him. The signs of latent depression which he had just confided to Titus were suddenly transformed into a kind of nightmare in which he saw his family dead, Constance being tortured, and his childhood friends either wounded or completely vanished. All this while he himself (I borrow Chopin's own words) remained shamefully inactive, physically incapable of bearing arms and champing at the bit, while he played the piano in a foreign town where, to crown everything, public opinion was hostile to the cause of his fellow countrymen.

He was haunted by a state of acute anguish which was later to inspire those wild self-reproaches, his dumbfounded indignation at the announcement of the fall of Warsaw, feverishly written down in a notebook he kept while in Stuttgart.

The sudden revelation of patriotic feeling, which until then had been nothing more than the notion of a traditional and respectable outlook on life, broke upon the young musician in such an overwhelmingly dramatic atmosphere, in such desperate conditions, that it became an incurable torment, an ever-open wound, that was to remain with him for the rest of his life. The work which bears eternal witness to this feeling for his country was always more readily nourished by the meditative expression of tragedy or sorrow than by hopeful visions of a proud and vengeful future. Only in the heroic rhythms of a few of the Polonaises do we find the exalted aspirations of a people who do not admit defeat.

Chopin left Vienna as soon as he could, still not knowing in what town, or even in what country he would work out his fate—a fate which he now knew was to be that of an exile without a homeland, and not simply that of a traveler moving from place to place as he had hoped.

He tried Munich, passed through Stuttgart and Strasbourg, and finally arrived in Paris—noted on his passport as a stopping place on a journey which was to have taken him to London—but where, in fact, he was to stay for eighteen years. If, during these eighteen years, the development of his character and the progress of his illness had been plotted on a graph, the two curves would have been found to be very closely related. For, after Chopin the precocious child and Chopin the adolescent discovering life with newly awakened sensitivity, we now encounter Chopin battling for his genius against the sickness which was eating into him more deeply every day. He was no longer a being able to do as he wished, but a creature condemned to suffering.

However, one must recognize the fact that the sympathy aroused in France for the misfortunes of his country played no small part in inducing a momentary semblance ·of calm in his impressionable nature which was inclined to go from one extreme to the other on the slightest pretext.

The place had novelty. The habits of the people were friendly. His modest apartment was pleasant; in fact he imagined it to be of the most luxurious elegance. In actuality this elegance consisted of nothing more than a piano, a bunch of violets, and a glimpse of the Boulevard Poissonnière from his windows, which opened, according to him, on the "most beautiful view in the world."

Above all, he made contact with people of great impor' tance in the musical world—people from whom he might hope to receive useful advice concerning the development of his career. For virtuosi of every nationality and degree of merit, Paris, at the beginning of the nineteenth century, was still the musical Mecca of Europe.

All this helped to counteract the severe moral strain to which Chopin had just been subjected, and for a few weeks kept him in a state of cheerful animation.

His physical and mental tone at that time is indicated in a most characteristic fashion by an entirely unexpected piece of behavior. Because he had some assurance of his completely original quality as a pianist and as a person, he firmly declined the long term tutelage which Kalkbrenner wished to impose on him.

It was an act of independence and a sign of self-confidence which could not have been expected from him during the preceding months, when he was so predisposed to despondency and so lacking in morale owing to the disastrous prolongation of his stay in Vienna.

The welcome he received from the high society of Paris, and from those aristocratic Polish families who had migrated to the French capital, did much to foster a state of well-being, but it was a state which occurred seldom during his adult life.

To define the exceptional nature of the sympathy by which Chopin was then surrounded, one cannot do better than quote the words of the Marquis de Custine: "Not only do we love him, we love ourselves in him."

Without any doubt it was the happiest time of his life. Spontaneous outbursts of gaiety and the pranks which had been a habit with him during his childhood, but which had been forgotten during his adolescence, reappeared without any apparent effort on his part to induce them. Alas, this brief clearing of his mental outlook passed like a flash, and melancholy was not long in weaving her darkening veil around him once more.

It was only a few weeks later that his favored confidant, Titus Woyciechowski, received a letter containing the following piteous confessions: "Outwardly I am gay, especially among my own, I mean by 'my own' all the Poles. But, at the root of my being I am suffering an indefinable torment —full of presentiments, uneasinesses, nightmares, when it is not insomnia. Sometimes I feel indifferent to everything and sometimes a prey to the most intense homesickness. I long to live as much as to die and sometimes I feel a sort of complete numbness which incidentally is not without a certain pleasure but which makes me feel away from everything. Then suddenly vivid memories arise and torture me; hatred, bitterness, a frightful mixture of unhealthy sensations which attack me and leave me exhausted."

This confused gathering together of vague dreams, anxious aspirations, unreasoning eagerness, and overwhelming discouragement, reveals the Polish *zall* in Chopin which can best be rendered into English by the word *spleen*. Musset was to call it *mal du siècle,* and after that every adherent of the budding romantic movement adopted the pose of disenchantment during the passage from adolescence to maturity. Manfred, Chatterton, Overman, and the rest held that it was the crucial point, the most discouraging in man's existence. But this state of affairs, that Chopin subjects to a sort of clinical analysis which is not unimpressive, reveals the germ of a psychic disorder that is far removed from the languors of the world of fashion.

The very depths of his nature are affected, and it is only too easy to observe the characteristic threats of neurasthenia and the initial symptoms of tuberculosis which were to increase with the years. One cannot prevent oneself from being overcome by pity at this exhibition of physical ills and mental sufferings struggling to undermine that youthful promise which showed itself to be so instinctively alert to the eager calls of life. Not only did they affect his musical inspiration, which was affected by his personal torments, but they exerted a destructive influence over his relationship with other human beings.

As in Vienna, Chopin's only appearances were those he made in the aristocratic drawing rooms he so assiduously attended. In reality he went to them only as a means of providing himself with a temporary diversion, to enable him to put up with the wearisome slavery of teaching by which he earned his daily bread.

No matter what compliments he might receive on ac count of his elegant appearance or personal charm—and the desire to please was sometimes of more interest to him than to be liked—whatever enthusiasm the magic of his talent might arouse, whatever imaginative dream might be evoked in the wake of some fascinating feminine apparition, the few efforts at lighthearted caricature which he gave there— fugitive recollections of those burlesque mimicries which formed the greater part of his childhood's fun—always, ac' cording to what George Sand said, took on a touch of bitter' ness. He never gave the smallest part of his own personality, and when the sound of the applause died down, the excite' ment of a moment of forgetfulness at an end, he would find himself alone once more with a homesick, unapproachable Chopin, a Chopin who was unknown to himself.

His intimate friends often reproached him for, to use Montaigne's expression, this "fluctuating and unstable" at' titude. He hid his real personality by a systematic retreat behind a protective screen of excessive courtesy. "One does not know what his thoughts are," people said of him.

Marie d'Agoult has acidly defined this evasive behavior as "that of an oyster sprinkled with sugar"; she also made it a pretext for saying that with Chopin "there was nothing permanent except his cough." Liszt, who so often used his generous powers of appreciation on behalf of his comrade's brilliant qualities, could not withhold the comment that "Chopin's character is composed of a thousand shades which in crossing one another become so disguised as to be indistinguishable."

As the biographer Louis Esnault has remarked, not without some perspicacity, "he lent himself sometimes but gave himself never." This variable behavior, which Marie d'Agoult has unkindly attributed to two-facedness, must have been accentuated by Chopin's constant anxiety as to his state of health.

Without wishing to attach too great an importance to the unkind remarks with which Fétis plasters his obituary notice of Chopin in the *Biographie Universelle des Musiciens,* it has to be admitted that Chopin's immediate circle was inclined to interpret this characteristic combination of an external affability and a fundamental indifference as a sort of involuntary two-facedness, and its unexpected eddies were often apparent in his relationship with others. George Sand has described the phenomenon of Chopin's double nature in a phrase to which we shall have occasion to return. She says: "As he had charmingly polite manners one was apt to take as a friendly courtesy what in him was only frigid disdain, if not an insuperable dislike." One must add to this a suspicious disposition which he derived from his Polish origins and his terror of being deceived. We find its parallel in Mérimée's description of Stendhal's behavior.

Any sympathy shown to Chopin by a newcomer was made the excuse for an instinctive mental withdrawal and he illustrates this in a letter that he wrote during the first few months of his stay in Paris: "I am more and more on the lookout for circumstances that will enable me to avoid seeing anyone for the whole day through."

Although he permitted himself a certain amount of super-ficial social contact, he resolutely refused to have anything to do with intimate personal relationships. By giving up his independence he was afraid that he might suffer some loss or that he might complicate his way of life, which until the end of his life was dependent on minute observations curiously like those of an old bachelor.

Add to this his horror of every kind of familiarity, moral as well as physical—his fear of material responsibility, his total disregard of human reactions, "he did not understand or would not understand anything that was not personal to himself," as George Sand put it, and we have the elements of his character in a nutshell.

It was this negative outlolok, this fugitive quality that aroused bitter criticism, and, aggravated by his illness, other mental peculiarities made their appearance, the evidence for which, unfortunately, was to grow as the years went by.

Chopin recognized these symptoms himself in that intro-spective inventory he made of his difficulties of character in the letter to his friend Titus to which I have already re-ferred.

Hidden beneath those simple euphemisms, one cannot fail to detect that serious variability of temper over which his defective physical organism no longer had control. That he subconsciously dismissed anything likely to disturb his way of life is no longer in question. As he grew older, irrepressible outbursts of rage, induced by the slightest contradiction and so violent that they sometimes left him in a state of complete collapse for several days, became the outward signs of a growing mental intolerance.

The greater number of his pupils witnessed these outbursts of fury, which often ended disastrously for the piece of furniture nearest to his hand. One of the last of his pupils, Georges Mathias, was still frightened, years after Chopin's death, by the memory of incidents of this kind that used to occur during his lessons. George Sand, who had numerous opportunities of observing them, if not personally suffering from the effects of these sudden storms, said that "Chopin in a rage was terrifying."

His anger did not always appear to be the result of a nervous disorder; it took other, more subtle forms, but was nonetheless overwhelming.

George Sand has described them in her novel, *Lucrezia Floriani*; she writes:

As he was extremely polite and reserved no one was ever able to understand what was going on in his mind. The more exasperated he became, the colder his manner; one could only judge the depth of his fury by the iciness of his polite behavior.

It was then that he became really impossible, because he tried to argue and submit the realities of life, which he had never understood, to principles which he could not define. And so he showed a charm, a charm which was false and glittering, with which he tortured those who loved him. He was flippant, stiff, affected, and bored with everything. He had the air of one who bites gently for the pleasure of doing it and his bite went deep. Or, if he had not the courage to argue and joke, he would shut himself up in a sorrowful silence, in a horrible fit of the sulks. Everything seemed strange and uninteresting, he held aloof from everything, every opinion, every idea. "I do not understand that!" When he made that answer to the affectionate approaches of a conversationalist who was trying in vain to offer him some distraction, one could be certain that he heartily despised all that had been said to him and all that could be said.

This analysis must naturally be treated with caution. It should be borne in mind that, by giving free rein to her writing, the novelist of Nohant hoped, if not to hasten the breaking off of this torturing relationship by means of savage allusions—Chopin incidentally pretended not to recognize himself in them—to prepare public opinion for the rupture while placing herself in the most favorable light.

However, arguing a case though she may be, her description clothes her character with a psychological versimilitude to which a purely imaginative piece of fiction could not correspond with the same incisive detail. One can find, moreover, from the same pen, in *Mémoires de ma Vie,* an additional summing up which confirms this oblique reference: "No temper was more uncertain, no imagination darker or more wild, no susceptibility more impossible of satisfaction."

Liszt, who cannot be accused of consistent partiality, does to a certain extent confirm the accusations of this woman, who no longer loved Chopin and was anxious to recover her freedom.

In a book in memory of Chopin, Liszt agrees that "never was there a nature more imbued with whims, caprices, and abrupt eccentricities. His imagination was fiery, his emotions violent, and his physical being feeble and sickly." He ends with this question, charged with affectionate pity: "Who can possibly plumb the suffering deriving from such a contradiction?"

If one understands Liszt correctly, he does not hold Chopin's illness to be entirely responsible for a behavior that made any intercourse with him increasingly difficult. In fact, he asks himself whether this exaggerated instability, this spasmodic mentality, and this irritability, which showed itself sometimes in wild outbursts and sometimes by any icy reserve, are not the signs of a psychic indisposition which existed before the morbid symptoms of tuberculosis made their appearance. That is, did Chopin inherit at birth what is popularly known as a difficult character or should this spiritual intolerance, which became more marked as the years went by, be charged to his physical deficiency? It goes without saying that the second of these two theses, which is in accord with the well known development of tuberculosis, will be taken into consideration by those who have any medical knowledge.

But, if we set aside Liszt's opinion in the matter, that is to say the disassociation of the conflicting elements, it is nonetheless certain that in his contact with human beings and with ideas, Chopin carried within himself this "innate respect for everything that was most strictly conventional," as George Sand puts it. From this we understand that Chopin did not believe that it was possible to depart from a blind obedience to certain moral obligations and rules of life, which were the outcome of his upbringing, based, as it was, on a priori convictions. Any questioning of these roused him to furious anger or icy contempt.

He was not unaware of the unusual character of these sudden changes of temper, as the following sentences show. "As for my sentiments, I am always at sixes and sevens with everyone else." Again—and this is full of bitter discouragement: "It is not my fault if I am like a bad mushroom which poisons whoever tastes it."

Things tended to get more and more out of proportion, to such an extent that Chopin began to live in an atmosphere of gloomy suspicion, ready to complain bitterly at the least act or gesture that disturbed him. This became particularly noticeable during his last visits to Nohant. For if he was ready to declare that he fled society in order that people should not be upset by coming into contact with his bad temper, he was nevertheless ready to attribute the responsibility for his black moods to others, that is his intimates, for he was quite able to restrain himself in the presence of strangers.

Already difficult to understand, he now became difficult to live with. He was the victim of a sort of latent malady which, aggravated as much by his efforts to rid himself of it as by his weaknesses, slowly permeated to the core of his oversensitized being. Liszt had every reason for suspecting "the sufferings which derived from such a contradiction."

This examination of Chopin's character has been undertaken not so much to underline his whims as to express sympathy for one who, without the bodily strength to fight against these tyrranical torments, had no other recourse than to the miraculous message of music.

Rollinat, a frequent visitor at Nohant, has said that the pathetic episodes in the beautiful *Fantaisie in F minor,* which was composed almost under his eyes, reflect the ups and downs of a quarrelsome scene between the disillusioned lovers. If it does contain the echoes of those evil states of feverish exaltation, we can see that, at the same time, some of the most moving of his divine themes, to which the very voice of love itself seems to have lent the secret of ecstasy, also grew beneath the fingers of this musician of genius.

These personal idiosyncrasies of Chopin lead us to an

investigation of the behavior he exhibited toward those rare beings to whom he accorded what one might define as the "vital minimum" of his feelings of affection.

His family was the object of an exclusive cult, a tender idealized memory, over which neither time nor absence had any power and which always played a part in Chopin's ardent imagination during his exile. He was on terms of passionate intimacy with his childhood friends, Titus Woycie-chowski, Jean Matuszyucki, and Jean Bioloblocki, who were the chosen confidants of the wild and lovely outbursts of his youth in Warsaw, and, on a less exalted plane, we have Marcelline Czartoryska and the Countess Delphine Potocka.

The list of his chosen comrades whose friendship was a necessity to him ends here with the exception, of course, of the heroines of his love affairs, Constance, Marie, and George Sand. With the exception of George Sand, they were all of Polish descent.

From the moment when he left his own country he was always on his guard with people, as though he had a treasure to defend which was already destined for an unknown purpose. Even within that circle of friends, particularly attractive to him on the score of culture, fortune, and birth, which formed around him directly after his arrival in Paris, he was not known to have become involved in any attachment which overstepped the conventional limits of social usage.

When dealing at close quarters with such a fickle person as Chopin, the relentless logic of Montaigne, the "because it was he and because it was I," has no place. Chopin was always ready to say to friendship: "Thus far and no further," except—one cannot help observing this, and chapter and verse have been given in drawing attention to it—with regard to Polish refugees. In contact with them he was immediately at home. Like his own, their exile was made the pretext for interminable conversations in which Warsaw, what people were doing and thinking there, was the invariable center of interest. However flattering the growing fame with which he was being endowed by the admiration and affection of the cream of Parisian society may have been to him, it was by the opinions of the *Warsaw Gazette* and the comments of the musical circles in the capital of his youth— which in his dreams had become the center of the universe— that he measured his renown.

His two isolated friendships with Frenchmen, Eugène Delacroix and the cellist Franchomme, only serve to give greater weight to this exclusive racial fixation.

Curious as it may seem, he was attracted to Delacroix because of a common interest in details of dress rather than by any particular artistic affinity. Chopin viewed with distaste the innovations of contemporary French painting. He preferred the academic studies of David, the historical subjects of Baron Gros, and the traditional style exemplified in the portraits of Ingres. As George Sand points out, "conventional taste" was a characteristic element in Chopin's intellectual outlook, strangely at variance with his musical aspirations which were imbued with an affinity of originality.

Delacroix accepted this contradiction in principle with good grace, and it did not interfere with the frequency of their meetings or the range of their discussion. Painting apart, their points of contact were numerous. Bach and Mozart both held a privileged place in their admiration, and, though he never frequented the concert hall, and the theater only rarely, the success or failure of new compositions or of singers on the road to fame was a subject of great interest to Chopin.

Without malice, if not without irony, they discussed the

doings and behavior of the drawing rooms well known to them, together with the most recent perfumes and their makers.

A subject which gave rise to more serious discussion and closer agreement between them was their condemnation of liberal doctrines, or libertarianism as it was called. In this they saw the threat of political and social revolution, from which they expected the worst.

It was a lively exchange of ideas, largely promoted by their obvious similarity of outlook rather than by a sentimental intimacy based on emotion and personal attraction, and if we are to judge from passages in Delacroix's Journal, Chopin received rather more than he gave. It cannot be doubted, however, that Chopin brought to these meetings the very qualities, which were so often deliberately lacking in other directions, human warmth and understanding.

We have to consider the nature of his relationship with Franchomme from quite another angle, from which it is difficult to eliminate certain considerations of a strictly utilitarian order.

This excellent cellist, for whom Chopin was to write the last published work of his lifetime—the attractive but unequal Sonata, Op. 65—did not limit his friendship to the exhibition of a genuine admiration. He surrounded the composer, who was so easily discouraged by all the practical details of everyday life, with the beneficial qualities of a man of affairs, ready and able to do anything for him. As the circumstances arose, we find him playing the part of secretary and copyist, of business man and proofreader; he even undertook the removals from house to house, which with their harassing complications darkened the last years of a life already overburdened with the symptoms of disease. Above all, in the demands made on him as the inflexible intermediary at meetings with Chopin's publishers, Franchomme was tireless. For Chopin, publishers were never more than shameless exploiters of his "torture writings," as he called his compositions. Inclined as he was to gestures of generosity, and ever ready to lend his talent to performances in aid of charity, and this is a side of his character that we must stress, Chopin was not to be moved when it was a question of his interests as an author, so much so that he devoted the greater part of his correspondence to them.

One has to admit, therefore, that, while allowing for his affectionate gratitude, which cannot have been lacking, in return for the service, devoid of any self-interest, rendered by Franchomme, Chopin's recognition of his help, that freed him from material drudgery, was not entirely unselfish.

The list of Chopin's associates would not be complete without the name of Camille Pleyel. He was not only the first French publisher to accept Chopin's works, but commissioned the immortal *Préludes* and also manufactured the pianos which Chopin preferred to all others.

Some writers have sought to establish that, because he shared the melancholy honor of accompanying the great composer's funeral cortege with Delacroix and Franchomme, a long-standing intimacy existed between them.

But, while the relationship between Chopin and Pleyel went beyond pleasant business formalities, and though Pleyel certainly accompanied Chopin on a journey to London, becoming in consequence aware of the great unhappiness Chopin endured as the result of the breaking off of his engagement with Marie Wodzinska, there was no real cordiality in their companionship.

At the same time that Chopin was expressing his

inalienable gratitude to Pleyel, both by letter and by word of mouth, he was making most disparaging statements about him to third parties.

This unwitting duplicity is of a similar nature to that which Liszt's Egérie stigmatized. It was a changeability that derived from the unpredictable vacillation which has been freely denounced by so many of his friends.

Be that as it may, we should be careful to avoid anything that leads to the conclusion that this relationship with Pleyel was anything other than a casual acquaintanceship wholly dependent on chance circumstances and not one of Chopin's seeking.

The name of his pupil Gutmann, the kindly German giant, whose deep affection for his beloved master resulted in his receiving as a melancholy reward the composer's last words and sighs, brings to an end the list of the only "foreigners" for whom Chopin relaxed his attitude of suspicious reserve and instinctive distrust. An exception must be made, however, in favor of Bellini, whose work and character bore evident affinities to his own, and who, like himself, lacked the opportunity of developing his genius to the full owing to the unhappy life he endured.

The relationship between Chopin and the well known musicians of his generation, who were the avowed sponsors of the romantic movement, does not appear to have gone very deep. Indeed, they exerted no particular influence on his essential outlook or his musical style, which was rooted in the classics and derived from no contemporary school of thought.

He was not on intimate terms with Berlioz, and while the latter was unrestrained in his expressions of admiration and heartfelt sympathy, his explosive genuis disconcerted Chopin to the point of making him feel ill.

Both Mendelssohn and Schumann greeted him with generous enthusiasm during his brief visits to Germany. Though Chopin mocked at the tenor of Schumann's article, it must not be forgotten that it was the legendary "Hats off, gentlemen" that set him on the road to European fame, and, before he had met Chopin in person, Schumann was the enthusiastic torch-bearer of the unknown genuis.

But Chopin retained no pleasant memories of either Mendelssohn or Schumann, nor did he derive any artistic stimulus from their works; for him they remained casual acquaintances. He left the roll of music that contained the work dedicated to him by Schumann unopened on his piano for several months, and one cannot help feeling that, in view of the debt Chopin owed to the enthusiastic admiration of his first admirer, he was ungrateful and extremely discourteous.

On the other hand, his friendship with Liszt might have been expected to ripen into intimacy. From the musical point of view, everything seemed to indicate the probability of a lasting and perfect friendship between the two inspired virtuosi, who, each in his own way, were to transform the accepted traditions of the art of piano playing.

The one a poet, the other a magician, free from the least suspicion of professional jealousy, since both were assured of a brilliant career, they were engaged in similar love affairs that took them outside the usual range of middle-class conventionality, a factor which led them to offer a united front to the outraged critics and, at the outset, formed a strong bond between them.

The sudden break in their friendship is usually assigned

to a disagreement between their respective mistresses, one of those vague quarrels which the feminine nature so often construes as an irreparable insult to self-esteem.

Others, however, suppose that the inflammable author of *Indiana*, in her search for new sensations, may not have remained as insensible to the vivid aura that emanated from the vigorous personality of Liszt that her friendship with Marie d'Agoult demanded, a doubtful hypothesis, since the break between them took place at a time when George Sand was completely wrapped up in her new infatuation and was entirely devoted to Chopin.

At a later date, Liszt, without going into any details regarding the episodes which led up to the attitude adopted by the two women, limited himself to saying that "the two knights took up positions to defend their queens."

Chopin, on the other hand, showed himself to be exceedingly bitter about the matter and, according to some, outrageously indelicate.

In spite of his careful observance of the conventions, indelicacy should not be excluded from coming within the range of Chopin's instinctive reactions, and, after reading some of his letters, the reader will not be surprised to hear of some coarseness of language.

But, whatever the cause, he took up too decided an attitude in the matter for there to be the slightest possibility of any reconciliation between the four of them.

While the precise reason for the break remains in doubt, there are three other things which may have had some bearing on the cooling off in the sympathetic admiration Chopin felt for Liszt at the beginning of their friendship.

In the first place, Liszt had used Chopin's rooms, during his absence, as a meeting place with a girl. Secondly, a cadenza that Liszt had introduced into his transcription of Beethoven's *Adelaide* had, in Chopin's view, done violence to the expressive significance of the touching Cantilena, And finally, a grievance unconsciously inspired by the delicate nature of his own physique, the fact that his Hungarian rival enjoyed a robust and powerful constitution, which Chopin ridiculed in a burlesque which has remained famous, but which was so sadly lacking in himself.

The fact remains that, either from indifference or force of circumstances, Chopin remained at a distance from all those of his contemporaries who showed themselves most willing to applaud his genius. He remained aloof from the evidence of their brotherly sympathy, insensible if not hostile to their creative personalities, and took no interest in their aesthetic speculations, which carried them forward to the same glorious future. It was this spiritual inhibition which stultified his efforts and led him to prefer the indefinable enchantment of a solitude peopled with self-induced dreams, rather than to risk dealing with other ideas and human relationships.

No account of Chopin's friendships would be complete without some mention of his attitude toward women.

By this I do not mean his love affairs, which I propose to discuss at a later point in this essay, but his friendships with women which remained, with perhaps one doubtful exception, purely platonic.

He was attracted to two ladies of Polish society, the Princess Marcelline Czartoryska and the Countess Delphine Potocka, by his wholly natural predilection for his own countrywomen, and they were accorded the privilege of ranking among his best pupils on that account.

The attractive Countess Delphine kept the Paris society

gossips busy, and it has been suggested that Chopin was not wholly indifferent to her charms, a supposition which, while there is no evidence to confirm it, and, while it is useless to expect Chopin to have overcome his determined reticence sufficiently to confide a secret of this nature to anyone, may not have been entirely without foundation. For, even if we refuse to admit that this attachment was a sentimental infatuation, it is difficult to reconcile the outspoken free-dom of the letters Chopin wrote to this young society girl to a friendship without any of that intimacy wherein maidenly reserve may be considered superfluous.

Of course, this is assuming that we can rely on that part of Chopin's correspondence, which has already been published, to a greater extent than on the bogus dairy, which a certain M. Knosp foisted on Edouard Ganche or on the so-called Méthode, reproduced in extenso in an earlier part of this essay, from which Mme. Janotha managed to deduce some learned principles.

Chopin rarely expressed himself in prose, and, on account of this, he has been made a convenient peg on which to hang artistic theories even to the point of subterfuge.

In this case, however, the general tone of the correspondence must be held to bear the stamp of truth. It would appear that Chopin, while by nature chaste and continent, had been subject to an uncontrollable sensual impulse, a momentary madness, whichever way we look at it, that could only have been of brief duration.

The Count Potocka nipped this and other amorous adventures in the bud by removing the inflammable Countess from the scene in which her fatal attractions had had so marked an effect.

Like Heine's Lorelei, this Polish enchantress combined a

lovely voice with her feminine seductiveness, and if her feelings for Chopin went deeper than a friendship based on a mutual love of music, they were to receive a symbolical sanctification, as it were, during the composer's last moments.

The evening before Chopin's death, while he was in the throes of an overwhelming agony, the Countess, the composer's sister, and the Princess Czartoryska were impotent and sorrowing witnesses at his bedside. Chopin turned to her and asked her to sing, a song by either Stradella or Bellini it is said to have been, thus making this temptress of a moment's madness the messenger of his last farewell to music.

No doubt can be thrown on the relationship that Marcelline Czartoryska maintained with this genius of a fellow country-man, and no scandal can cast a shadow over the limpid clarity of their mutual attachment.

She was not only his best pupil—indeed the only one according to him, and by general consent of their contemporaries could play his works in the way he wished. She was equally his most faithful and solicitous supporter, and indulgent of his uncertain temper as she was, as able to show a complete understanding of his physical worries. It was to her lasting affection that Chopin turned for consolation when, with his pride mortally wounded by the rejection of his love, he was distracted by the harassing details of his daily life.

She was the only woman, apart from his mother and sisters, whom Chopin never thought to criticize. Very few of his friends enjoyed the trust that Chopin placed in Marcelline Czartoryska, and he had many occasions to be thankful for her warm human understanding.

He would, perhaps, have been inclined to view his friendship with Jane Stirling, whose admiration and devotion became all-embracing during the last years of his life, in a similiar light, had she not added to her generous care of the composer the idea of matrimony. Chopin learned of this through a third party, and was so horrified that, on the most flimsy excuses, he began to make plans for a concert in London in order to hasten his departure from this luxurious Scottish residence and a hospitality which had become embarrassing.

For some time past he had described himself as being literally overwhelmed by the excess of care with which his hostess surrounded him, even going so far as to attempt to convert him to her own religious beliefs, a task she pursued with an incorrigible persistence. The news that she contemplated marrying him brought matters to a head.

For one who had been obliged to come into daily contact with the established local gentry around Calder House, who thought of nothing but horses, dogs, whisky and whist, and who represented all that was most distasteful to an ailing and supersensitive musician, the idea of marriage seemed the last straw. He unburdened himself to his pupil Gutmann in terms that leave no doubt as to his attitude: "I am about as much that way inclined as if it was suggested that I should marry death."

Even after his return to Paris—where the occasional lessons he was able to give while resting on his bed did not provide sufficient money to pay his doctor—he considered the substantial gift, sent him by his pathetic and tactless admirer, in an attempt to lessen his burden of financial care, to be an intolerable interference in his private affairs. This simple soul's embarrassing devotion, which precipitated Chopin's sudden departure from Scotland, was not to be recompensed until after the death of her beloved composer. It was to her that

Chopin left the task of dividing among his few intimate friends those personal belongings, possession of which was to perpetuate his memory, and, in accomplishing the melancholy request, she was able to create the illusion that she was the composer's widow.

To the end of her days she gave evidence of a fervent devotion to Chopin's memory. Her letters to the dead man's sisters bear witness to an unshakable fidelity. It seems as though she wished to prove herself the perfect counterpart of all a loving woman should be.

It would be unwise to suggest that similar virtues were behind the intimacy, association is perhaps a more suitable word, that existed between Chopin and George Sand's daughter Solange. "She did evil because of her love of art," a servant observed after that obscure chain of events that caused them to leave Nohant for good.

There is no doubt that, in order to spite her mother, for whom she had no affection and who returned this dislike, she had several years earlier practiced her youthful powers of seduction on Chopin. For the moment, and there is good reason for believing it, Chopin succumbed, though he could not have been unaware of Solange's insincerity. It was a flirtation that helped to relieve the tedium of days that were saturated with an atmosphere of growing hatred.

But at the period we are considering, this unhealthy, ambigious state of mind no longer existed to prey on Chopin's distraught imagination. It certainly did not exist for Solange, recently married and violently in love with the insipid beauty of the sculptor whom she had just rescued from the clutches of her insatiable mother; nor did she attempt to continue the perverse behavior she had indulged in as a seductress of fifteen.

It seems highly probable that this curious relationship had its roots in an instinctive desire to present a united front in the face of public opinion, which was beginning to seek a reason for this sensational parting. This relationship was due to circumstances rather than to any real depth of feeling and aroused the sympathy of all those who were aware of the drama.

Solange's husband, whom Chopin disliked, and who by the irony of fate was to be entrusted with the task of immortalizing his rival's feature's in the second-rate statue that now adorns the composer's tomb in Père-Lachaise, was quite incapable of undertaking the affair, which had been carried on largely by letter. Chopin, who was so easily thrown off his balance by the least change in his daily existence, thought, perhaps ingenuously, that by this correspondence he might repair the break in their former intimacy that had lasted for over eight years.

The names of his two assistants, Mlles. de Rozières and Vera de Kolognivof, completes the list of Chopin's feminine associates.

Vera de Kolognivof became the wife of the artist Rubio who painted, for reasons I have stated in an earlier chapter, the most lifelike of Chopin's portraits.

Both of these ladies were daily visitors at Chopin's places of residence in Paris, and, in addition to the musical assistance they rendered, had the unenviable position of being the recipients of the composer's most intimate confidences. Indeed, because of the peculiar nature of their relationship with the master of the house, which covered every moment and event in his intimate dealings with men and affairs, nothing could escape them. In consequence, they were better informed than any of his friends of the details of his private life, and Mlle.

de Rozières was the only person, outside the inner circle of Chopin's friends, who knew the real reasons which led to his break with George Sand.

They obtained a very clear picture of the unhappy and preoccupied Chopin who, at a later date, accused them both of abusing his confidence by recounting a whole tissue of untrue anecdotes about himself.

No one was more aware of the unpredictable changes of mind that assailed this unstable character who, once aroused by some quite trivial incident, took so long to revert to normal, than were these two unfortunate assistants.

Except in the case of Marcelline Czartoryska, and the few men friends he made during his long stay in Paris, there can be little doubt that except as they ministered to his needs Chopin took little interest in human beings for their own sake.

If we examine the evidence of Chopin's legendary love affairs, we find that they mark three stages in the melancholy progress of his emotional life. The first two of these, although they remained unfulfilled dreams, fired his hypersensitive nature with the most ardent aspirations, while the third, extending, as it did, over a number of years, reached its tragic climax in an irreparable misunderstanding.

The memory of these discouraging experiences, which throw light on so many dissimilar aspects of his mental outlook, was to prompt him to these words of disillusionment: "I have never been loved as I would have liked to have been."

His first meeting with Constance Gladkowska, a young singer and fellow student at the Warsaw Conservatoire, made so deep an impression on Chopin that for a time he seems to have lost all sense of reality.

He was drunk with mystic exaltation and transported with ecstasy which, with his imaginative and sensitive temperament, went much deeper than any promptings of the flesh. Even to touch the dress of his adored one with trembling fingers would for him have been sacrilege. The very thought of declaring his love rendered him speechless. Though he saw her every day and dreamed of her every night for six months, Constance knew nothing of his consuming passion.

While she remained in ignorance, the letters with which Chopin inundated Titus Woyciechowski and Jean Matusinski are full of a lover's delirium. It was in an attempt to earn a smile of encouragement from the object of his passion that he arranged for her to take part in a concert he had organized, and it was for her that he wrote that quivering message, full of expectant happiness and jealous uncertainty, the *Adagio du Concerto en F.*

A waltz dedicated to Constance, the manuscript of which he sent to Titus, contains a passage marked by a cross. While this probably refers to some insignificant trifle, to Chopin's imagination it becomes "the most beautiful moment of his life."

Writing to Matuzynski from Vienna, at the commencement of his exile, he says: "As long as my heart beats I shall not cease to adore her. Even after my death I should like my ashes to be scattered at her feet." His obsession with "what people will think" prompted him to add: "If my letter were to fall into the hands of strangers what would they think of her?"

The only consolation that Vienna had to offer for his separation from her, which moved him to the verge of tears, was his friendship with a family in which one of the daughters bore the same Christian name as his adored one and who marked her handkerchiefs "Constantia."

Ranging from extravagant passion to a tender romanticism, Chopin's love, as one might expect of a youth who had forged the fetters of an indescribable torment for himself, had the effect of intensifying his imaginative life to the point where, for the moment, it became the only breathable atmosphere. It is only too easy to forecast the ending of this one-sided love affair.

A short while after the departure of her silent lover Constance married a small country squire, with whom she lived a quiet conventional life devoid of surprise. At the end of her days, having become both blind and a widow, her attention was drawn to a book by Karazowski. In it the author hints at the flame she had inspired in Chopin and the place that her image had occupied in the dreams of her fellow student. Indifferent to the immortality which quite unknown to herself the refusal of his adoration had conferred on her, she remarked: "After all, it is probable that Chopin would not have been as good a husband as my worthy Joseph."

Chopin invested his passion for Constance with all the force of his imagination. Inspired by illusory dreams, he, like, Pygmalion, brought the image of his love to life. His second experience of love was on a rather different level, and was steeped in a tenderness which he hoped would develop into a lifetime of harmonious comradeship.

He had known Marie Wodzinska, who was five years his junior, from childhood. She had filled the happy days of their holidays, passed in the hospitable home of her parents in the company of her brothers, who shared with Chopin the lax discipline of his father's school, with her vivacity and roguishness. He was to meet her again at Carlsbad in 1835, where he had gone to meet his father, who was undergoing a cure there.

The companion of his childhood was now a witty and attractive young lady, keenly interested in music and painting.

Chopin began to realize that the Marie of his youth had never ceased to occupy his thoughts. Until now, his out' pourings of tender phantasy had been an undefined passion, an ecstasy which, though he had been unaware of it, had its roots in those childish escapades they shared together. Schumann had undergone a very similar experience during his romance with Clara.

The maternal warmth of the Countess Wodzinski's greeting and the geniality of Marie's brothers reminded Chopin of the carefree years of his childhood in Warsaw. The intimate evenings spent in the family circle which encouraged him to improvise at the piano, and above all the marked interest that Marie seemed to attach to his person and his talent formed an ideal background for the flowering of this dream that had so suddenly arisen from the strange distillations of the past. A rose broken from a bouquet at the moment of parting, the two words "Be Happy" that he wrote in her album as a souvenir of the days which had passed too quickly, were to become the symbols of a secret spiritual camaraderie during the sadness of his solitary existence.

During the long winter months of 1835, when the hours seemed to pass with almost desperate slowness, Chopin would relive those enchanting moments beside the girl with whom he hoped to pass his future.

At last, during the following summer, he was able to rejoin the "well-beloved afar," who had just inspired the feverish outpouring of the *Ballade in G minor*, at Marienbad.

Encouraged by the evident emotion which accompanied their joyful reunion, awaited, so it seemed to him, with an impatience the equal of his own, emboldened by long con' versations during the dusk of summer evenings, with a trembling heart he dared to ask the question that was to settle his fate. And with the answer "Yes," Chopin experienced in that instant, which is worth all eternity, the only undiluted happiness of his whole pitiful existence.

But while the Countess Wodzinska had been won over and was prepared to give her consent to the union, she insisted that her husband, who was in Poland, should be consulted before the engagement was made public.

Once again the specter of uncertainty, which never ceased to cast its evil shadow over every event in Chopin's life, stood between him and the happiness he longed for so ardently.

He returned to his solitary existence in Paris to wait anxiously for the verdict which was to decide his fate. The weeks of waiting were filled with the sad and tedious monotony of teaching pupils who were unaware of the dream he carried in his heart.

The letters that passed between the lovers seem charged with a mutual embarrassment; no allusion is made to the promises they have exchanged or to the happiness they hope to share in the future. Even the word "Dusk," by which they had agreed to refer to the love which bound them one to another, is contained in phrases of no particular significance. The tenderest passage in one of these rare letters of Marie's is to tell "Chopena" that she has kept the pencil he left behind on the piano at Marienbad as a precious memento.

For his part, Chopin does no more than write the sorrowful air of a *largo con gran espressione* which he had composed some time before for his sister Ludwika in the album Marie had entrusted to him, and in reply she sent him a pair of embroidered slippers.

Then came her father's decision, humiliating and final,

supported by vague and embarrassing hints concerning Chopin's state of health and his uncertain financial position.

The real reason for the refusal, the family's opposition to the marriage of a musician of plebeian origin with the heiress of a well known palatine family, is passed over in complete silence.

Marie, bowing to the family will, wounded the unhappy Chopin still further by her icy farewell: "Rest assured that I shall always be grateful to you for your kindness."

Like Constance, Marie was not long in forgetting the sentimental adventure on which she had so boldly embarked, now that it had been vetoed by her father. A few months later she married Count Scharbeck, lord of the manor at Zelazowa-Wola where, twenty-seven years earlier, the musician who had dared to aspire to the hand and, who knows, perhaps to the inheritance of this daughter of Count Wodzinski, had been born.

Chopin made no protest nor did he write any reproach. As so often related, he contented himself by putting her letters from Marienbad and the dead rose from Dresden in an envelope tied with a faded ribbon—the tomb of an unfulfilled dream and a wounded heart. On the envelope, in the handwriting of a distracted being, he wrote the epitaph of his ruined happiness two Polish words, the meaning of which tells equally of a material loss of an infinite spiritual distress: *Moja Bieda.*

In his long association with George Sand, we find Chopin in an entirely different guise from that in which we have seen him in his affairs with Constance and Marie. There is no longer any question of sentimental dreams, ecstatic excitement, or delicate abandon. Instead, we find a long relationship sustained amid the prosaic realities of everyday life, which lacked the convincing impulse of mutual affection from first to last.

So far as Chopin was concerned, the commencement of their affair was due to a misunderstanding, a surprise attack on his senses which, unwisely prolonged, led to their living together, rather than as a consequence of any irresistible affection.

Chopin was still suffering from the blow of his broken engagement to Marie Wodzinska when, at the express request of George Sand, Liszt arranged a meeting at the house of a mutual friend, Mme. Marlian, who was later to play an important part in their relationship.

At an earlier encounter, the celebrated author of *Indiana* had made such an unfavorable impression that Chopin remarked: "What an antipathy this George Sand arouses! Is she really a woman? It seems doubtful to me."

But now, in an effort to restore his self-confidence and heal his wounded pride, he fell an easy victim to feminine flattery.

In spite of the fact that Chopin showed himself most unwilling to receive proof to the contrary, his doubts as to George Sand's sex were not long in being disproved.

Fastening on her prey, George Sand, who had loved so many men, brought about a physiological shock that for eight years completely changed the habits of the young artist, who, up to that moment, had been singularly uninterested in the appetites of the flesh. A feeling of responsibility, coupled with an illusory belief in this passion, led Chopin to abandon his material independence for the doubtful benefits of this ill assorted union.

Few human beings could have been less suited to attempt a life of domesticity than these highly strung artists, and inevitably the constraints of this existence gradually became intolerable for both of them.

Already a woman of considerable experience, imbued with vague philanthropic theories and half-baked libertarianism, which she made the excuse for her insatiable sexual appetite, George Sand made Chopin a party to an association by which he shared her favors with her son's tutor, the insignificant Mallefille.

Harnessed to her pen, as the ploughman to his furrow, she was a powerful, vital machine incapable of discernment or discrimination. She was repelled neither by vulgarity nor mediocrity, and felt no shame at the indiscriminate bestowal of her favors which, indeed, she deemed an honor.

It is difficult to imagine anyone less fitted to struggle against these circumstances than Chopin. For him, incapable of taking the initiative, every decision became the source of a distressing internal conflict. He was weak, instinctively introverted, and the slave to an unhealthy sensitivity from which flowed the nostalgic accents of his genius.

As Baudelaire says: "The artist's greatest honor is to accomplish what he has set out to do," and with Chopin, accomplishment was the result of precise and desperately concentrated perseverance which never ceased to astonish George Sand.

Physically, of course, Chopin's health was already undermined by the disease he had contracted during his youth, and his powers of resistance were slight. From childhood onward he was the slave of tradition, and contact with the most sophisticated Parisian society did nothing to shake his almost superstitious regard for the conventions.

And now, as the result of a chance affair, which George Sand regarded as no more than a passing adventure, these two personalities, diametrically opposed to one another, were to be parties to a kind of mock marriage, played on the out-skirts of conventional morality, with the parts normally played by man and woman reversed.

By nature inclined to be excessively scrupulous and im-bued with an almost feminine hesitancy, there can be no doubt that Chopin realized the difficulties which would face him once he had definitely resigned himself to this double existence.

His feeling for religion, which he had acquired from his mother rather than from any metaphysical convictions of his own, led him to fear the threat of punishment ascribed by the Church to all those who transgress the laws of chastity outside the bonds of holy matrimony.

Further, he was pursued by an indefinable feeling of guilt that he was profaning the memory of those he had loved so chastely by surrendering himself to the expert embrace of a mistress who had been enjoyed by so many others.

Finally, he could not rid himself of his terror of "what will people say." This fear had been with him since child-hood, and as I have already pointed out, he refers to it in a letter from Warsaw: "I am prepared to do anything on earth, so long as public opinion cannot contribute to my misfortune."

He was well aware of the false position in which he found himself, and in his letters to his parents and friends in Poland he attempted to disguise the true nature of his relationship with George Sand by referring to it as brotherly affection. It was not long, of course, before the affair became the sub-ject for gossip in the drawing rooms, and now that he had been caught up in the wake of this novelist, who disguised herself as a man and was referred to as a revolutionary blue-stocking, he appeared there less frequently than before.

We know of no love letters that passed between Chopin and George Sand, and the short notes written from either Paris or Nohant during their brief periods of separation contain no hint of their intimate relationship. George Sand's letters to Chopin, on the other hand, are believed to have been destroyed in Poland by Alexander Dumas *fils* at her request. A solitary sheet of paper, probably sent to Chopin during the course of an evening at Mme. Marliani's, containing the words "Someone adores you," is the only written evidence we have of a love to which legend has ascribed every conceivable emotional upheaval.

It is only from letters addressed to friends in times of emotional stress, notably at the beginning and end of their affair, that we obtain some insight into the motives underlying their reactions to one another.

We have Chopin's sorrowful letter to Delacroix, written on the day following their final separation, and from George Sand come the two messages she sent to Chopin's childhood friend, Gryzmala, in which she appears as counsel for the defence.

Justly famous for the light it throws on the mentality of an ageing and blasé woman excited at the prospect of capturing an innocent young man, the first of these two messages to Gryzmala is an attempted justification of her efforts to overcome the natural hesitancy of the young artiste whom she covets as prey.

While it appears that Chopin, whether from physical indifference or moral aversion, refuses to participate in what is referred to as "fleshly coarseness," George Sand attributed "an angelic sanctity" and "divine purity" to "that act which has no name save in heaven."

Eight years later the same correspondent is given her reasons for insisting on their separation, which in essence is a re-capitulation of the accusations she levels at Chopin in her scandalous book, *Lucrezia Floriani*.

Reading these two letters, it is impossible to find in them any of the marks of a true love affair. They amount to little more than a collection of verbose and contradictory argu-ments written entirely without shame and full of bitter re-crimination prompted by wounded feminine vanity.

No matter how deeply we probe for evidence to the con-trary, the life they led together for eight years brought neither party any real happiness. As they lived together they became accustomed to a relationship that amounted to mutual in-difference, with Chopin occupying the position of a distant relative who had been tacitly accepted in the family circle.

And shortly after their return from Majorca, either as the result of medical advice or perhaps because of a gradual cooling of her ardor, George Sand ceased to enjoy the physical pleasures she had shared with Chopin, for which he had sacrificed the privilege of his independence.

While she informs her correspondent that "the poor child is dying of the insane affection which he has for me," she also refers to Chopin by the gruesome title of "her dear corpse," and in an attempt to satisfy her feminine pride she casts herself in the role of nurse.

One can almost hear an echo of the cry of disillusionment uttered by his predecessor, Musset: "You believed yourself to be my mistress, but you were only my mother."

George Sand's numerous love affairs can perhaps be ex-cused on the grounds that she was always to remain unful-filled, but once her sensual curiosity had evaporated, or proved abortive, she sought to surround her lovers with those cares and attentions most in character with her role of "The Good Lady of Nohant."

We would be doing her an injustice, however, if we did not concede that her "original conduct," a virtue she applauds while deploring the restrictions, did not play a part in prolonging by several years a life which had already been threatened in Majorca.

But this ascetic restraint, far from calming Chopin, exasperated him, rather like withholding the drug from a morphia addict. On the one hand, George Sand accused him of contravening her hygienic regulations by seeking consolation in the arms of her maid, and on the other he experienced the bitter humiliation of realizing once more "that it was not for him to be able to live like anyone else."

Far from curing him of his tendency to neurasthenia, his daily contact with George Sand and her children, Maurice and Solange, served only to make him sensitive to the point of becoming unendurable. The care he received undermined his character and aroused him to a dark ferment of unconscious maliciousness.

His abnormally placid temperament gave place to moods of suppressed irritability and icy rage, while his uneasy relationship with Maurice, who had always regarded him as an "intruder" collected by his mother, now became one of open enmity.

For Chopin, George Sand's republican ideals which, with her aesthetic theories, formed the chief topic of conversation at Nohant, were subversive, and any gesture of friendship toward a visitor or an impolite word from Maurice was sufficient to arouse him. He had become jealous of everyone and suspicious of every intimacy from which he felt excluded.

A door left ajar or closed too loudly, a rebuke to a ser-

vant, the moving of a piece of furniture, all these gave rise
to a state of irritability, bordering on the dictatorial, which
led him to attempt to order his hosts' behavior and interfere
in their affairs.

In Chopin's eyes, the manners displayed at Nohant were
deplorable, and, since the ménage was conducted in such an
irregular fashion, he may have considered that his association
with George Sand entitled him to assume the role of head
of a family that had lacked male authority for so long.

On the other hand, his outrageous demands and exhibitions
of bad temper may have been further symptoms of the disease that was daily gaining its hold over him. But, whatever
the reason, the embarrassing scenes and the resultant ill will
became all-embracing, leaving nothing but hatred between the
two unhappy lovers whom affection had deserted.

At the time of the break between them, Mickiewicz, who
one would have expected to side with his compatriot, did
not hesitate to say that for several years "the poor woman"—
meaning George Sand—"had been the victim of a pitiless
tormentor."

Even allowing for some exaggeration on the part of the
Polish writer, one is forced to admit that Chopin's behavior
regarding family and domestic problems had become ill-tem-
pered meddling in affairs which were properly the responsibility of his hostess.

The decisive attitude that Chopin took during the unhappy
arguments that centered round Solange's engagement gave
George Sand the opportunity she had sought for some time
of breaking the bonds, which, so far as she was concerned,
were held together by force of habit.

While Chopin pretended not to recognize himself as the
hero of *Lucrezia Floriani,* and went so far as to say that he

admired "the sincerity and poetry which adorn this beautiful book," to those already partly in the know, its publication was the sign that the break was imminent.

And so the exhausting ordeal, which had taken up almost a quarter of Chopin's brief existence and brought out the very worst in his character, came to an end. Without anticipating the bitter irony of her suggestion, George Sand had advised Balzac a few years previously to entitle the book he was thinking of devoting to the love affair between Liszt and Marie d'Agoult, *Les Galériens ou Les Amours Forcés.*

The story of her own adventure with Chopin, the conflict which finally broke the chains of two beings bound to one another by circumstance, the ever-present thought of separation while neither dared look the possibility of freedom in the face, would have fitted that very title.

It was only later, in her *Histoire de ma Vie,* that George Sand found the courage to ask: "Why does not some combination of events beyond our control separate us from one another before it is too late?"

Relieved of the constant irritation that arose from his daily contact with a family who, if not openly hostile, were apathetic toward him, Chopin, in spite of ever more threatening symptoms of his illness, was to enjoy a more tranquil existence during the two long years before his death.

A more realistic philosophy—the Nitchevo of the Slav— for which his two early love affairs had prepared an unhappy background, was to support him in his rediscovered solitude.

He made vague plans for the future, gave further thought to the idea of going to America; then, in a moment of comparative good health and at the pressing and affectionate insistence of Jane Stirling, his recently acquired Scottish pupil, he decided on the journey to England, which, so his friend assured him, would provide him with the funds necessary to relieve his pressing financial embarrassment.

We know only too well to what extent the depressing climate, his profitless existence, coupled with a continual round of fatiguing receptions, contributed to the further undermining of his health, and when he returned to France, toward the end of November, 1848, he knew within himself that there was no hope of recovery.

The death of the only doctor, a Pole, in whom he had confidence, affected him deeply, and he felt so desperately lonely that he begged his sister to come and join him in Paris.

He could no longer walk, gave no more lessons, and, most alarming symptom of all, felt no desire to compose. His inspiration had shriveled within him, and his cry of: "I can scarcely remember how they sing in the country!"—coming from the very heart of his being—throws a revealing light on the mental outlook of the dying composer.

If we are to understand the real, the immortal Chopin, we must seek the explanation in the Poland of his childhood. Everything he stood for, everything that emanated from him was insistently, devotedly Polish. His true friendships, his true love affairs, Constance and Marie, his beliefs, his superstitions, his habits of life, his prejudices, even his illness, were formed before he left the banks of the Vistula.

And, above all, linked mysteriously in an incessant interplay between nostalgic folk song and the vivid national rhythms which never ceased to crowd his imagination, towered his musical genius.

He worked to no preconceived artistic creed, but obeyed a vital spiritual urge. In his inspired outpourings he sought to re-create the atmosphere of a childhood full of wonder and alive to the promise of the future. In addition to his physical misery, not the least of his sorrows was the longing for his country. His whole being longed for those places which he endowed with every delight and surrounded with a regret that he expressed in a letter to his parents: "I dream constantly that I am on my way to you across the unknown wastes that separate us. I know that they are the wastes of my imagination and that our reunion will remain an illusion. But does not the Polish proverb say: "The crown is only reached by means of the imagination?'—as for me I am a pure Mazovian."

This *cri de coeur* is the light by which we must examine everything in Chopin's character likely to affect his personal behavior, which, as Jane Stirling puts it, so often exceeded the normal.

While it is usual to describe his outbursts of ill temper, his ungovernable rages, his weakness of will, his secret bitterness, for he was incapable of hating openly like an ordinary man, as symptoms of the disease that was to prove fatal, they cannot be said to account for the whole of his behavior. To all these we must add the rancor of his exile; while his body was in France, his heart was in Poland.

Not until his death was this heart of his, that had pulsed with such constant affection for the land of his youth, to find a final resting place in the parish church where he had listened to Mass at his mother's side.

From his eighteenth year onward his personality underwent little further development, and, in truth, the rest of his life was spent in the dream world of his youth.

As we have seen, the praises Paris sang in celebration of his triumphs meant little to him; it was what Warsaw wrote and thought that really mattered.

Ways of life, opinions, and principles were accepted without question, so long as they sprang from Polish origins. One
can hear the ring of pride in his claim, "as for me I am a
pure Mazovian." If we find evidence of a mistrust of speculative thinking, if his notions of good and evil reflect an elementary dogmatism that George Sand referred to as a "narrow-
ness of soul," and if his aversions as well as his enthusiasms
appear as reflex instincts in which argument plays no part,
it is to the ineradicable influences of his childhood that we
must look if we are to account for his intolerance and those
exhibitions of arbitrary behavior.

A kind of second Chopin, unheard by those around him,
must have coexisted with the fashionable young artist that
appeared in the flesh, a being lost, as he tells us, amid mysterious and nameless wastes which separate him from his own
people and across which he reaches in the vain endeavor to
recapture his childhood.

Doctors have invented the barbarous name of schizophrenia
to describe this state of imaginative and spiritual isolation
which in Chopin's case was exaggerated by the special characteristics of his basic physical disease. Indeed, Chopin's illness seems almost to have intensified that side of his character
which attracts our devotion.

Tuberculosis certainly had the deplorable effect of exaggerating his faults and weaknesses in everyday life, but it is with
that secret being who had no contact with material things,
who was able to escape from himself into the world of un-
reality, that one feels oneself to be in a state of complete
spiritual affinity.

It is this legendary Chopin that we must cherish. By dis-
regarding the deprecatory facts of his daily life, but going to the
heart of the essential truth, we preserve the image of a Chopin

who answers all our aspirations, a Chopin who existed in a world created by his imagination, who had no other existence save that of his dreams, no other desire than to relive the enchantments of the past, who by the outpourings of his genius was able to immortalize the dreams and longings of countless human souls.

REFERENCE
SECTION

BIBLIOGRAPHY

ABRAHAM, GERALD. *Chopin's Musical Style.* London: Oxford University Press, 1939. 116 pp.

ANONYMOUS: *Chopin, Thumb-Nail Sketches of Great Composers.* London: Paxton, 1926. 14 pp.

ANONYMOUS. *Frédéric Chopin, sa vie, son oeuvre.* Paris: Bernard Grasser, 1938. 38 pp.

AUDLEY, MME. A. *Frédéric Chopin, sa vie et ses oeuvres.* Paris: E. Plon et Cie, 1880. 245 pp.

BANDROWSKI, JULJUSZ. *Zycie Chopina.* Warsaw: Gebethner i Wolff, 1938. 129 pp.

BARBAG, SEWERYN. *Studjuim o Piesniach Chopina.* Warsaw: Wydarrnictivo Zakaldu Narodowego Im, Ossolinskich, 1927. 60 pp.

BARBEDETTE, HIPPOLYTE. *Chopin.* Paris: Leiber, 1861. 68 pp.

BAROJA Y NESSI, PIO. *Chopin y Jorge Sand.* Barcelona: Ediciones Pallas Bartrés, 1941. 243 pp.

BARRY, KEITH. *Chopin and His Fourteen Doctors.* Sydney: Australasian Medical Publishing Co., 1934.

BENNET JOSEPH. *Frédéric Chopin.* London: Novello, Ewer & Co., 1884. 71 pp.

BIDOU, HENRI. *Chopin.* Paris: Félix Alcan, 1925. 244 pp.

BIDOU, HENRI. *Chopin.* (Translated by Catherine Alison Phillips.) New York: Alfred A. Knopf, 1927. 267 pp.

BINENTAL, LEOPOLD. *Chopin. Dokumente und Erinnerungen aus seiner Heimatstadt.* Leipzig: Breitkopf und Härtel, 1932. 193 pp.

BINENTAL, LEOPOLD. *Chopin.* Paris: Les Editions Rieder, 1934. 122 pp.

BINENTAL, LEOPOLD. *Chopin.* Warsaw: Wydawnictwo Ksiegarni F. Hoesicka, 1937. 172 pp.

BOHME, CHARLES. *Frédéric Chopin, l'homme et l'oeuve*. Nancy: L. Stoquert, 1924.

BONNEFON, MARIE FRANCOIS JOSEPH JEAN DE. *Triptyque d'âmes*. Paris: Picart, 1926. 78 pp.

BORDES, MARC. *La maladie et l'oeuvre de Chopin*. Lyon: Bose Frères, 1932.

BOSCH, CARLOS. *Chopin*. Madrid: Ediciones Mercurio, 1929. 134 pp.

BOSCHOT, ADOLPHE. *Musiciens poètes (Bach, Beethoven, Schubert, Liszt, Chopin)*. Paris: Librairie Plon, 1937. 202 pp.

BRONARSKI, LUDWIG. *Harmonika Chopina*. Warsaw: Towarzystwo Wydawnicze Muzyki Polskiev, 1935. 480 pp.

BRONARSKI, LUDWIG. *Etudes sur Chopin. Vol. I.* Lausanne: Editions La Concorde, 1944. 175 pp.

BRONARSKI, LUDWIG. *Etudes sur Chopin. Vol. II.* Lausanne: Editions La Concorde, 1946. 175 pp.

BRONARSKI, LUDWIG. *Chopin et l'italie* (Preface by D. E. Inghelbrecht). Lausanne: Editions La Concorde, 1947. 149 pp.

BROOKSHAW, SUSANA. *Concerning Chopin in Manchester*. (On a concert at which Chopin played, held in Manchester, August 28, 1848.) Manchester: Richard Bates, 1937. 27 pp.

CAPLAIN, FERNAND. *La vie amoureuse de George Sand*. Paris: Pédépradé, 1936. 188 pp.

CHANTAVOINE, JEAN. *Musiciens et poètes. L'italianisme de Chopin*. Paris: F. Alcan, 1912. 220 pp.

CHOPIN, FRÉDÉRIC FRANCOIS. *Souvenirs inédits de Frédéric Chopin*. (Collected by Mieczyslaiw Karlowicz. Translated by Laure Disière.) Paris: Librairie Universitaire, 1904. 224 pp.

CHOPIN, FRÉDÉRIC FRANCOIS. *Lettres de Frédéric Chopin à Jean Bialoblocki*. (Edited by Stanislas Pereswiet.) Warsaw: Soltan, L'Union Nationale des Etudiants de Pologne, 1926. 80 pp.

CHOPIN, FRÉDÉRIC FRANCOIS. *Gesammelte Briefe*. (Translated and edited by Dr. A. V. Guttry.) Munich: George Muller Verlag, A. G., 1928. 464 pp.

CHOPIN, FRÉDÉRIC FRANCOIS. *Lettres*. (Edited by Henri Opienski; translated by Stéphane Danysz; Foreword by Ignace Jan Paderewski.) Paris: Société française d'editiones Litteraires et Techniques, 1933. 591 pp.

CHOPIN, FRÉDÉRIC FRANCOIS. *Letters.* (Collected and edited by Dr. Henryk Opienski.) Warsaw: Nakladem Jaroslawa Iwaszkiewicza i "Wiadomosci Literackich," 1937. 373 pp.

CHOISY, FRANK. *Frédéric Chopin.* Geneva: Conservatoire populaire de musique, 1923. 72 pp.

COATES, HENRY. *Chopin.* London: Novello & Co., Ltd., 1940. 16 pp.

CORTOT, ALFRED. *Aspects de Chopin.* Paris: Editions Albin Michel, 1949. 324 pp.

DAHMS WALTER. *Chopin.* Munich: O. Halbreiter, 1924. 81 pp.

DAVISON, JAMES WILLIAM. *An Essay on the Works of Frédéric Chopin.* London: Wessel & Stapleton, 1843. 18 pp.

DAVISON, JAMES WILLIAM. *Frédéric Chopin.* London: William Reeves, 1843. 18 pp.

DELACROIX, EUGÈNE. *Journal* (3 vols. Edited by André Joubin.) Paris: Librairie Plon, 1932. Vol. I, 503 pp.; Vol. II, 483 pp.; Vol. III, 518 pp.

DELACROIX, EUGÈNE. *The Journal.* (Translated by Walter Pach.) London: Jonathan Cape, 1938. 731 pp.

DEMANGE, CHARLES. *Chopin.* Paris: Bibliothéque des Marches de l'est, 1911.

DOUMIC, RENÉ. *George Sand. Dix conférences sur sa vie et son oeuvre* Paris: 1900. 363 pp.

DOUMIC, RENÉ. *George Sand. Some Aspects of Her Life and Writings.* (Translated by Alys Hallard.) London: Chapman & Hall, 1910. 309 pp.

DUNN, JOHN PETRIE. *Ornamentation in the Works of Frédéric Chopin.* London: Novello & Co., Ltd., 1921. 75 pp.

DRY, WAKELING. *Chopin.* London: John Lane, the Bodley Head, Ltd., 1926. 118 pp.

EGERT, PAUL. *Fredrich Chopin.* Potsdam, 1936. 128 pp.

ENAULT, LOUIS. *Frédéric Chopin.* Paris: E. Thunot, 1936. 47 pp.

FERRA I PERELLO, BARTOMEU. *Chopin and George Sand in the Cartuja de Valldemosa.* (Translated by James Webb.) Palma de Mallorca: 1932. 39 pp.

FINCK, HENRY T. *Chopin and Other Musical Essays.* London: T. Fisher Unwin, 1889.

GANCHE, EDOUARD. *Frédéric Chopin. Sa vie et ses oeuvres, 1810-1849.* Paris: Mercure de France, 1913. 462 pp.

GANCHE, EDOUARD. *Dans le souvenir de Frédéric Chopin.* Paris: Mercure de France, 1925. 274 pp.

GANCHE, EDOUARD. *Souffrances de Frédéric Chopin. Essaie de médecine et psychologie.* Paris: Mercure de France, 1935. 287 pp.

GARIEL, EDWARD. *Chopin, la traditional de sa musica.* Mexico: 1895.

GEDDO, ANGELO. *Chopin.* Brescia: Giulio Vannini, 1937. 215 pp.

GIDE, ANDRE. *Notes on Chopin.* (Translated by Bernard Frechtman.) New York: The Philosophical Library, 1949. 126 pp.

GILLINGTON, MAY CLARISSA. *A Day with Frédéric Chopin.* London: Hodder & Stoughton, 1911. 47 pp.

HADOW, SIR WILLIAM HENRY. *Studies in Modern Music, Vol.* 2, Frederick Chopin. pp 79-170. London: Seeley & Co., Ltd., 1895.

HADDEN, J. CUTHBERT. *Chopin.* London: J. M. Dent & Sons, Ltd., 1903. 248 pp.

HEDLEY, ARTHUR. *Chopin.* London: J. M. Dent & Sons, Ltd., 1947. 214 pp.

HILLMAN, ADOLF. *Chopin.* Stockholm: Wahlstrom and Widstrand, 1920. 175 pp.

HIPKINS, ALFRED JAMES. *How Chopin Played.* London: J. M. Dent & Sons, Ltd., 1937. 39 pp.

HOESICKA, FERDYNAND. *Fryderyk Chopin. Zarys Biograficzny.* Petersburg: Nakladem Ksiegarni K. Grendynszyskieg, 1899. 107 pp.

HOESICKA, FERDYNAND. *Chopin. Zycie i Tworczosc* (3 vols.). Warsaw: Nakladem Ksiegarni F. Hoesicka, 1904. 881 pp.

HOESICKA, FERDYNAND. *Chopin. Zycie i Tworczosc* (3 vols.). Warsaw: Nakladem Ksiegarni F. Hoesicka, 1910-11. Vol. 1, 347 pp.; Vol. 2, 532 pp.; Vol. 3, 561 pp.

HOESICKA, FERDYNAND. *Chopiniana* (Vol. 1). *Korespondencya Chopina.* Warsaw: Nakladem Ksiegarni F. Hoesicka, 1912. 469 pp.

HUEFFER, FRANCIS. *Musical Studies.* Edinburgh: A. & C. Black, 1880. 258 pp.

HUNEKER, JAMES. *Chopin, the Man and his Music.* London: William Reeves, 1921. 415 pp.

HUNEKER, JAMES. *Mezzotints in Modern Music.* (Critical Essays on Brahms, Tchaikovsky, Chopin, Strauss, Liszt, and Wagner.) London: William Reeves, 1928. 318 pp.

HUTSCHENRUIJTER, WOUTER. *Frédéric Chopin.* s'-Gravenhage: 1939. 104 pp.

INVERNIZZI, FRANCO. *Chopin.* Milan: Edizioni Aurora, 1935. 255 pp.

IWASZKIEWICZ, JAROSLAV. *Summer at Nohant.* (A play in three acts. Translated by Celina Wieniewska.) London: Minerva Publishing Company, 1942. 72 pp.

JACHIMECKI, ZDZISLAW. *Fryderyk Chopin.* Cracow: Rys Zycia Tworczosci Nakladem i czcionkami drunkarni narodowej, 1927. 165 pp.

JACHIMECKI, ZDZISLAW. *Frédéric Chopin et son oeuvre.* (Preface by Edouard Ganche.) Paris: Librairie Delagrave, 1930. 244 pp.

JANKOWSKI, JOZEF. *Milose Artysty. Szopen i pani Sand.* Warsaw: Naklad Gebethnera I Wolffa, 1927. 145 pp.

JONSON, GEORGE CHARLES ASHTON. *A Handbook of Chopin's Works.* London: William Heinemann, 1905. 200 pp.

JONSON, GEORGE CHARLES ASHTON. *A Handbook of Chopin's Works.* (Second edition, revised). London: William Heinemann, 1908. 287 pp.

KARASKOSKI, MORITZ. *Friedrich Chopin. Sein Leben, Seine Werke und Briefe.* (2 Vols.) Dresden: F. Ries, 1877. Vol. I, 228 pp.; Vol. II, 206 pp.

KARASKOSKI, MORITZ. *Frédéric Chopin, His Life and Letters.* (Translated by Emily Hill.) London: William Reeves, 1938. 479 pp.

KARENINE, WLADIMIR. *George Sand, sa vie et ses oeuvres.* (4 Vols.) Paris: Plon, 1899-1926.

KARLOWICZ, MIECZYSLAW. *Souvenirs inédits de Frédéric Chopin.* (H. Welter). Paris: Librairie Universitaire, 1904. 224 pp.

KARLOWICZ, MIECZYSLAW. *Pamiatki po Chopinie.* Warsaw. Sklad Glowny w Ksiergarni Jana Fiszera, 1904. 403 pp.

KELLEY, EDGAR STILLMAN. *Chopin the Composer. His Structural Art and Its Influence on Contemporaneous Music.* New York and London: G. Schirmer, 1913. 190 pp.

KLECZYNSKI, JEAN. *Frédéric Chopin. De l'interpretation de ses oeuvres.* Paris: A. Noël, 1880. 95 pp.

KLECZYNSKI, JEAN. *The Works of Frederic Chopin. Their Proper Interpretation.* (Translated by Alfred Whittingham.) London: William Reeves, 1882. 75 pp.

KLECZYNSKI, JEAN. *Chopin's Greater Works. How They Should Be Understood.* (Translated with additions by Natalie Janotha.) London: William Reeves, 1896. 115 pp.

KOCZALSKI, RAOUL. *Frédéric Chopin. Betrachungen, Skizzen, Analysen.* Cologne: 1936. 221 pp.

LANDOWSKA, WANDA L. *Frédéric Chopin et Gabriel Fauré.* Paris: Richard-Masse, 1946. 222 pp.

LANGE, INA. *Skilda Tiders Musixmästare* (Händel, Beethoven, Chopin, Sibelius). Stockholm: P. A. Norstedt & Söners Förlag, 1913. 205 pp.

LANGE, INA. *Frédéric Chopin och Hans Alskade.* Stockholm: Lavs, Hökerbergs Bokförlag, 1921. 226 pp.

LEE, ERNEST MARKHAM. *Chopin.* London: Chappell & Company, Ltd., 1948. 28 pp.

LEGOUVÉ, ERNEST. *Soixante ans de souvenirs.* (2 Vols.). Paris: Hetzel et cie, 1886-87.

LEICHTENTRITT, HUGO. *Frédéric Chopin.* Berlin: Verlag "Harmonie," 1905. 144 pp.

LEICHTENTRITT, HUGO. *Analyse von Chopins Klavierwerken.* (2 Vols.). Berlin: Max Hesses Verlag. Vol. 1, 1921; Vol. 2, 1922. Vol. 1, 281 pp.; Vol. 2, 280 pp.

LENZ, WILHELM VON. *Die grossen Pianoforte-Virtuosen unserer Zeit.* (Liszt, Chopin, Tausig, Henselt.) Berlin: B. Behrs Buchhandlung, 1872. 111 pp.

LISZT, FRANZ. *F. Chopin.* Paris: M. Escudier, 1852. 206 pp.

LISZT, FRANZ. *Life of Chopin.* (Translated from the French by Martha Walker Cook.) Boston: Oliver Ditson, 1872. 202 pp.

LISZT, FRANZ. *Fr. Chopins Individualität.* Leipzig: Breitkopf und Härtel, 1880. 56 pp.

LISZT, FRANZ. *Life of Chopin.* (Translated in full for the first time by John Broadhouse.) London: William Reeves, 1899. 240 pp.

LISZT, FRANZ. *Chopin.* (Translated by Dr. A. Chybinskiego.) Welwowie: Nakladem Ksiegarni H. Altenberga, 1924. 118 pp.

LOUCKY, ROBERT. *Chopin.* Básrúk Tónu Nakladetelske Druztro Maje v Praze, 1947. 353 pp.

MAINE, BASIL. *Chopin.* London: Duckworth, 1933. 140 pp.

MARIOTTI, GIOVANNI. *Chopin.* Florence: Rinascimento del Libro, 1933. 353 pp.

MARVASI, ROBERTO. *Chopin Conferenza di Roberto Marvasi.* Naples: Riccardo Marghieri di Giuseppe, Galena Umberto, 1899.

MAUCLAIR, CAMILLE. *Le religion de la musique. Une causerie sur Chopin.* Paris: Fischbacher, 1928.

MAUROIS, ANDRÉ. *Frédéric Chopin.* Montreal: Les Editions Variétés, 1942. 91 pp.

MIOMANDRE, FRANCIS DE. *Mallorca.* Grenoble: B. Arthaud, 1933. 64 pp.

MULLER, IVAN. *Friedrich Chopin.* Erlangen: Verlag von Andreas Deichert, 1879. 24 pp.

MURDOCH, WILLIAM. *Chopin, His Life.* London: John Murray, 1934. 410 pp.

NIECKS, FREDERICK. *Frederick Chopin, as a Man and Musician.* (2 Vols.). London: Novello, Ewer & Co., 1888. Vol. 1, 340 pp.; Vol. 2, 375 pp.

NIGGLI, ARNOLD. *Friedrich Chopins Leben und Werke.* Leipzig: 1879.

NOWACZYNSKI, ADOLF. *Mlodose Chopina.* Warsaw: Iowarzystwo Wydawnicze Roj, 1939. 231 pp.

OLDMEADOW, ERNEST J. *Chopin: Bell's Miniature Series of Musicians.* London: George Bell & Sons, 1905. 65 pp.

OPIENSKI, HENRYK. *Chopin.* Warsaw: E Wende i Spolka, 1910. 139 pp.

OPIENSKI, HENRYK. *Le style musical polonais ancien et moderne.* Paris: Alcan, 1918. 107 pp.

PADEREWSKI, IGNACE JAN. *Chopin, un discours.* (Translated from the Polish by Laurence Alma Tadema.) London: W. Adlington, 1911. 30 pp.

PADEREWSKI, IGNACE JAN. *A la mémoire de Frédéric Chopin.* (Translated by Paul Cazin.) Paris: Agence Polonaise de Presse, 1911. 14 pp.

PALOMER, MOSSEN JOSEPH. *Chopin a Arenys de Mar.* Arenys de Mar: J. Folch i Torres, 1921. 44 pp.

PASKHALOV, VYACHESLAV. *Shopen.* Moscow: Gosudarstrennoe Muzuika 'noe Isdatelstvo, 1941. 74 pp.

PLAISANT, MARCEL. *Chopin.* Paris: A. Durand et Fils, 1926. 37 pp.

POIRÉE, ELIE. *Chopin.* Paris: Libraire Renouard, 1907. 125 pp.

POLINSKI, ALEKSANDER. *Dzieeje muzyki polskiej.* Warsaw: Sklad glowny w ksiegarni H. Albenberga we Lwowie Warszara E Wende i Spolka, 1907. 280 pp.

POLINSKI, ALEKSANDER. *Chopin.* Warsaw: 1914.

PORTE, JOHN FRANCIS. *Chopin the Composer and His Music.* London: William Reeves, 1935. 193 pp.

POURTALES, GUY DE. *Chopin ou le poéte.* Paris: Librairie Gallimard, 1927. 254 pp.

POURTALES, GUY DE. *Liszt et Chopin. Deux abrégés sans musique.* Cahiers de la Quinzaine. Paris: L'Artisan du Livre, 1929. 75 pp.

PRINCET, MAURICE, *Frédéric Chopin.* Paris: Réveil Economique, 1932. 79 pp.

PRZYBYSZEWSKI, STANISLAW. *Sur la psychologie individuelle Chopin et Nietszche.* Berlin: F. Fontane & Co., 1892. 48 pp.

PRZYBYSZEWSKI, STANISLAW. *Szopen a Narod.* Cracow: "Ksiazka," 1910. 53 pp.

PUGNO, RAOUL. *The Lessons of Raoul Pugno.* (Includes a short biography of Chopin by M. Michel Delines. Translated by Ethel Colburn Mayne.) London: Boosey & Co., 1911. 71 pp.

RAYSON, ETHEL. *Polish Music and Chopin Its Laureate.* London: William Reeves, 1916. 64 pp.

REES, CATHERINA FELICIA VAN. *Frederik Chopin.* Amsterdam: Van Kampen et Zoon, 1880.

REDENBACHER, ELSE. *Frédéric François Chopin.* Leipzig: Reclam, 1923.

ROBERT, PAUL LOUIS. "Etudes sur Boieldieu, Chopin, et Liszt." Published in the *Bulletin de la Société libre d'emulation de Rouen.* Rouen: 1912, pp. 169-243.

ROCHEBLAVE, SAMUEL. *George Sand et sa fille.* Paris: C. Lévy, 1905. 200 pp.

SAND, AURORE. *Journal intime de George Sand.* Paris: Calmann-Lévy, 1926. 232 pp.

SAND, GEORGE. *Un hiver à Majorque.* Paris: Calmann-Lévy, 1842.

SAND, GEORGE. *Historie de ma vie.* (4 Vols.). Paris: Cadot, 1854-55.

SAND, GEORGE. *Correspondance, 1812-1876.* (6 Vols.). Paris: Calmann-Lévy, 1882-84.

SCHALLENBERG, EVERT WILLEM. "Chopinologie." An Essay. Pp. 86-98 of *Muziekhistorische Perspectieven.* Amsterdam: N. V. De Spieghel, 1932. 154 pp.

SCHALLENBERG, EVERT WILLEM. *Frédéric Chopin.* (Translated from the Dutch by M. Smedts.) London: Sidgwick & Jackson, 1949. 57 pp.

SCHARLITT, BERNARD. *Friedrich Chopins gesammelte Briefe.* Leipzig: Brietkopf und Härtel, 1919. 289 pp.

SCHMIDT, HANS: "Stufeniweise geordnetes Verzeichnis" *Sammtlicher Kompositionen* von Friederich Chopin. Vienna: Wessely.

SCHNEIDER, LOUIS. *Une heure de musique avec Chopin.* Paris: Aux editions cosmopolites, 1930. 62 pp.

SCHUCHT, JEAN. *Friederich Chopin und seine Werke.* Leipzig: C. F. Kahnt, 1897. 68 pp.

SCHUMANN, ROBERT ALEXANDER. *Musik und Musiker.* (4 Vols.). Leipzig: George Wigans Verlag, 1854. Vol. 1, 328 pp.; Vol. 2, 286 pp.; Vol. 3, 293 pp.; Vol. 4, 304 pp.

SCHUMANN, ROBERT ALEXANDER. *Music and Musicians.* (Translated by Fanny Raymond Ritter.) London: William Reeves, 1880. 540 pp.

SCHUMANN, ROBERT ALEXANDER. *Musik und Musiker.* (2 Vols.). (Edited by Martin Kreisig) Leipzig: Breitkopf und Härtel, 1914. Vol. 1, 511 pp.; Vol. 2, 561 pp.

SEGUEL, MANIA. *Chopin's Tempo Rubato.* Altham, Accrington: The Old Parsonage Press, 1928. 26 pp.

SOLENIERE, EUGÈNE DE. *Notules et impressions musicales.* Paris: Seven et Rey, 1902.

SOWINSKI, ALBERT. *Les musiciens polonais et slaves.* Paris: Librairie Adrien Le Clerc et Cie, 1857. 599 pp.

STRACHEY, MARJORIE. *The Nightingale.* London: Longmans Green & Co., 1925. 305 pp.

STRENGER, HENRYK. *O Zycin Chopina, gienjuszu i duchu jego muzyki.* Warsaw: Nakladem Autova, 1910. 124 pp.

STRZELECKI, ADOLF. *Karty z zycia Chopina.* Cracow: Ksiegarnia Gebethnera i Spolki, 1901, 132 pp.

SZULC, MAROIN ANTONI. *Fryderyk Chopin.* Poznan: Nakladem Ksiegarni Jana Konstantego Zupanskiego, 1873. 293 pp.

TARCZYNSKI, TADEUSZ ALF. *Homage to Chopin.* Glasgow: The Polish Library, 1942. 31 pp.

TARNOWSKI, STANISLAW. *Chopin i Grollger.* Cracow: Spolka wydawnicza Polska, 1892.

TARNOWSKI, STANISLAW. *Chopin as Revealed by Extracts from His Diary.* (Translated from the Polish by Natalie Janotha.) London: William Reeves, 1906. 69 pp.

UMNISKA, ZOFIA, and Kennedy, Harriette Eleanor. *Chopin, the Child and the Lad.* London: Methuen & Co., Ltd., 1925, 91 pp.

VALETTA, IPPOLITO. *Chopin, La Vita, Le Opere.* Turin: Fratelli Bocca, 1909. 433 pp.

VOLKMANN, HANS. *Chopin in Dresden. Neue Daten zu seiner Lebens und Leibesgeschichte.* (Sonderabruck aus der Wissenschaftlichen Bellage des Dresdner Anziegers vom 18 und 25 April und 9 mai Dresden.) 1933, 51 pp.

VUILLERMOZ, EMILE. *La vie amoureuse de Chopin.* Paris: Flammarion, 1927. 185 pp.

WEISSMANN, ADOLF. *Chopin.* Berlin: Schuster und Loeffler, 1919. 187 pp.

WHEELER, OPAL. *Frédéric Chopin, Son of Poland.* London: Faber & Faber, Ltd., 1949. 156 pp.

WILLEBY, CHARLES. *Frédéric François Chopin.* London: Sampson Low, Marston & Company, 1892. 316 pp.

WODZINSKI, ANTONI. *Les trois romans de Frederic Chopin.* Paris: Calmann Lévy, 1886, 342 pp.

WOJCIK, BRONISLAWA. *La polyphonie de Chopin* (Essay). Kwartalnik Muzyczny. Vol. 1, No. 3, 1929, pp. 251-259.

WOJCIKOWNA, BRONISLAWA, *Sur la litterature relative à Chopin en Pologne restaurée* (Essay). Kwartalnik Muzyczny. Vol. 1, No. 4, 1929, pp. 412-428.

WOJCIK-KEUPRUILIAN, BRONISLAWA. *Melodyka Chopina.* Lwów: 1930. 304 pp.

WOOD, CHARLES. *Letters from Majorca.* London: Bentley & Sons, 1888. 410 pp.

WSZELACZYNSKI, WLADYSLAW. *Fryderyka Chopina.* Tarnopol: Naklad Ksiegarni Leopolda Gileczka, 1885. 93 pp.

ZUKOWSKI OTTEN MIECZYSLAW. *Fryderyk Chopin.* Warsaw: 1910.

PERIODICALS:

Musica. (Paris. Special Chopin Number. July, 1908.)

Die Musik. (Berlin. Special Chopin Number. 1909-10.)

Le Courrier Musical. (Paris. Special Chopin Number. 1910.)

La Revue Musicale. (Paris. Special Chopin Number. Dec., 1931.)

Musyka. (Warsaw. Special Chopin Number. 1932.)

Journal of the Instytut Fryderyka Chopina. (Warsaw. Vol. 1, Nos. 1-2, 1937.)

DISCOGRAPHY

List of Frederic Chopin's published works in chronological order, including a discography, compiled by Cyril Clarke.

1825.

Op. 1 *Premier Rondean pour le piano.* In C Minor. Dedicated to *Mine de Linde.* Published by *Brezina,* Warsaw. *Adolph Martin Schlesinger,* Berlin. *Maurice Schlesinger,* Paris.

NOT RECORDED

1830-1834.

Op. 2 *La ci darem le mano, varié pour le piano, avec accompagnement d'orchestre.* In B flat major. Dedicated to *M. Woyciechowski.* Published by *Tobias Haslinger,* Vienna. *Maurice Schlesinger,* Paris.

NOT RECORDED

1833-1835.

Op. 3 *Introduction et Polonaise brillante, pour piano et violoncelle.* In C major. Dedicated to *M. Joseph Merk.* Published by *Pietro Mechetti,* Vienna. *Simon Richault,* Paris.

NOT RECORDED

1833-1835.

Op. 4 *Sonate pour le piano.* In C minor. Dedicated to *M. Joseph Elsner.* Published by *Carl Haslinger,* Vienna. Simon Richault, Paris.

The manuscript was in Haslinger's hands in 1828, but was not published until 1851.

NOT RECORDED

1836.

Op. 5 *Rondean à la Mazur, pour le piano.* In F major. Dedicated to *Mlle. la Comtesse Alexandrine de Mariolles.* Published by *Brezina*, Warsaw. *Friedrich Hofmeister*, Leipzig. *Schonenberger*, Paris.

NOT RECORDED

1832-1834.

Op. 6 *Quatre Mazurkas pour le piano.* In F sharp minor, C sharp minor, E major, and E flat minor. Dedicated to *Mlle. le Comtesse Pauline Plater.* Published by *Probst-Kistner*, Leipzig. *Maurice Schlesinger*, Paris.

RECORDINGS

No. 1 F sharp minor: *Arthur Rubinstein*, Victor—15779.
No. 2 C sharp minor: Victor—15779.
No. 4 E flat minor: Victor—15780, U.S.A. His Master's Voice: No. 1—DB3802, No. 2—DB3802, No. 3—DB3802, No. 4—DB3803.

1832-1834.

Op. 7 *Cinq Mazurkas pour le piano.* In B flat major, A minor, F minor, A flat major and C major. Dedicated to *Mr. Johns.* Published by *Probst-Kistner*, Leipzig. *Maurice Schlesinger*, Paris.

RECORDINGS

No. 1 B flat major: *Alexander Brailowsky*, Polydor—95324, France, Germany, and Switzerland. *Ignaz Friedman*, Columbia—72059D, U.S.A. *José Iturbi*, Victor, 10-1284, U.S.A. *Arthur Rubinstein*, Victor—15781, U.S.A. His Master's Voice—DB3804, Great Britain.

No.2 A minor: *Ignaz Friedman*, Columbia—72059D, U.S.A. *Arthur Rubinstein*, Victor—15779, U.S.A. His Master's Voice—DB3802, Great Britain.

No. 3 F minor: *Ignaz Friedman*, Columbia—72059D, U.S.A. *Vladimir Horowitz*, His Master's Voice—DA1305, Great Britain. *Nicolas Orloff*, Decca—K1424, Great Britain and U.S.A. *Arthur Rubinstein*, Victor—15780, U.S.A. His Master's Voice—DB3803, Great Britain.

No. 4 A flat major: *Arthur Rubinstein*, Victor—15780, U.S.A. His Master's Voice, DB3803, Great Britain.

No. 5 C major: *Arthur Rubinstein*, Victor—15780, U.S.A. His Master's Voice—DB3803, Great Britain.

1833. Published without Opus number
Grand duo Concertant pour piano et violoncelle sur des Thèmes de Robert le Diable. Written in collaboration with *Auguste Franchomme.* Published by *Adolph Martin Schlesinger,* Berlin. *Maurice Schlesinger,* Paris.

NOT RECORDED

1833-1834.
Op. 8 *Premier pour piano violon, et violoncelle.* In B flat minor. Dedicated to *Prince Antoine Radziwill.* Published by *Probst-Kistner,* Leipzig. *Maurice Schlesinger,* Paris.

NOT RECORDED

1833-1834.
Op. 9 *Trois Nocturne pour le piano.* In B flat minor, E flat major, and B major. Dedicated to *Mme. Camille Pleyel.* Published by *Probst-Kistner,* Leipzig. *Maurice Schlesinger,* Paris.

RECORDINGS

No. 1 B flat minor: *Leopold Godowsky,* Columbia—112, U.S.A. *Arthur Rubinstein,* Victor—14961, U.S.A. His Master's Voice—DB3186, Great Britain.

No. 2 E flat major: *Alexander Brailowsky,* Polydor—95143, France, Germany, and Switzerland. *Alfred Cortot,* His Master's Voice—DB1321, Great Britain. *Jacob Gimpel,* Vox—604, U.S.A. *Leopold Godowsky,* Columbia—112, U.S.A. *Mark Hambourg,* His Master's Voice—C2587, Great Britain. *Eileen Joyce,* Parlophone—E11448, Great Britain. *Raoul Koczalski,* Polydor—67246, France, Germany, and Switzerland. *Oscar Levant,* Columbia—72107D, U.S.A. *Benno Moiseiwitsch.* His Master's Voice—C3197, Great Britain. *Leo Nadelmann,* His Master's Voice—DB10073, Great Britain. *Ignace Paderewski,* Victor—7416, U.S.A. *Serge Rachmanioff,* Victor—6731, U.S.A. *Solomon,* His Master's Voice—C3345, Great Britain. *Willi Stech,* Telefunken—A1914, Germany. *Johanne Stockmarr,* His Master's Voice—DB5261, Great Britain.

No. 3 B major: *Arthur Rubinstein,* Victor—14962, U.S.A. His Master's Voice—DB3187, Great Britain.

1833.

Op. 10 *Douze Grandes Etudes pour le piano.* In C major, A minor, E major, C sharp minor, G flat major, E flat minor, C major, F major, F minor, A flat major, E flat major, and C minor. Dedicated to *Franz Liszt.* Published by *Probst-Kistner,* Leipzig. *Maurice Schlesinger,* Paris.

RECORDINGS

No. 1 C major: *Wilhelm Backhaus,* His Master's Voice–DB928, Great Britain. *Alexander Brailowsky,* Victor–II-9885, U.S.A. *Alfred Cortot,* Victor–14558, U.S.A. His Master's Voice–DB2027, Great Britain. *Jeanne-Marie Darré, Pathé*–PDT93, France. *Edward Kilenyi,* Columbia–P72063D, U.S.A., Great Britain. Pathé–PAT105, France. *Raoul Koczalski,* Polydor–67263, France, Germany, and Switzerland. *Robert Lortat,* Columbia–LFX135, U.S.A., Great Britain. *Otakar Vondrovic,* Esta–F5189, Czechoslovakia.

No. 2 A minor: *Wilhelm Backhaus,* His Master's Voice–DB928, Great Britain. *Alexander Brailowsky,* Victor–II-9885, U.S.A. *Alfred Cortot,* Victor–14558, U.S.A. His Master's Voice–DB2027, Great Britain. *Jeanne-Marie Darré,* Pathé–PDT93, France. *Edward Kilenyi,* Columbia–P72063D, U.S.A., Great Britain. Pathé–PAT105, France. *Raoul Koczalski,* Polydor–90030, France, Germany, and Switzerland. *Robert Lortat,* Columbia–LFX135, U.S.A., Great Britain.

No. 3 E major: *Alexander Brailowsky,* Victor–II-9886, U.S.A. Polydor–95323, France, Germany, and Switzerland. *Alfred Cortot,* Victor–14559, U.S.A. His Master's Voice–DB2028, Great Britain. *France Ellegard,* Polydor–67919, France, Germany, and Switzerland. *O. Frugoni,* Elite–7031, Switzerland. *Eileen Joyce,* Columbia–DX1002, U.S.A., Great Britain. *Edward Kilenyi,* Columbia–P72064D, U.S.A., Great Britain. Pathé–PAT106, France. *Raoul Koczalski,* Polydor– 67262, France, Germany, and Switzerland. *Oscar Levant,* Columbia –72106D, U.S.A., Great Britain. *Hans Leygraf,* Son–K9516, Germany. *William Murdoch,* Decca–K704, Great Britain, U.S.A. *Ignace J. Paderewski,* Victor–6628, U.S.A. His Master's Voice–DB1037, Great Britain. *Solomon,* His Master's Voice–C3433, Great Britain.

No. 4 C sharp minor: *Alexander Brailowsky,* Victor–II-9886, U.S.A. Polydor–35012, France, Germany, and Switzerland. *Alfred Cortot,* Victor–14558, U.S.A., His Master's Voice–DB2027, Great Britain.

Vladimir Horowitz, Victor–14140, U.S.A. His Master's Voice–DB2788, Great Britain. *Edward Kilenyi*, Columbia–P72064D, U.S.A., Great Britain. Pathé–PAT106, France. *Raoul Koczalski*, Polydor–67262, France, Switzerland, Germany. *Oscar Levant*, Columbia–72109D, U.S.A., Great Britain. *Robert Lortat*, Columbia–LFX136, U.S.A., Great Britain. *Nicolas Orloff*, Decca–K1426, Great Britain, U.S.A.

No. 5 G flat major: *Alexander Brailowsky*, Victor–II-9887, U.S.A. Polydor–D95140, France, Germany, and Switzerland. *Alfred Cortot*, Victor–14558, U.S.A. His Master's Voice–DB2027, Great Britain. *Jeanne-Marie Darré*, Pathé–PDT93, France. *Vladimir Horowitz*, Victor–14140, U.S.A. His Master's Voice–DB2788, Great Britain. *Edward Kilenyi*, Columbia–P72065D, U.S.A., Great Britain. Pathé–PAT107, France. *Raoul Koczalski*, Polydor–67263, France, Germany, and Switzerland. *Oscar Levant*, Columbia–71890D and 72106D, U.S.A., Great Britain. *Nicolas de Magaloff*, Radiola–RZ3044, Hungary. *Vladimir de Pachmann*, His Master's Voice DA1302, Great Britain. *Irene Scharrer*, His Master's Voice–D1303, Great Britain.

No. 6 E flat major: *Alexander Brailowsky*, Victor–II-9887, U.S.A. *Alfred Cortot*, Victor–14559, U.S.A. His Master's Voice–DB2028, Great Britain. *Edward Kilenyi*, Columbia–P72065D, U.S.A., Great Britain. Pathé–PAT107, France. *Raoul Koczalski*, Polydor–67262 and 90028, France, Germany, and Switzerland. *Robert Lortat*, Columbia–LFX136, U.S.A., Great Britain.

No. 7 C major: *Wilhelm Backhaus*, His Master's Voice–DB929, Great Britain. *Alexander Brailowsky*, Victor–II-9885, U.S.A. *Alfred Cortot*, Victor–14558, U.S.A. His Master's Voice–DB2027, Great Britain. *Edward Kilenyi*, Columbia–P72063D, U.S.A., Great Britain. Pathé–PAT105, France. *Raoul Koczalski*, Polydor–67263, France, Germany, and Switzerland. *Robert Lortat*, Columbia–LFX137, U.S.A., Great Britain.

No. 8 F major: *Alexander Brailowsky*, Victor–II-9888, U.S.A. *Alfred Cortot*, Victor–14560, U.S.A. His Master's Voice–DB2029, Great Britain. *Jacob Gimpel*, Vox–164, U.S.A. *Edward Kilenyi*, Columbia–P72064D, U.S.A., Great Britain. Pathé–PAT106, France. *Raoul Koczalski*, Polydor–67264, France, Germany and Switzerland. *Robert Lortat*, Columbia–LFX137, U.S.A., Great Britain. *Nicolas de Magaloff*, Radiola–RZ3044, Hungary. *Nicolas Orloff*, Decca–K1426, Great Britain. U.S.A. *Solomon*, Columbia–DX669, U.S.A., Great Britain. *Carlo*

Zecchi, Telefunken—A1948, Germany, Italy, Sweden, Switzerland.
No. 9 F minor: *Alexander Brailowsky,* Victor—II-9886, U.S.A. *Alfred Cortot,* Victor—14560, U.S.A. His Master's Voice—DB2029, Great Britain. *Edward Kilenyi,* Columbia—P72063D, U.S.A., Great Britain. Pathé—PAT105, France. *Raoul Koczalski,* Polydor—67264, France, Germany, and Switzerland. *Robert Lortat,* Columbia—LFX137, U.S.A., Great Britain. *Solomon,* His Master's Voice—C3345, Great Britain.

No. 10 A flat major: *Alexander Brailowsky,* Victor—II-9885, U.S.A. *Alfred Cortot,* Victor—14560, U.S.A. His Master's Voice—DB2029, Great Britain. *Edward Kilenyi,* Columbia—P72065D, U.S.A., Great Britain. Pathé—PAT107, France. *Raoul Koczalski,* Polydor—67264, France, Germany, and Switzerland. *Robert Lortat,* Columbia—LFX137, U.S.A., Great Britain. *Otakar Vondrovic*—Esta—F5188, Czechoslovakia.

No. 11 E flat major: *Alexander Brailowsky,* Victor—11-9888, U.S.A. *Alfred Cortot,* Victor—14559, U.S.A. His Master's Voice—DB2028, Great Britain. *Samson François,* Decca—K1399, Great Britain, U.S.A. *Edward Kilenyi,* Columbia—P72063D, Great Britain, U.S.A. Pathé—PAT 105, France. *Raoul Koczalski,* Polydor—67263, France, Switzerland, Germany. *Josef Lhevinne,* DISC—774, U.S.A. *Robert Lortat,* Columbia—LFX138, U.S.A., Great Britain

No. 12 C minor: *Wilhelm Backhaus,* His Master's Voice—DB928, Great Britain. *Alexander Brailowsky,* Victor—11-9888, U.S.A. *Alfred Cortot,* Victor—14560, U.S.A. His Master's Voice—DB2029, Great Britain. *Jacob Gimpel,* Vox—604, U.S.A. *Louis Kentner,* Columbia—DX1083, U.S.A., Great Britain. *Edward Kilenyi,* Columbia—P72065D, U.S.A., Great Britain. Pathé—PAT107, France. *Raoul Koczalski,* Polydor—67264, France, Germany and Switzerland. *Oscar Levant,* Columbia—71890D and 72106D, U.S.A., Great Britain. *Ignace J. Paderewski,* Victor—1387, U.S.A. His Master's Voice—DA1047, Great Britain. *Emile Von Sauer,* Columbia—LW38, U.S.A., Great Britain. *Irenne Scharrer,* Columbia—DX456, U.S.A., Great Britain.

1833.
Op. 11 *Grand Concerto pour le piano avec orchestre.* In E minor. Dedicated to *Friedrich Kalkbrenner.* Published by *Probst* *Kistner,* Leipzig. *Maurice Schlesinger,* Paris.

DISCOGRAPHY

RECORDINGS

Alexander Brailowsky and The Berlin Philharmonic Orchestra, con-
ducted by *Julius Prüwer*, Polydor–66753-6, France, Germany, and
Switzerland. Vox–452, U.S.A. *Edward Kilenyi* and The Minneapolis
Symphony Orchestra, conducted by *Dimitri Mitropoulos*, Columbia–
CM515, U.S.A., Great Britain. *Arthur Rubinstein* and The London
Symphony Orchestra, conducted by *Sir John Barbirolli*, Victor–VM418,
U.S.A. His Master's Voice–DB3201-4, Great Britain.

1834.
Op. 12 *Variations brillantes pour le piano sur le Rondeau favori
de Ludovic de Hérold: Je vends des Scapulaires.* In B flat
minor. Dedicated to *Mlle. Emma Horsford.* Published by
Breitkopf & Hartel, Leipzig. *Maurice Schlesinger,* Paris.

RECORDINGS

Wilfrid Maggiar, Pathé–PTD101, France.
1834.
Op. 13 *Grande Fantaisie sur des airs polonais, pour le piano avec
orchestre.* In A minor. Dedicated to *Johann Peter Pixis.*
Published by *Probst-Kistner,* Leipzig. *Maurice Schlesinger,*
Paris.

NOT RECORDED

1834.
Op. 14 *Krakowiak, Grand Rondeau de Concert pour le piano avee
orchestre.* In F major. Dedicated to *Princesse Adam
Czartoryska.* Published by *Probst-Kistner,* Leipzig. *Maurice
Schlesinger,* Paris.

RECORDINGS

An Orchestral arrangement by Auber, forming part of the music to
the ballet La Nuit Ensorcelée, has been recorded by the Paris Conservatory Orchestra under Charles Münch. His Master's Voice–
DB11100-2, Great Britain.

1834.
Op. 15 *Trois Nocturnes pour le piano.* In F major, F sharp major,
and G minor. Dedicated to *Ferdinand Hiller.* Published
by *Breitkopf & Hartel,* Leipzig. *Maurice Schlesinger,* Paris.

⊰ 237 ⊱

In Search of Chopin

RECORDINGS

No. 1 F major: *Harriet Cohen*, Columbia–DX1231, U.S.A., Great Britain. *Leopold Godowsky*, Columbia–CM112, U.S.A., Great Britain. *Arthur Rubinstein*, Victor–14962, U.S.A. His Master's Voice–DB3187, Great Britain.

No. 2 F sharp major: *Alexander Brailowsky*, Victor–II-9009, U.S.A. *Jacques Dupont*, Pathé–PG21, France. *Myrtle C. Eaver*, Victor–24796, U.S.A. *Leopold Godowsky*, Columbia–CM112, U.S.A., Great Britain. *Myra Hess*, Columbia–DB1232, U.S.A., Great Britain. *Vladimir Horowitz*, Victor–II-9842, U.S.A. *Raoul Koczalski*, His Master's Voice–DA4430, Great Britain. *Oscar Levant*, Columbia–72107D, U.S.A. *Mischa Levitzki*, His Master's Voice–D1721, Great Britain. *Bronislaw Malaizynski*, Columbia–LX975, U.S.A., Great Britain. *Ignace J. Paderewski*, His Master's Voice–DB3711, Great Britain. *Arthur Rubinstein*, Victor–14963, U.S.A. His Master's Voice–DB3187, Great Britain. *Raymond Trouard*, Odeon–123844, Germany, Sweden, and France.

1834.

Op. 16 *Rondeau pour le piano*. In E flat major. Dedicated to *Mlle. Caroline Hartmann*. Published by *Breitkopf & Hartel*, Leipzig. *Maurice Schlesinger*, Paris.

NOT RECORDED

1834.

Op. 17 *Quatre Mazurkas pour le piano*. In B flat major, E minor, A flat major, and A minor. Dedicated to *Mme. Lina Freppa*. Published by *Breitkopf & Hartel*, Leipzig. *Maurice Schlesinger*, Paris.

RECORDINGS

No. 1 B flat major: *Arthur Rubinstein*, Victor–15781, U.S.A. His Master's Voice–DB3804, Great Britain.

No. 2 E minor: *Arthur Rubinstein*, Victor–15781, U.S.A. His Master's Voice–DB3804, Great Britain.

No. 3 A flat major: *Arthur Rubinstein*, Victor–15782, U.S.A. His Master's Voice–DB3805, Great Britain.

No. 4 A minor: *Robert Casadesus*, Columbia–LFX75, U.S.A., Great Britain. *Walter Gieseking*, Columbia–LWX304, U.S.A., Great Britain. *Edward Kilenyi*, Columbia–P69671D, U.S.A., Great Britain. Pathé–PAT82, France. *Boutet de Monvel*, His Master's Voice–L1045, Great

Britain. *Marie Panthès,* Columbia–DF1919, U.S.A., Great Britain. *Carlo Zecchi,* Cetra–CB20359, Italy, U.S.A.

1834.

Op. 18 *Grande Valse pour le piano.* In E flat major. Dedicated to *Mlle. Laura Horsford.* Published by *Breitkopf & Hartel,* Leipzig. *Maurice Schlesinger,* Paris.

RECORDINGS

Jacques Abram, Musicraft–76, U.S.A. *Wilhelm Backhaus,* His Master's Voice–DB1131, Great Britain. *Alexander Brailowsky,* Victor– 18383, U.S.A. His Master's Voice–DB3706, Great Britain. *Alfred Cortot,* His Master's Voice–DB2311, Great Britian. *Robert Goldsand,* Decca–23191, Great Britain, U.S.A. *Edward Kilenyi,* Columbia– 72066D, U.S.A., Great Britain. *Raoul Koczalski,* Polydor–95201, France, Germany, and Switzerland. *Lubka Kollesa,* His Master's Voice– DB4654, Great Britain. *Robert Lortat,* Columbia–LFX214, U.S.A., Great Britian. *Ignace J. Paderewski,* Victor–6877, U.S.A. *Otakar Vondrovic,* Esta–F5187, Czechoslovakia.

1834.

Op. 19 *Bolero pour le piano.* In B minor. Dedicated to *Mlle. la Comtesse de Flahault.* Published by *Peters,* Leipzig. *Phillip et cie,* Paris.

RECORDINGS

Lilly Dymont, Polydor–27041, France, Germany, and Switzerland.

1835.

Op. 20 *Premier Scherzo pour le piano,* In B minor. Dedicated to *M. T. Albrecht.* Published by *Breitkopf & Hartel,* Leipzig. *Maurice Schlesinger,* Paris.

RECORDINGS

Anatole Kitain, Columbia–DX885, U.S.A., Great Britain. *Raoul Koczalski,* His Master's Voice–DB4474, Great Britain. *Niedzieldski,* His Master's Voice–K7797/8, Great Britain. *Arthur Rubinstein,* Victor–78855, U.S.A. His Master's Voice–DB1915, Great Britain. *Cyril Smith,* Columbia–DX1382, Great Britain, U.S.A.

1836.

Op. 21 *Second Concerto pour le piano avec orchestre.* In F minor. Dedicated to *Mme. la Comtesse Delphine Potocka.* Published by *Breitkopf & Hartel,* Leipzig. *Maurice Schlesinger,* Paris.

RECORDINGS

Alfred Cortot and Symphony Orchestra, conducted by *Sir John Barbirolli.* Victor–567, U.S.A. His Master's Voice–DB2612–25, Great Britain. *Marguerite Long* and Paris Conservatory Orchestra, conducted by *Phillipe Gaubert,* Columbia–143 U.S.A., Great Britain. *Bronislaw Malcuzynski* and Philharmonic Orchestra, conducted by *Paul Kletzki,* Columbia–LX1013/6, Great Britain, U.S.A. *Arthur Rubinstein* and N.B.C. Symphony Orchestra, conducted by *Steinberg,* Victor–1012, U.S.A. *Arthur Rubinstein* and London Symphony Orchestra, conducted by *Sir John Barbirolli,* His Master's Voice–128, Great Britain.

1836.

Op. 22 *Grande Polonaise brillante précédée d'un Andante spianato, pour le piano avec orchestre.* In E flat major. Dedicated to *Mme. la Baronne d'Est.* Published by *Breitkopf & Hartel,* Leipzig. *Maurice Schlesinger,* Paris.

RECORDINGS

An arrangement for pianoforte solo has been recorded by *Arthur Rubinstein,* Victor–14287-8, U.S.A. His Master's Voice– DB2499-500, Great Britain. *Vladimir Horowitz,* Victor–11-9043-4, U.S.A.

1836.

Op. 23 *Ballade pour le piano.* In G minor. Dedicated to *M. le Baron de Stockhausen.* Published by *Breitkopf & Hartel,* Leipzig. *Schlesinger,* Paris.

RECORDINGS

Alexander Brailowsky, Polydor–95325, France, Germany, and Switzerland. *Robert Casadesus,* Columbia–D15076, Great Britain, U.S.A. *Alfred Cortot,* Victor–14651, U.S.A. His Master's Voice– DB2023, Great Britain. *Jean Doyen,* His Master's Voice–DB5145, Great Britain. *Samson François,* Decca–K1398, Great Britain, U.S.A. *Vladimir Horowitz,* Victor–11-9841, U. S. A. *Eileen Joyce,* Columbia– DX1084, Great Britain, U.S.A. *Julian von Karolyi,* Polydor–68089, France, Germany, and Switzerland. *Louis Kentner,* Columbia–DX 1391, Great Britain, U.S.A. *Raoul Koczalski,* Polydor–67528, France,

Germany, and Switzerland. *Anna Kremarova,* Esta—F5213, Czechoslovakia. *Victor Schioler,* Tono—A103, Denmark.

1836.

Op. 24 *Quatre Mazurkas.*. In G minor, C major, A flat major, and B minor. Dedicated to *M. le Comte de Perthuis.* Published by *Breitkopf & Hartel,* Leipzig. *Maurice Schlesinger,* Paris.

RECORDINGS

No. 1 G minor: *Arthur Rubinstein,* Victor—15783, U.S.A. His Master's Voice—DB3806, Great Britain.

No. 2 C major: *Arthur Rubinstein,* Victor—15783, U.S.A. His Master's Voice—DB3806, Great Britain.

No. 3 A flat major: *Arthur Rubinstein,* Victor—15780, U.S.A. His Master's Voice—DB3803, Great Britain.

No. 4 B minor: *Ignaz Friedman,* Columbia—72060D, Great Britain, U.S.A. *Bronislaw Malaizynski,* Columbia—LX1028, U.S.A., Great Britain. *Arthur Rubinstein,* Victor—15907, U.S.A. *Otokar Vondrovic,* Esta—F5186, Czechoslovakia.

1837.

Op. 25 *Douze Etudes pour le piano.* In A flat major, F minor, F major, A minor, E minor, G sharp minor, C sharp minor, D flat major, G flat major, B minor, A minor, and C minor. Dedicated to *Mme. la Comtesse d'Agoult.*. Published by *Breitkopf & Hartel,* Leipzig. *Maurice Schlesinger,* Paris.

RECORDINGS

No. 1 A flat major: *Alexander Brailowsky,* Victor—11-9889, U.S.A. *Alfred Cortot,* His Master's Voice—DB2308, Great Britain. *Jeanne-Marie Darré,* Pathé—PDT92, France. Jacques Dupont, Pathé—PG9, France. *Edward Kilenyi,* Columbia—72074D, Great Britain, U.S.A. *Raoul Koczalski,* Polydor—67243, France, Germany, and Switzerland. *Robert Lortat,* Columbia—LFX139, Great Britain, U.S.A. *Irene Scharrer,* Columbia—DB1348, Great Britain, U.S.A. *Solomon,* Columbia—LX314, Great Britain, U.S.A. *I. Ungar,* Radiola—RBM103, Hungary. *Otakar Vondrovic,* Esta—F5188, Czechoslovakia.

No. 2 F minor: *Alexander Brailowsky,* Victor—11-9889, U.S.A. Polydor—95140, France, Germany, and Switzerland. Cetra—OR5082, Italy, U.S.A. *Alfred Cortot,* His Master's Voice—DB2308, Great Britain.

Colin Horsley, Decca–K1405, Great Britain, U.S.A. *Edward Kilenyi*, Columbia–72074D, Great Britain, U.S.A. Pathé–PG93, France. *Raoul Koczalski*, Polydor–67243, France, Germany, and Switzerland. *Robert Lortat*, Columbia–LFX139 Great Britain, U.S.A. *Solomon*, His Master's Voice–C3345, Great Britain.

No. 3 F major: *Wilhelm Backhaus*, His Master's Voice–DB928, Great Britain. *Alexander Brailowsky*, Victor–11-9889, U.S.A. Polydor –35012, France, Germany, and Switzerland. *Alfred Cortot*, His Master's Voice–DB2309, Great Britain. *Edward Kilenyi*, Columbia–72074D, Great Britain, U.S.A. *Raoul Koczalski*, Polydor–67245, France, Germany, and Switzerland. *Robert Lortat*, Columbia–LFX139, Great Britain, U.S.A. *Vladimir de Pachmann*, His Master's Voice–DB860, Great Britain. *Solmon*, His Master's Voice–C3345, Great Britain.

No. 4 A minor: *Alexander Brailowsky*, Victor–11-9889, U.S.A. *Alfred Cortot*, His Master's Voice–DB2309, Great Britain. *Colin Horsley*, Decca–K1405, Great Britain, U.S.A. *Edward Kilenyi*, Columbia–72074D, Great Britain, U.S.A. Pathé–PG93, France. *Raoul Koczalski*, Polydor–67245, France, Germany, and Switzerland. *Robert Lortat*, Columbia–LFX139, Great Britain, U.S.A.

No. 5 E minor: *Alexander Brailowsky*, Victor–11-9890, U.S.A. *Alfred Cortot*, His Master's Voice–DB2309, Great Britain. *Edward Kilenyi*, Columbia–72075D, Great Britain, U.S.A. *Raoul Koczalski*, Polydor–67242 France, Germany, and Switzerland. *Robert Lortat*, Columbia–LFX140, Great Britain, U.S.A.

No. 6 G sharp minor: *Alexander Brailowsky*, Victor–11-9890, U.S.A. *Alfred Cortot*, His Master's Voice–DB2309, Great Britain. *Jeanne-Marie Darré*, Pathé–PDT92, France. *France Ellegard*, Polydor–62839, France, Germany and Switzerland. *Colin Horsley*, Decca–K1405, Great Britain, U.S.A. *Edward Kilenyi*, Columbia–72075, Great Britain, U.S.A. *Raoul Koczalski*, Polydor–67245, France, Germany and Switzerland. *Robert Lortat*, Columbia–LFX140, Great Britain, U.S.A.

No. 7 C sharp minor: *Alexander Brailowsky*, Victor–11-9891, U.S.A. *Alfred Cortot*, His Master's Voice–DB2310, Great Britain. *Edward Kilenyi*, Columbia–72075D, Great Britain, U.S.A. *Raoul Koczalski*, Polydor–67242, France, Germany, and Switzerland. *Robert Lortat*, Columbia–LFX141, Great Britain, U.S.A. *Otakar Vondrovic*, Esta– F5188 Czechoslovakia.

No. 8 D flat major: *Alexander Brailowsky*, Victor–11-9889, U.S.A. *Alfred Cortot*, His Master's Voice–DB2309, Great Britain. *Jeanne-Marie Darré*, Pathé–PDT93, France. *Colin Horsley*, Decca–K1405, **Great**

Britain, U.S.A. *Edward Kilenyi*, Columbia–72076D, Great Britain, U.S.A. *Raoul Koczalski*, Polydor–67243, France, Germany, and Switzerland. *Robert Lortat*, Columbia–LFX140, U.S.A., Great Britain.

No. 9 G flat major: *Alexander Brailowsky*, Victor–11-9890, U.S.A. Polydor–90197, France, Germany, and Switzerland. *Alfred Cortot*, His Master's Voice–DB2310, Great Britain. *Jeanne-Marie Darré*, Pathé –PDT93, France. *Myrtle C. Eaver*, Victor–24796, U.S.A. *Edward Kilenyi*, Columbia–72076D, U.S.A., Great Britain. *Raoul Koczalski*, Polydor–67243, France, Germany, and Switzerland. *Josef Lhevinne*, Disc–774, U.S.A. *Robert Lortat*, Columbia–LFX138, U.S.A., Great Britain. *Nikita de Magaloff*, Radiola–RZ3044, Hungary. *Ignace J. Paderewski*, His Master's Voice–DA470, Great Britain. *Irene Scharrer*, Columbia–DB1348, Great Britain, U.S.A. *I. Ungar*, Radiola–RBM103, Hungary.

No. 10 B minor: *Alexander Brailowsky*, Victor–11-9891, U.S.A. *Alfred Cortot*, His Master's Voice–DB2308, Great Britain. *Samson François*, Decca–K1399, Great Britain, U.S.A. *Edward Kilenyi*, Columbia– 72076D, Great Britain, U.S.A. *Raoul Koczalski*, Polydor–67242, France, Germany, and Switzerland. *Robert Lortat*, Columbia–LFX141, Great Britain, U.S.A.

No. 11 A minor: *Alexander Brailowsky*, Victor–11-9892, U.S.A. Polydor–95323, France, Germany, and Switzerland. Cetra–RR8029, Italy, U.S.A. *Alfred Cortot*, His Master's Voice–DB2310, Great Britain. *Jacques Dupont*, Pathé–PG9, France. *Edward Kilenyi*, Columbia– 72076D, Great Britain, U.S.A. *Raoul Koczalski*, Polydor–67244, France, Germany, and Switzerland. *Robert Lortat*, Columbia–LFX142, Great Britain, U.S.A.

No. 12 C minor: *Alexander Brailowsky*, Victor–11-9888, U.S.A. Polydor–95423, France, Germany, and Switzerland. *Alfred Cortot*, His Master's Voice–DB2308, Great Britain. *Edward Kilenyi*, Columbia– 72074D, Great Britain, U.S.A. *Raoul Koczalski*, Polydor–67245, France, Germany, and Switzerland. *Robert Lortat*, Columbia–LFX142, U.S.A., Great Britain. *Dirk Schafer*, Columbia–DHX15, U.S.A., Great Britain. *Otakar Vondrovic*, Esta–F5185, Czechoslovakia.

1836.
Op. 26 *Deux Polonaises pour le piano.* In C sharp minor and E flat minor. Dedicated to *M. Joseph Dessauer.* Published by *Breitkopf & Hartel*, Leipzig. *Maurice Schlesinger*, Paris.

RECORDINGS

No. 1 C sharp minor: *Arthur Rubinstein*, Victor—14281, U.S.A. His Master's Voice—DB2493, Great Britain. *Hanna Schwab*, Polydor—15175, France, Germany, and Switzerland.

No. 2 E flat minor: *Ignace J. Paderewski*, His Master's Voice— DB-5897, Great Britain. *Arthur Rubinstein*, Victor—14282, U.S.A. His Master's Voice, DB2494, Great Britain.

1836.

Op. 27 Deux Nocturnes pour le piano. In C sharp minor and D flat major. Dedicated to *Mme. la Comtesse d'Appony.* Published by *Breitkopf & Hartel,* Leipzig. *Maurice Schlesinger,* Paris.

RECORDINGS

No. 1 C sharp minor: *Leopold Godowsky.* Columbia—112, U.S.A., Great Britain. *William Murdoch*, Decca—K691, Great Britain, U.S.A. *Arthur Rubinstein,* Victor—14964, U.S.A. *Winfried Wolf,* His Master's Voice—DB7605, Great Britain.

No. 2 D flat major: *Yvonne Gelbibert,* His Master's Voice—DB5159, Great Britain. *Leopold Godowsky,* Columbia—112, U.S.A., Great Britain. *Raoul Koczalski,* Polydor—95172, France, Germany, and Switzerland. *Dinu Lipatti,* Columbia—LB63, Great Britain, U.S.A. *Vladimir de Pachmann,* His Master's Voice—DB860, Great Britain. *Solomon,* His Master's Voice—C3308, Great Britain.

1839.

Op. 28 Vingt-quatre Préludes pour le piano. In C major, A minor, G major, E minor, D major, B minor, A major, F sharp minor, E major, C sharp minor, B major, G sharp minor, F sharp major, E flat minor, D flat major, B flat minor, A flat major, F minor, E flat major, C minor, B flat major, G minor, F major, D minor. Dedicated to *Camille Pleyel* (in the French and English editions), and to *Joseph Christoph Kessler* (in the German edition). Published by *Breitkopf & Hartel,* Leipzig. *Catelin et Cie,* Paris. The French edition was published in two parts with an opus number.

RECORDINGS

No. 1 C major: *Wilhelm Backhaus,* His Master's Voice—DB2059, Great Britain. *Alfred Cortot,* Victor—8813, U.S.A. His Master's Voice—DB2015, Great Britain. *Andor Földes,* Continental—22, U.S.A. *Nicolas*

Orloff, Decca–K1425, Great Britain, U.S.A. *Egon Petri*, Columbia–71402D, Great Britain, U.S.A.

No. 2 A minor: *Alfred Cortot*, Victor–8813, U.S.A. His Master's Voice –DB2015, Great Britain. *Nicolas Orloff*, Decca–K1425, Great Britain, U.S.A. *Egon Petri*, Columbia–71402D, Great Britain, U.S.A.

No. 3 G major: *Alexander Brailowsky*, Polydor–95423, France, Germany, and Switzerland. *Alfred Cortot*, Victor–8813, U.S.A. His Master's Voice–DB2015, Great Britain. *Nicolas Orloff*, Decca–K1425, Great Britain, U.S.A. *Egon Petri*, Columbia–71402D, Great Britain, U.S.A. *Moritz Rosenthal*, His Master's Voice–DB2772, Great Britain.

No. 4 E minor: *Alfred Cortot*, Victor–8813, U.S.A. His Master's Voice–DB2015, Great Britain. *Lili Kraus*, Polydor–R20451, France, Germany, and Switzerland. *Egon Petri*, Columbia–71402D, Great Britain, U.S.A.

No. 5 D major: *Alfred Cortot*, Victor–8813, U.S.A. His Master's Voice–DB2015, Great Britain. *Egon Petri*, Columbia–71402D, Great Britain, U.S.A.

No. 6 B minor: *Alexander Brailowsky*, Polydor–95423, France, Germany, and Switzerland. *Alfred Cortot*, Victor–8813, U.S.A. His Master's Voice–DB2015, Great Britain. *Edward Kilenyi*, Pathé–PG93, France. *Vladimir de Pachmann*, His Master's Voice–DA1302, Great Britain. *Egon Petri*, Columbia–71402D, Great Britain, U.S.A. *Moritz Rosenthal*, His Master's Voice–DB2772, Great Britain. *I. Ungar*, Radiola–RBM104, Hungary.

No. 7 A major: *Alfred Cortot*, Victor–8814, U.S.A. His Master's Voice–DB2016, Great Britain. *Raoul Koczalski*, Odeon–4761, Germany, Sweden, France. *Egon Petri*, Columbia–71403D, Great Britain, U.S.A. *Moritz Rosenthal*, His Master's Voice–DB2772, Great Britain. *I. Ungar*, Radiola–RBM104, Hungary.

No. 8 F sharp minor: *Alfred Cortot*, Victor–8814, U.S.A. His Master's Voice–DB2016, Great Britain. *Egon Petri*, Columbia–71403D, Great Britain, U.S.A.

No. 9 E major: *Alfred Cortot*, Victor–8814, U.S.A. His Master's Voice–DB2016, Great Britain. *Raoul Koczalski*, Polydor–67506, France, Germany, and Switzerland. *Egon Petri*, Columbia–71403D, Great Britain, U.S.A.

No. 10 C sharp minor: *Alfred Cortot*, Victor–8814, U.S.A. His Master's Voice–DB2016, Great Britain. *Raoul Koczalski*, Polydor–67506, France, Germany, and Switzerland. *Egon Petri*, Columbia–71403D, Great Britain, U.S.A.

No. 11 B major: *Alfred Cortot*, Victor—8814, U.S.A. His Master's Voice—DB2016, Great Britain. *Raoul Koczalski*, Polydor—90038, France, Germany, and Switzerland. *Egon Petri*, Columbia—7140D, Great Britain, U.S.A.

No. 12 G sharp minor: *Alfred Cortot*, Victor—8814, U.S.A. His Master's Voice—DB2016, Great Britain. *Raoul Koczalski*, Polydor—67506, France, Germany, and Switzerland. *Egon Petri* Columbia—71403D, Great Britain, U.S.A.

No. 13 F sharp major: *Alfred Cortot*, Victor—8814, U.S.A. His Master's Voice—DB2016, Great Britain. *Raoul Koczalski*, Polydor—67506, France, Germany, and Switzerland. *Egon Petri*, Columbia—71403D, Great Britain, U.S.A.

No. 14 E flat minor: *Alfred Cortot*, Victor—8814, U.S.A. His Master's Voice—DB2016, Great Britain. *Raoul Koczalski*, Polydor—67506, France, Germany, and Switzerland. *Egon Petri*, Columbia—71403D, Great Britain, U.S.A.

No. 15 D flat major: *Alexander Brailowsky*, Polydor—35012, France, Germany, and Switzerland. *Alfred Cortot*, Victor—8815, U.S.A. His Master's Voice—DB2017, Great Britain. *Leo Nadelmann*, His Master's Voice—DB10073, Great Britain. *Ignace J. Paderewski*, Victor—6847, U.S.A. His Master's Voice—DB1272, Great Britain. *Egon Petri*, Columbia—71404D, Great Britain, U.S.A. *Mary-Jo Turner*, Decca—K652, Great Britain, U.S.A.

No. 16 B flat minor: *Alfred Cortot*, Victor—8815, U.S.A. His Master's Voice—DB2017, Great Britain. *Samson François*, Decca—K1399, Great Britain, U.S.A. *Egon Petri*, Columbia—7140D, Great Britain, U.S.A.

No. 17 A flat major: *Alfred Cortot*, Victor—8815, U.S.A. His Master's Voice—DB2017, Great Britain. *Samson Francois*, Decca—K1399, Great Britain, U.S.A. *Mark Hambourg*, His Master's Voice, C2064, Great Britain. *Raoul Koczalski*, Polydor—95174, France, Germany, and Switzerland. *Ignace J. Paderewski*, Victor—6847, U.S.A. His Master's Voice—DB1272, Great Britain. *Egon Petri*, Columbia—71404D, Great Britain, U.S.A. *I. Ungar*, Radiola—RBM105, Hungary.

No. 18 F minor: *Alfred Cortot*, Victor—8815, U.S.A. His Master's Voice—DB2017, Great Britain. *Egon Petri*, Columbia—7140D, Great Britain, U.S.A.

No. 19 E flat major: *Alfred Cortot*, Victor—8816 U.S.A. His Master's Voice—DB2018, Great Britain. *Egon Petri*, Columbia—71405D, Great Britain, U.S.A.

No. 20 C minor: *Alfred Cortot*, Victor—8816, U.S.A. His Master's

Voice—DB2018, Great Britain. *Raoul Koczalski*, Polydor—90030, France, Germany, and Switzerland. *Egon Petri*, Columbia—71405D, Great Britain, U.S.A.

No. 21 B flat major: *Alfred Cortot*, Victor—8816, U.S.A. His Master's Voice—DB2018, Great Britain. *Egon Petri*, Columbia—71405D, Great Britain, U.S.A.

No. 22 G minor: *Alfred Cortot*, Victor—8816, U.S.A. His Master's Voice—DB2018, Great Britain. *Egon Petri*, Columbia—71405D, Great Britain, U.S.A.

No. 23 F major: *Alfred Cortot*, Victor—8816, U.S.A. His Master's Voice—DB2018, Great Britain. *Walter Gieseking*, Columbia—17079D, Great Britain, U.S.A. *Egon Petri*, Columbia—71405D, Great Britain, U.S.A. *I. Ungar*, Radiola—RBM105, Hungary.

No. 24 D minor: *Alfred Cortot*, Victor—8816, U.S.A. His Master's Voice—DB2018, Great Britain. *Egon Petri*, Columbia—71405D, Great Britain, U.S.A.

1838.
  Op. 29 *Impromptu pour le piano.* In A flat major. Dedicated to *Mlle. la Comtesse de Loban.* Published by *Breitkopf & Hartel*, Leipzig. *Maurice Schlesinger*, Paris.

RECORDINGS

Alexander Brailowsky, Victor—11-8643, U.S.A. *Alfred Cortot*, His Master's Voice—DB2021, Great Britain. *Ania Dorfmann*, Columbia—DX818, U.S.A., Great Britain. *Louis Kentner*, Columbia—DX1081, Great Britain, U.S.A. *Nicolas Orloff*, Decca—K1424, Great Britain, U.S.A. *Irene Scharrer*, His Master's Voice—D1087, Great Britain. *Hanna Schwab*, Polydor—15175 France, Germany, and Switzerland.

1838.
  ..*Op.* 30 *Quatre Mazurkas pour le piano.* In C minor, B minor, D flat major, and C sharp minor. Dedicated to *Mme. la Princesse de Wurtemberg.* Published by *Breitkopf & Hartel*, Leipzig. *Maurice Schlesinger*, Paris.

RECORDINGS

No. 1 C minor: *Arthur Rubinstein*, Victor—15781, U.S.A. His Master's Voice—DB3804, Great Britain.

No. 2 B minor: *Maryla Jonas*, Columbia—72099D, U.S.A., Great

Britain. *Arthur Rubinstein*, Victor–17297, U.S.A. His Master's Voice –DB3807, Great Britain.

No. 3 D flat minor: *Arthur Rubinstein*, Victor– 15783, U.S.A. His Master's Voice–DB3806, Great Britain.

No. 4 C sharp minor: *Vladimir Horowitz*, Victor–1327, U.S.A. *Arthur Rubinstein*, Victor–15907, U.S.A. His Master's Voice–DB3808, Great Britain. *Carlo Zecchi*, Cetra–CB20346, Italy, U.S.A.

1838.

Op. 31 *Deuxième Scherzo pour le piano.* In B flat minor. Dedicated to *Mlle. la Comtesse Adèle de Furstenstein.* Published by *Breitkopf & Hartel,* Leipzig. *Maurice Schlesinger,* Paris.

RECORDINGS

Hans Bund, Telefunken–E2011, Germany, Italy, Sweden, Switzerland. *Marcel Ciampi,* Columbia–D15225, U.S.A., Great Britain. *Raoul Koczalski,* His Master's Voice–DB4474, Great Britain. *Marguerite Long,* Columbia–LFX513, Great Britain, U.S.A. *Arturo Michaelangeli,* His Master's Voice–DB5355, Great Britain. *Benno Moisewitsch,* His Master's Voice–D1065, Great Britain. *Arthur Rubinstein,* Victor–7856, U.S.A. His Master's Voice–DB1916, Great Britain. *Irene Scharrer,* Columbia–DX433, Great Britain, U.S.A. *Otakar Vondrovic,* Esta– F5184, Czechoslovakia.

1837.

Op. 32 *Deux Nocturnes pour le piano.* In B major and A flat major. Dedicated to *Mme. la Baronne de Billing.* Published by *Adolph Martin Schlesinger,* Berlin. *Maurice Schlesinger,* Paris.

RECORDINGS

No. 1 B major: *Leopold Godowsky,* Columbia–112, U.S.A., Great Britain. *Eileen Joyce,* Parlophone–E11448, Great Britain. *Louis Kentner,* Columbia–DX1147, Great Britain, U.S.A. *Raoul Koczalski,* Polydor –67534, France, Germany, and Switzerland. *Arthur Rubinstein,* Victor –14967, U.S.A. His Master's Voice–DB3192, Great Britain.

No. 2 A flat major: *France Ellegaard,* Polydor–67841, France, Germany, and Switzerland. *Arthur Rubinstein,* Victor–14967, U.S.A. His Master's Voice–DB3192, Great Britain.

1838.

Op. 33 *Quatre Mazurkas pour le piano*. In G sharp minor, D major, C major, and B minor. Dedicated to *Mlle. la Comtesse Mostowska*. Published by *Breitkopf & Hartel*, Leipzig. *Maurice Schlesinger*, Paris.

RECORDINGS

No. 1 G sharp minor: *Arthur Rubinstein*, Victor—17298, U.S.A. His Master's Voice—DB3808, Great Britain.

No. 2 D major: *Ignaz Friedman*, Columbia—72059D, Great Britain, U.S.A. *Ignace J. Paderewski*, His Master's Voice—DA1245, Great Britain. *Arthur Rubinstein*, Victor—15908, U.S.A. His Master's Voice—DB3839, Great Britain.

No. 3 C major: *Arthur Rubinstein*, Victor—15908, U.S.A. His Master's Voice—DB3840, Great Britain.

No. 4 B minor: *Ignaz Friedman*, Columbia—72060D, Great Britain, U.S.A. *Raoul Koczalski*, Polydor—90031, France, Germany, and Switzerland. *Leonio Kreutzer*, Polydor—90034, France, Germany, and Switzerland. *Marie Panthès*, Columbia—DFX216, Great Britain, U.S.A. *Arturo Michaelangeli*, Telefunken—SKB3289, Germany, Italy, Sweden, and Switzerland. *Arthur Rubinstein*, Victor—15909, U.S.A. His Master's Voice—DB3840, Great Britain.

1839.

Op. 34 *Trois Valses brillantes pour le piano*. In A flat major, A minor, and F minor. Dedicated to *Mlle. de Thun-Hohenstein, Mme. G. d'Ivri, Mlle. A. d'Eichthal*.. Published by *Breitkopf & Hartel*, Leipzig. *Maurice Schlesinger*, Paris.

RECORDINGS

No. 1 A flat major: *Jacques Abram*, Musicraft—76, U.S.A. *Alexander Brailowsky*, Victor—18383, U.S.A. Polydor—67247, France, Germany, and Switzerland. *Alfred Cortot*, His Master's Voice—DB2311, Great Britain. *Myrtle Eaver*, Victor—24796, U.S.A. *Rudolph Ganz*, Victor—7290, U.S.A. *Edward Kilenyi*, Columbia—72066D, Great Britain, U.S.A. *Raoul Koczalski*, Polydor—67247, France, Germany, and Switzerland. *Robert Lortat*, Columbia—LFX214, Great Britain, U.S.A. *Arthur Rubinstein*, His Master's Voice—DB1160, Great Britain.

No. 2 A minor *Jacques Abram*, Musicraft—76, U.S.A. *Alexander Brailowsky*, Victor—18384, U.S.A. *Alfred Cortot*, His Master's Voice—

DB2312, Great Britain. *Valdimir Horowitz*, Victor—11—9044, U.S.A. *Edward Kilenyi*, Columbia—72067D, Great Britain, U.S.A. *Raoul Koczalski*, Polydor—95201, France, Germany, and Switzerland. *Robert Lortat*, Columbia—LFX215, Great Britain, U.S.A. *Margarita Mirimanowa*, Columbia—GQX16448, Great Britain, U.S.A. *Leo Nadelmann*, His Master's Voice—DB10056, Great Britain.

No. 3 F major: *Jacques Abram*, Musicraft—76, U.S.A. *Alexander Brailowsky*, Victor—18385, U.S.A. *Alfred Cortot*, His Master's Voice—DB2312, Great Britain. *Edward Kilenyi*, Columbia—72067D, Great Britain, U.S.A. *Raoul Koczalski*, Polydor—67553, France, Germany, and Switzerland. *Robert Lortat*, Columbia—LFX215, Great Britain, U.S.A. *Nicolas Orloff*, Decca—K1424, Great Britain, U.S.A., *Emil von Sauer*, Columbia—LW38, U.S.A., Great Britain. *Robert Frouard*, Odeon—188947, Germany, Sweden, France.

1840. Published without Opus number.

> *Trois Nouvelles Etudes—Etudes de Perfection de la Methode des Methodes de Moscheles et Fétis.* In F minor, A flat major, and D flat major. Published by *Adolph Martin Schlesinger*, Berlin. *Maurice Schlesinger*, Paris.

RECORDINGS

No. 1 F minor: *Alexander Brailowsky*, Victor—11-9892, U.S.A. *Harriet Cohen*, Columbia—DX1231, Great Britain, U.S.A. *Raoul Koczalski*, Polydor—67244, France, Germany, and Switzerland. *Robert Lortat*, Columbia—LFX142, Great Britain, U.S.A.

No. 2 D flat major: *Alexander Brailowsky*, Victor—11-9892, U.S.A. *Raoul Koczalski*, Polydor—67244, France, Germany, and Switzerland. *Robert Lortat*, Columbia—LFX142, Great Britain, U.S.A.

No. 3 A flat major: *Alexander Brailowsky*, Victor—11-9822, U.S.A. *Raoul Koczalski*, Polydor—67244, France, Germany, and Switzerland. *Harriet Cohen*, Columbia— DX1231, Great Britain, U.S.A. *Robert Lortat*, Columbia—LFX140, Great Britain, U.S.A.

1840.

> Op. 35 *Sonate pour le piano*. In B flat minor. Published by *Breitkopf & Hartel*, Leipzig. *Eugène Troupenas et Cie*, Paris

RECORDINGS

Paul Baumgartner, His Master's Voice—DB10026-8, Great Britain. *Alexander Brailowsky*, Vox—453, U.S.A. Polydor—95480-1, France

Germany, and Switzerland. *Robert Casadesus*, Columbia–698, Great Britain, U.S.A. *Alfred Cortot*, His Master's Voice–DB2019-20, Great Britain. *Percy Grainger*, Columbia–GQX10303-5, U.S.A., Great Britain. *Edward Kilenyi*, Columbia–378, U.S.A., Great Britain. *Robert Lortat*, Columbia–D15092-3, U.S.A., Great Britain. *Serge Rachmaninoff*, His Master's Voice–151, Great Britain. *Arthur Rubinstein*, Victor–1082, U.S.A.

1840.
Op. 36 *Deuxième Impromptu pour le piano*. In F sharp minor. Published by *Breitkopf & Hartel*, Leipzig. *Eugène Troupenas et Cie*, Paris.

RECORDINGS
Alfred Cortot His Master's Voice–DB2021, Great Britain. *Louis Kentner*, Columbia–DX997, Great Britain, U.S.A. *Raoul Koczalski*, Polydor–67248, France, Germany, and Switzerland. *Lili Krauss*, Parlophone–R20451, Great Britain.

1840.
Op. 37 *Deux Nocturnes pour le piano*. In G minor and G major. Published by *Breitkopf & Hartel*, Leipzig. *Eugène Troupenas et Cie*, Paris.

RECORDINGS
No. 1 G minor: *Leopold Godowsky*, Columbia–112, Great Britain, U.S.A. *Arthur Rubinstein*, Victor–14964, U.S.A. His Master's Voice–DB3189, Great Britain.
No. 2 G major: *Leopold Godowsky*, Columbia–112 Great Britain, U.S.A. *Mark Hambourg*, His Master's Voice–C2516, Great Britain. *Arthur Rubinstein*, Victor–14966, U.S.A. His Master's Voice–DB3191, Great Britain.

1840,
Op. 38 *Deuxième Ballade pour le piano*. In F major. Dedicated to *Robert Schumann*. Published by *Breitkopf & Hartel*, Leipzig. *Eugène Troupenas et Cie*, Paris.

RECORDINGS

Robert Casadesus, Columbia—LFX166, Great Britain, U.S.A. *Alfred Cortot,* Victor—14562, U.S.A. His Master's Voice— DB2024, Great Britain. *Jean Doyen,* His Master's Voice—DB5146, Great Britain. *Raoul Koczalski,* Polydor—67531, France, Germany, and Switzerland. *Anna Kremarova, Esta*—F5214, Czechoslovakia. *Benno Moisewitsch,* His Master's Voice—C3685, Great Britain.

1840.
Op. 39 *Troisième Scherzo pour le piano.* In C sharp minor. Dedicated to *Adolph Gutmann.* Published by Breitkopf & Hartel, Leipzig. *Eugène Troupenas et Cie,* Paris.

RECORDINGS

Claudio Arrau, Parlophone—R20428, Great Britain. *Jacques Dupont,* Pathé—X98071, France. *France Ellegaard,* Polydor—67918, France, Germany, and Switzerland. *Arthur Rubinstein,* Victor—7857, U.S.A. His Master's Voice—DB1917, Great Britain.

1840.
Op. 40 *Deux Polonaises pour le piano.* In A major and C minor. Dedicated to *Julius Fontana.* Published by *Breitkopf & Hartel,* Leipzig. *Eugène Troupenas et Cie,* Paris.

RECORDINGS

No. 1 A major: *Suzanne Gyr,* His Master's Voice—DB10074, Great Britain. *Mark Hambourg,* His Master's Voice—C1292, Great Britain. *Louis Kentner,* Columbia—DX1083, Great Britain, U.S.A. *Raoul Koczalski,* Polydor—90031, France, Germany, and Switzerland. *Oscar Levant,* Columbia—72108D, U.S.A., Great Britain. *Iris Loveridge,* Columbia—DX1234, Great Britain, U.S.A. *Ignace Paderewski,* His Master's Voice—DB375, Great Britain. *Arthur Rubinstein,* Victor—14283, U.S.A. His Master's Voice—DB2495, Great Britain.

No. 2 C minor: *Arthur Rubinstein,* Victor—14283, U.S.A. His Master's Voice, DB2495, Great Britain.

1840.
Op. 41 *Quatre Mazurkas pour le piano.* In C sharp minor, E minor, B major, and E flat major. Dedicated to *Etienne Witwicki.* Published by *Breitkopf & Hartel,* Leipzig. *Eugène Troupenas et Cie,* Paris.

RECORDINGS

No. 1 C sharp minor: *Ignaz Friedman*, Columbia–72061V, Great Britain, U.S.A. *Arthur Rubinstein*, Victor–15909, U.S.A. His Master's Voice–DB3840, Great Britain.

No. 2 E minor: *Vladimir Horowitz*, His Master's Voice–DA1353, Great Britain. *Arthur Rubinstein*, Victor–15783, U.S.A. His Master's Voice– DB3806, Great Britain.

No. 3 B major: *Arthur Rubinstein*, Victor–15909, U.S.A. His Master's Voice–DB3840, Great Britain.

No. 4 A flat major: *Arthur Rubinstein*, Victor–15780, U.S.A. His Master's Voice–DB3803, Great Britain.

1840.
Op. 42 *Valse pour le piano.* In A flat major. Published by *Breitkopf & Hartel*, Leipzig. *Pacini*, Paris.

RECORDINGS

Simone Barère, His Master's Voice–DB2166, Great Britain. *Alexander Brailowsky*, Victor–18385, U.S.A. *Alfred Cortot*, His Master's Voice–DB2313, Great Britain. *Ania Dorfmann*, Columbia–DX818, Great Britain, U.S.A. *France Ellegaard*, Polydor–67841, France, Germany, and Switzerland. *Edward Kilenyi*, Columbia–72068D, U.S.A., Great Britain. *Robert Lortat*, Columbia–LFX216, U.S.A., Great Britain. *Ignace J. Paderewski*, His Master's Voice–DB380, Great Britain. *Moritz Rosenthal*, His Master's Voice–DB2772, Great Britain. *Solomon*, His Master's Voice–C3433, Great Britain. *Carlo Zecchi*, Cetra–CB20351, Italy.

1841. Published without Opus number.
Variation VI from the Hexameron: Morceau de Concert Grandes Variations de bravoure sur la Marche des "Puritains" de Bellini. Composed for a charity concert given by Mme. la Princesse Belgiojoso by *Liszt, Thallerg, Pixis, Hertz, Czerny,* and *Chopin.* Published by *Tobias Haslinger*, Vienna. *Eugène Troupenas et Cie*, Paris.

NOT RECORDED

1841.
Op. 43 *Tarantelle pour le piano.* In A flat major. Published by *Julius Schubert & Co.*, Leipzig. *Troupenas et Cie*, Paris.

RECORDINGS

Alfred Cortot, Victor—8251, U.S.A.   His Master's Voice—DB2032,
Great Britain.   *Noel Mewton-Wood,* Decca—K1064, Great Britain,
U.S.A.

1841.
   Op. 44 *Polonaise pour le piano.* In F sharp minor. Dedicated to
   Mlle. la Princesse Charles de Beavau. Published by *Pietro
   Mechetti,* Vienna. *Maurice Schlesinger,* Paris.

RECORDINGS

Arthur Rubinstein, Victor—14285, U.S.A.   His Master's Voice—
DB2496, Great Britain.

1841.
   Op. 45 *Prélude pour le piano.* In C sharp minor. Dedicated to
   Mlle. la Princesse Elisabeth Czermicheff. Published by
   Pietro Mechetti, Vienna. *Maurice Schlesinger,* Paris.

RECORDINGS

Raoul Koczalski, Polydor—95174 France, Germany, and Switzerland.

1842. Published without Opus number.
   Mazurka pour piano. In A minor. Published by *Schotts
   Sohne.*

RECORDINGS

Arthur Rubinstein, Victor—17298, U.S.A.   His Master's Voice—
DB3845, Great Britain.

1842.
   Op. 46 *Allegro de Concert pour le piano.* In A major. Dedicated
   to *Mlle. Friederike Müller.* Published by *Breitkopf &
   Hartel,* Leipzig. *Maurice Schlesinger,* Paris.

NOT RECORDED

1842.
   Op. 47 *Troisiéme Ballade pour le piano.* In A flat major. Dedi-
   cated to *Mlle. P. de Noailles.* Published by *Breitkopf &
   Hartel,* Leipzig. *Maurice Schlesinger,* Paris.

Claudio Arrau, Parlophone—R20443, Great Britain. *Robert Casadesus,* Columbia—LFX131, U.S.A., Great Britain. *Alfred Cortot,* Victor—14563, U.S.A. His Master's Voice—DB2025, Great Britain. *Jean Doyen,* His Master's Voice—DB5147, Great Britain. *Eileen Joyce,* Columbia—DX976, Great Britain, U.S.A. *Raoul Koczalski,* Polydor—67529, France, Germany, and Switzerland. *Anna Kremarova,* Esta—F5215, Czechoslovakia. *Benno Moisewitsch,* His Master's Voice—C3100, Great Britain. *Leo Nadelmann,* His Master's Voice—DB10050, Great Britain. *Guiomar Novaës,* Columbia—72345D, U.S.A., Great Britain. *C. M. Savery,* Tono—A124, Denmark.

1842.

Op. 48 *Deux Nocturnes pour le piano.* In C minor and F sharp minor. Dedicated to *Mlle. L. Duperré.* Published by *Breitkopf & Hartel,* Leipzig. *Maurice Schlesinger,* Paris.

No. 1 C minor: *Raoul Koczalski,* Polydor—67534, France, Germany, Switzerland. *Arthur Rubinstein,* Victor—14968, U.S.A. His Master's Voice—DB3193, Great Britain.

No. 2 F sharp minor: *Jacques Dupont,* Pathé—PG21, France. *Leopold Godowsky,* Columbia—112, U.S.A., Great Britain. *Arthur Rubinstein,* Victor—14968, U.S.A. His Master's Voice—DB3193, Great Britain. *William Worden,* Decca—F3053, Great Britain, U.S.A.

1842.

Op. 49 *Fantaisie pour le piano.* In F minor. Dedicated to *Mlle la Princesse de Souzzo.* Published by *Breitkopf & Hartel,* Leipzig. *Maurice Schlesinger,* Paris.

Alfred Cortort, His Master's Voice—DB2031-2, Great Britain. *Solomon,* Columbia—DX668-9, Great Britain, U.S.A.

1842.

Op. 50 *Trois Mazurkas pour le piano.* In G major, A flat major, and C sharp minor. Dedicated to *M. Leon Szmitkowski.* Published by *Pietro Mechetti,* Vienna. *Maurice Schlesinger,* Paris.

No. 1 G major: *Arthur Rubinstein*, Victor—15910, U.S.A. His Master's Voice, DB3841, Great Britain.
No. 2 A flat major: *Ignaz Friedman*, Columbia—72061D, Great Britain, U.S.A. *Arthur Rubinstein*, Victor—15910, U.S.A. His Master's Voice—DB3841.
No. 3 C sharp minor: *Vladimir Horowitz*, Victor—14140, U.S.A. His Master's Voice—DB2788, Great Britain. *Nicolas de Magaloff*, Radiola—RZ3031, Hungary. *Bronislaw Malcuzynski*, Columbia—LX1028, Great Britain, U.S.A. *Nicolas Orloff*, Decca—K1426, Great Britain, U.S.A. *Otakar Vondrovic*, Esta—F5185, Czechoslovakia. *Arthur Rubinstein*, Victor—15911, U.S.A. His Master's Voice—DB3842, Great Britain.

1843.
Op. 51 *Allegro Vivace Troisiéme Impromptu pour le piano.* In G flat major. Dedicated to *Mme. la Comtesse Esterhazy.* Published by *Friedrich Hofmeister*, Leipzig. *Maurice Schlesinger*, Paris.

Alfred Cortot, Victor—8239, U.S.A. His Master's Voice—DB2022, Great Britain. *Arthur Rubinstein*, Victor—11-9301, U.S.A.

1843.
Op. 52 *Quatrième Ballade pour le piano.* In F minor. Dedicated to *Mme. la Baronne de Rothschild.* Published by *Breitkopf & Hartel*, Leipzig. *Maurice Schlesinger*, Paris.

Robert Casadesus, Columbia—LFX74-5, U.S.A., Great Britain. *Alfred Cortot*, Victor—14564, U.S.A. His Master's Voice—DB2026, Great Britain. *Jean Doyen*, His Master's Voice—DB5148-9, Great Britain. *Jacques Dupont*, Pathé—X98015-6, France. *Raoul Koczalski*, Polydor —67530, France, Germany, and Switzerland. *Anna Kremarova*, Esta—F5216, Czechoslovakia. *Solomon*, His Master's Voice—C3403, Great Britain.

1843.

Op. 53 *Huitième Polonaise pour le piano*. In A flat major. Dedicated to *M. August Leo*. Published by *Breitkopf & Hartel*, Leipzig. *Maurice Schlesinger*, Paris.

RECORDINGS

Paul Baumgartner, His Master's Voice—DB10033, Great Britain. *Alexander Brailowsky*, Polydor—90196, France, Germany, and Switzerland. *Alfred Cortot*, His Master's Voice—DB2014, Great Britain, *France Ellegaard*, Decca—K1600, Great Britain, U.S.A. *Yvonne Gellibert*, His Master's Voice—DA4932, Great Britain *Jacob Gimpel*, Vox—604, U.S.A. *Vladimir Horowitz*, Victor—11-9065, U.S.A. *José Iturbi*, Victor—11-8848, U.S.A., His Master's Voice, DB6288, Great Britain. *Raoul Koczalski*, His Master's Voice—DA4431, Great Britain. *Mischa Levizki*, His Master's Voice—DA1316, Great Britain. *Bronislaw Malcuzynski*, Columbia—LX982, U.S.A., Great Britain. *Ignace J. Paderewski*, Victor—14974, U.S.A. His Master's Voice—DB3134, Great Britain. *Egon Petri*, Columbia—17377D, Great Britain, U.S.A. *Arthur Rubinstein*, Victor—14285, U.S.A. His Master's Voice—DB2497, Great Britain. *Victor Schioler*, Tono—A104, Denmark. *Solomon*, Columbia—LX314, Great Britain, U.S.A. *Winfried Wolf*, His Master's Voice—DB7683, Great Britain.

1843.

Op. 54 *Scherzo No. 4 pour le piano*. In E major. Dedicated to *Mlle. J. de Caraman*. Published by *Breitkopf & Hartel*, Leipzig. *Maurice Schlesinger*, Paris.

RECORDINGS

Vladimir Horowitz, Victor—14634, U.S.A. His Master's Voice—DB3205, Great Britain. *Arthur Rubinstein*, Victor—7858, U.S.A. His Master's Voice—DB1918, Great Britain.

1844.

Op. 55 *Deux Nocturnes pour le piano*. In F minor and E flat major. Dedicated to *Miss Jane Stirling*. Published by *Breitkopf & Hartel*, Leipzig. *Maurice Schlesinger*, Paris.

RECORDINGS

No. 1 **F minor**: *Leopold Godowsky*, Columbia—112, U.S.A., Great

Britain. *Arthur Rubinstein*, Victor—14969, U.S.A. His Master's Voice—DB3194, Great Britain.

No. 2 E flat major: *Ignaz Friedman*, Columbia—DX781, Great Britain, U.S.A. *Yvonne Gellibert*, His Master's Voice—DB5159, Great Britain. *Arthur Rubinstein*, Victor—14969, U.S.A. His Master's Voice—DB31969, Great Britain.

1844.

Op. 56 *Trois Mazurkas pour le piano.* In B major, C major, and C minor. Dedicated to *Mlle. C. Maberby.* Published by *Breitkopf & Hartel*, Leipzig. *Maurice Schlesinger*, Paris.

RECORDINGS

No. 1 B major: *Arthur Rubinstein*, Victor—15911, U.S.A. His Master's Voice—DB3842, Great Britain.

No. 2 C major: *Arthur Rubinstein*, Victor—17295, U.S.A. His Master's Voice—DB3843, Great Britain.

No. 3 C minor: *Arthur Rubinstein*, Victor—17295, U.S.A. His Master's Voice—DB3843, Great Britain.

1845.

Op. 57 *Berceuse pour le piano.* In D flat major. Dedicated to *Mlle. Elise Gerard.* Published by *Breitkopf & Hartel*, Leipzig. *Joseph Meissonnier*, Paris.

RECORDINGS

Wilhelm Backhaus, His Master's Voice—DB1131, Great Britain. *Alexander Brailowsky*, Victor—15382, U.S.A. *Yvonne Gellibert*, His Master's Voice—W1523, Great Britain. *Walter Gieseking*, Columbia—LWX304, Great Britain, U.S.A. *Corde Groot*, Odeon—8776, Germany, Sweden, and France. *Suzanne Gyr*, His Master's Voice—DB10074, Great Britain. *Eileen Joyce*, Parlophone—E11432, Great Britain. *Raoul Koczalski*, Polydor—95202, France, Germany, and Switzerland. *Oscar Levant*, Columbia—72108D, U.S.A., Great Britain. *Arturo Michelangeli*, Telefunken—SKB3289, Germany, Italy, Sweden, and Switzerland. *Arthur Rubinstein*, Victor—11-9408, U.S.A. His Master's Voice—DB2149, Great Britain. *Solomon*—His Master's Voice—C3308, Great Britain. *Carlo Zecchi*, Cetra—CB20354, Italy, U.S.A.

1845.

Op. 58 *Sonate pour le piano.* In B minor. Dedicated to *Mme. la Comtesse de Perthuis.* Published by *Breitkopf & Hartel, Leipzig. Joseph Meissonier,* Paris.

RECORDINGS

Alexander Brailowsky, Victor—548, U.S.A. *Alfred Cortot,* His Master's Voice—DA1333-6, Great Britain. *Dinu Lipatti,* Columbia—LX994-6, U.S.A., Great Britain.

1846.

Op. 59 *Trois Mazurkas pour le piano.* In A minor, A flat major, and F sharp minor. Published by *Stern et Cie-Brandus et Cie,* Paris.

RECORDINGS

No. 1 A minor: *Arthur Rubinstein,* Victor—17295, U.S.A. His Master's Voice—DB3843, Great Britain.

No. 2 A flat major: *Ignace J. Paderewski,* His Master's Voice—DA1245, Great Britain. *Arthur Rubinstein,* Victor—17296, U.S.A. His Master's Voice—DB3844, Great Britain.

No. 3 F sharp minor: *Simon Barère,* Victor—14263, U.S.A. *Marguerite Long,* Columbia—67803D, Great Britain, U.S.A. *Arthur Rubinstein,* Victor—17296, U.S.A. His Master's Voice—DB3844, Great Britain.

1846.

Op. 60 *Barcarolle pour le piano.* In F sharp major. Dedicated to *Mme. la Baronne de Stockhausen.* Published by *Breitkopf & Hartel,* Leipzig. *Brandus et Cie,* Paris.

RECORDINGS

Alexander Brailowsky, Polydor—35014, France, Germany, and Switzerland. *Alfred Cortot,* His Master's Voice—DB2030, Great Britain. *Walter Gieseking,* Columbia—71026D, Great Britain, U.S.A. *Louis Kentner,* Columbia—DX1112, Great Britain, U.S.A. *Marguerite Long,* Columbia—LFX325, Great Britain, U.S.A. *Benno Moiseiwitsch,* His Master's Voice—C3229, Great Britain. *Arthur Rubinstein,* His Master's Voice—DB1161, Great Britain. *Carlo Zecchi,* Cetra—CB20349, Italy, U.S.A.

1846.
Op. 61 *Polonaise-Fantaisie pour le piano*. In A flat major. Dedicated to *Mme. A. Veyret*. Published by *Breitkopf & Hartel*, Leipzig. *Brandus et Cie*, Paris.

RECORDINGS

Louis Kentner, Columbia—DX1146-7, Great Britain, U.S.A. *Walter Rehberg*, Polydor—25137-8, France, Germany, and Switzerland. *Arthur Rubinstein*, Victor—14286-7, U.S.A. His Master's Voice—DB2498-9, Great Britain.

1846.
Op. 62 *Deux Nocturnes pour le piano*. In B major and E major. Dedicated to *Mlle. R. de Konneritz*. Published by *Breitkopf & Hartel*, Leipzig. *Brandus et Cie*, Paris.

RECORDINGS

No. 1 B major: *Raoul Koczalski*, Polydor—95172 France, Germany, and Switzerland. *Marie Panthés*, Columbia—DFX216, Great Britain, U.S.A. *Arthur Rubinstein*, Victor—14970, U.S.A. His Master's Voice—DB3195, Great Britain. *Erik Then-Bergh*, His Master's Voice—EH1306, Great Britain.

No. 2 E major: *Arthur Rubinstein*, Victor—14971, U.S.A. His Master's Voice—DB3196, Great Britain.

1847.
Op. 63 *Trois Mazurkas pour le piano*. In B major, F minor, and C sharp minor. Dedicated to *Mme. la Comtesse Czosnowska*. Published by *Breitkopf & Hartel*, Leipzig. *Brandus et Cie*, Paris.

RECORDINGS

No. 1 B major: *Arthur Rubinstein*, Victor—15908, U.S.A. His Master's Voice—DB3839, Great Britain.

No. 2 F minor: *Arthur Rubinstein*, Victor—15910, U.S.A. His Master's Voice—DB3841, Great Britain.

No. 3 C sharp minor: *Andor Földes*, Continental-22, U.S.A. *Ignaz Friedman*, Columbia—C72062D, Great Britain, U.S.A. *Edward Kilenyi*, Pathé—PG92, France. *Ignace J. Paderewski*, Victor—7416, U.S.A. His Master's Voice—DB1763, Great Britain. *Arthur Rubinstein*, Victor—

15910, U.S.A. His Master's Voice—DB3841, Great Britain.

1847.

Op. 64 *Trois Valses pour le piano*. In D flat major, C sharp minor, and A flat major. Dedicated to *Mme. la Comtesse Potocka*. *Mme. la Baronne de Rothschild. Mme. la Baronne Bronicka*. Published by *Breitkopf & Hartel*, Leipzig. *Brandus et Cie*, Paris.

RECORDINGS

No. 1 D flat major: *Jacques Abram*, Musicraft—76, U.S.A. *Wilhelm Backhaus*, His Master's Voice—DB929, Great Britain. *Alexander Brailowsky*, Victor—18385, U.S.A. *Alfred Cortot*, His Master's Voice—DB-2313, Great Britain. *Jean Doyen*, His Master's Voice—DB5149, Great Britain. *Walter Gieseking*, Columbia—17079D, Great Britain, U.S.A. *Robert Goldsand*, Decca—23191, Great Britain, U.S.A. *Mark Hambourg*, His Master's Voice—C2579, Great Britain. *José Iturbi*, Victor—10-1283, U.S.A. His Master's Voice—DA1848, Great Britain. *Edward Kilenyi*, Columbia—72068D, Great Britain, U.S.A. *Raoul Koczalski*, Polydor—9003, France, Germany, and Switzerland. *Robert Lortat*, Columbia—LFX217, Great Britain, U.S.A. *Nicolas de Magaloff*, Radiola —RZ3031, Hungary. *William Murdoch*, Decca—K682, Great Britain, U.S.A. *Vladimir de Pachmann*, His Master's Voice—DA761, Great Britain. *Raymond Trouard*, Odeon—188949, Germany, Sweden, and France. *Otakar Vondrovic*, Esta—F5189 Czechoslovakia. *Michael von Zadora*, Polydor—22120, France, Germany, and Switzerland.

No. 2 C sharp minor: *Jacques Abram*, Musicraft—76, U.S.A. *Alexander Brailowsky*, Victor—18386, U.S.A. Polydor—95140, France, Germany, and Switzerland. Cetra—OR5077, Italy, U.S.A. *Alfred Cortot*, His Master's Voice—DB2311, Great Britain. *Orazio Frugoni*, Elite—7031, Switzerland. *Jacob Gimpel*, Vox—604, U.S.A. *Robert Goldsand*, Decca—23193, Great Britain, U.S.A. *Cor de Groot*, Odeon—8776, Germany, Sweden, and France. *Mark Hambourg*, His Master's Voice—B3798, Great Britain. *Vladimir Horowitz*, Victor 11-9519, U.S.A. *Louis Kentner*, Columbia—DX1081, Great Britain, U.S.A. *Edward Kilenyi*, Columbia—72069D, Great Britain, U.S.A. *Raoul Koczalski*, Polydor—90038, France, Germany, and Switzerland. *Oscar Levant*, Columbia—72109D, U.S.A., Great Britain. *Robert Lortat*, Columbia—LFX216, U.S.A., Great Britain. *Bronislaw Malcuzynski*, Columbia—

LX975, U.S.A., Great Britain. *Margarita Mirimanowa,* Columbia—CQ102, Great Britain, U.S.A. *William Murdoch,* Decca—F7495, Great Britain, U.S.A. *Vladimir de Pachmann,* His Master's Voice—DB860, Great Britain. *Ignace J. Paderewski,* His Master's Voice—DB3711, Great Britain. *Serge Rachmaninoff,* Victor—1245, U.S.A. *Arthur Rubinstein,* His Master's Voice—DB1495, Great Britain. *Willi Stech,* Telefunken, A1914, Germany, Italy, Sweden, and Switzerland. *Johanne Stockmarr,* His Master's Voice—DB5261, Great Britain. *Raymond Trouard,* Odeon —188950, Germany, Sweden, and France. *Michael von Zadora,* Polydor—22120, France, Germany, and Switzerland.

No. 3 A flat major: *Jacques Abram,* Musicraft—76, U.S.A. *Alexander Brailowsky,* Victor—18386, U.S.A. *Alfred Cortot,* His Master's Voice—DB2314, Great Britain. *Edward Kilenyi,* Columbia—72067D, Great Britain, U.S.A. *Raoul Koczalski,* Polydor—67533, France, Germany, and Switzerland. *Robert Lortat*—Columbia—LFX218, Great Britain, U.S.A. *Serge Rachmaninoff,* Victor—1245, U.S.A.

1847.
Op. 65 *Sonate pour piano et violoncelle.* In G minor. Dedicated to *M. Auguste Franchomme.* Published by *Breitkopf & Hartel,* Leipzig. *Brandus et Cie,* Paris.
NOT RECORDED

1851. Published after the composer's death without Opus number. *Variations pour le piano sur un air allemand..* In E major. Composed *circa* 1824. Published *by Carl Haslinger,* Vienna. *Simon Richault,* Paris.
NOT RECORDED

1851. Published after the composer's death without Opus number. *Mazurka.* In G major. Composed *circa* 1825. Published by *J. Leitgeber-Gebethner & Wolff,* Warsaw.
NOT RECORDED

1851. Published after the composer's death without Opus number. *Mazurka.* In B flat major. Composed *circa* 1825. Published by *J. Leitgeber-Gebethner & Wolff,* Warsaw.

RECORDING
Maryla Jonas, Columbia—72099D, U.S.A., Great Britain.

1851. Published after the composer's death without Opus number. *Mazurkas.* In D major. Composed *circa* 1829-30. Published by *J. Leitgeber-Gebethner & Wolff,* Warsaw.

NOT RECORDED

1851. Published after the composer's death without Opus number. *Mazurka.* In A minor. Dedicated to *M. Emile Gaillard.* Published by *Bote & Bock.*

RECORDINGS

Arthur Rubinstein, Victor—17297, U.S.A. His Master's Voice—DB 3845, Great Britain.

1851. Published after the composer's death without Opus number. *Mazurkas.* In D major. Composed *circa* 1832. A revised version of the *Mazurka* composed *circa* 1829-30. Published by *J. Leitgeber-Gebethner & Wolff,* Warsaw.

NOT RECORDED

1851. Published after the composer's death without Opus number. *Mazurka.* In C major. Composed *circa* 1833. Published by *Gebethner & Wolff,* Warsaw.

NOT RECORDED

1855.
Op. 66 *Fantaisie Impromptu.* In C sharp minor. Composed *circa* 1834. Published after the composer's death by *Adolph Martin Schlesinger,* Berlin. *Joseph Meissonnier fils,* Paris.

RECORDINGS

Wilhelm Backhaus, His Master's Voice—DB2059, Great Britain. *Alexander Brailowsky,* Victor—12-0016, U.S.A. *Alfred Cortot,* Victor— 8239, U.S.A. His Master's Voice—DB2022, Great Britain. *Jacob Gimpel,* Vox—604, U.S.A. *José Iturbi,* Victor—10-1283, U.S.A. *Eileen Joyce,* Parlophone—E11432, Great Britain. *Louis Kentner,* Columbia— DX997, Great Britain, U.S.A. *Raoul Koczalski,* Polydor—67248, France, Germany, and Switzerland. *Iris Loveridge,* Columbia—DX1239, Great Britain, U.S.A. *Nicolas Orloff.* Decca—K1425, Great Britain, U.S.A. *Dirk Schaffer,* Columbia—DHX12, U.S.A., Great Britain. *Irene Scharrer,* Columbia—DX456, Great Britain, U.S.A. *Magda Tagliaferro,* Pathé— PAT22, France.

1855.

Op. 67 *Quatre Mazurkas.* In G major, G minor, C major, and A minor. No. 1 composed *circa* 1835, No. 2 *circa* 1849, No. 3 *circa* 1835, No. 4 *circa* 1846. Published after the composer's death by *Adolph Martin Schlesinger,* Berlin. *Joseph Meissonier fils,* Paris.

RECORDINGS

No. 1 G major: *Valdimir de Pachmann,* His Master's Voice—DA1302, Great Britain. *Arthur Rubinstein,* Victor—17296, U.S.A. His Master's Voice—DB3844, Great Britain.

No. 2 G minor: *Maryla Jonas,* Columbia—72099D, U.S.A., Great Britain. *Arthur Rubinstein,* Victor—17297, U.S.A. His Master's Voice—DB3807, Great Britain.

No. 3 C major: *Ignaz Friedman,* Columbia 72062D, Great Britain, U.S.A. *Arthur Rubinstein,* Victor—17297, U.S.A. His Master's Voice, DB3807, Great Britain.

No. 4 A minor: *Jean Francaix,* Telefunken—A2232, Germany, Italy Sweden, and Switzerland. *Ignaz Friedman,* Columbia—72062D, Great Britain, U.S.A. *Arthur Rubinstein,* Victor—17298, U.S.A. His Master's Voice— DB3808, Great Britain.

1855.

Op. 68 *Quatre Mazurkas.* In C major, A minor, F major, and F minor. No. 1 Composed *circa* 1830, No. 2 *circa* 1827, No. 3 *circa* 1830, No. 4 *circa* 1849. Published after the composer's death by *Adolph Martin Schlesinger,* Berlin. *Joseph Meissonnier fils,* Paris.

RECORDINGS

No. 1 C major: *Arthur Rubinstein,* Victor—17296, U.S.A. His Master's Voice—DB3844, Great Britain.

No. 2 A minor: *Ignaz Friedman,* Columbia—72062D, Great Britain, U.S.A. *John Hunt,* His Master's Voice—C2567, Great Britain. *Raoul Koczalski,* Polydor—90040, France, Germany, and Switzerland. *Arturo Michelangeli,* His Master's Voice—DA5371, Great Britain. *Arthur Rubinstein,* Victor—17297, U.S.A. His Master's Voice—DB3845, Great Britain. *Solomon,* His Master's Voice—C3509 Great Britain.

No. 3 F major: *Raoul Koczalski,* His Master's Voice—DA4430, Great Britain. *Arthur Rubinstein,* Victor—17298, U.S.A. His Master's Voice— DB3808, Great Britain.

No. 4 F minor: *Maryla Jonas*, Columbia—72099D, U.S.A., **Great Britain**, *Arthur Rubinstein*, Victor—15908, U.S.A. His Master's Voice— DB3839, Great Britain.

1855.
Op. 69 *Deux Valse*, In F minor and B minor. No. 1 composed *circa* 1836, No. 2 *circa* 1829. Published after the composer's death by *Adolph Martin Schlesinger*, Berlin. *Joseph Meissonnier fils*, Paris.

RECORDINGS

No. 1 F minor: *Alexander Brailowsky*, Victor—18367, U.S.A. Polydor 90197, France, Germany, and Switzerland. *Alfred Cortot*, His Master's Voice—DB2315, Great Britain. *Robert Goldsand*, Decca—23192, Great Britain, U.S.A. *Edward Kilenyi*, Columbia—72069D, Great Britain, U.S.A. *Raoul Koczalski*, Polydor— 67247, France, Germany, and Switzerland. *Robert Lortat*, Columbia—LFX217, Great Britain, U.S.A. *Arturo Michaelangeli*, His Master's Voice—DA5371, Great Britain. *Raymond Trouard*, Odeon—188950, Germany, Sweden, and France. *Otakar Vondrovic*, Esta—F5186, Czechoslovakia.

No. 2 B minor: *Alexander Brailowsky*, Victor—18387, U.S.A. *Alfred Cortot*, His Master's Voice—DB2315, Great Britain. *Edward Kilenyi*, Columbia—72068D, Great Britain, U.S.A. *Robert Lortat*, Columbia— LFX217, Great Britain, U.S.A.

1855.
Op. 70 *Trois Valses*. In G flat major, F minor, and D flat major. No. 1 composed *circa* 1835, No. 2 *circa* 1843, No. 3 *circa* 1830. Published after the composer's death by *Adolph Martin Schlesinger*, Berlin. *Joseph Meissonnier fils*, Paris.

RECORDINGS

No. 1 G flat major: *Alexander Brailowsky*, Victor—18388, U.S.A. *Alfred Cortot*, His Master's Voice—DB2316, Great Britain. *Jean Doyen*, His Master's Voice—DB5149, Great Britain. *Robert Goldsand*, Decca— 23193, Great Britain, U.S.A., *Mark Hambourg*, His Master's Voice— C2579, Great Britain. *Maryla Jonas*, Columbia—72101, Great Britain, U.S.A. *Edward Kilenyi*, Columbia—72070D, Great Britain, U.S.A. *Raoul Koczalski*, Polydor—67533, France, Germany, and Switzerland. *Oscar Levant*, Columbia—72109D, U.S.A., Great Britain. *Robert Lortat*,

Columbia—LFX218, Great Britain, U.S.A. *William Murdoch,* Decca—
K682, Great Britain, U.S.A., *Vladimir de Pachmann,* His Master's Voice—
DA761, Great Britain. *Raymond Trouard,* Odeon—188951, Germany,
Sweden, and France. *Otakar Vondrovic,* Esta—F5189, Czechoslovakia.
Wilfred Worden, Decca—F2708, Great Britain, U.S.A.
No. 2 F minor: *Alexander Brailowsky,* Victor—18388, U.S.A. *Alfred
Cortot,* His Master's Voice—DB2313, Great Britain. *Edward Kilenyi,*
Columbia—72070D, Great Britain, U.S.A. *Robert Lortat,* Columbia—
LFX218, U.S.A., Great Britain.
No. 3. D flat major: *Paul Baumgartner,* His Master's Voice—DB10012,
Great Britain. *Alexander Brailowsky,* Victor—18389, U.S.A. *Alfred
Cortot,* His Master's Voice—DB2316, Great Britain. *Maryla Jonas,*
Columbia—72101D, Great Britain, U.S.A. *Edward Kilenyi,* Columbia—
72070D, Great Britain, U.S.A. *Robert Lortat,* Columbia—LFX218,
Great Britain, U.S.A.

1855.
Op. 71 *Trois Polonaises.* In D minor, B flat major, and F minor.
No. 1 composed *circa* 1827, No. 2 *circa* 1828, No. 3 circa 1829.
Published after the composer's death by *Adolph Martin
Schlesinger,* Berlin. *Joseph Meissonier fils,* Paris.

RECORDING

No. 1 D minor: (*Not recorded*).
No. 2 B flat major: *Mark Hambourg,* His Master's Voice—C2579,
Great Britain. *Maryla Jonas,* Columbia—72101D, Great Britain, U.S.A.
Benno Moiseiwitch, His Master's Voice—C3485, Great Britain.
No. 3 F minor: (*Not recorded*).

1855.
Op. 72 *Nocturne.* In E minor. Composed *circa* 1827. *March
Funèbre.* In C minor. Composed *circa* 1829. *Trois Ecos-
saises.* In D major, G major, and D flat major. Composed
circa 1830. Published after the composer's death by *Adolph
Zadora,* Polydor—22120, France, Germany, and Switzerland.
Martin Schlesinger, Berlin. *Joseph Meissonier fils,* Paris.
Victor—17296, U.S.A. His Master's Voice—DB3844, Great Britain.

RECORDINGS

No. 1 Nocturne in E minor: *Leopold Gadowsky,* Columbia—112,
U.S.A., Great Britain. *Maryla Jonas,* Columbia—72100D, Great Britain,

U.S.A. *Leo Nadleman*, His Master's Voice—DB10056, Great Britain. *Arthur Rubinstein*, Victor—14971, U.S.A.

No. 2 Marche Funèbre in C minor: (*Not recorded*).

No. 3 Trois Ecossaises: *Alexander Brailowsky*, Victor—V15382, U.S.A. *Jacques Dupont*, Pathé—PG21, France. *Raoul Koczalski*, His Master's Voice—DA4430, Great Britain. *Raymond Trouard*, Odeon—188940, Germany, Sweden, France.

1855.
Op. 73 *Rondeau pour deux pianos*. In C major. Composed *circa* 1828, Published after the composer's death by *Adolph Martin Schlesinger*, Berlin. *Joseph Meissonier fils*, Paris.

RECORDING
Pierre Luboschutz and Genia Nemenoff, Victor—11-9137, U.S.A.

1855.
Op. 74 *Seventeen Polish Songs*. Composed between 1824-1844. German Translation by *Ferdinand Gumbert*. English Translation by *Rev. J. Troutbeck*. Published after the composer's death by *Adolph Martin Schlesinger*, Berlin. *Joseph Meissonier fils*, Paris.

RECORDINGS
No recordings are available of these works as songs. Three of them Nos. 1, 12, and 15, have been recorded as piano solos, arranged by *Franz Liszt*. No. 1 The Maidens Wish: *Margarita Mirimanows*, Columbia—CQX16447, Great Britain, U.S.A. *Serge Rachmaninoff*, Victor—11-8593, U.S.A. No. 12 My Joys: *Bernard Stavenhagen*, Odeon—4751, Germany, Sweden, and France. No. 15 The Return Home: *Serge Rachmaninoff*, Victor—11-8593, U.S.A.

1864. Published after the composer's death without Opus number. *Polonaise*. In G sharp minor. Dedicated to *Mme. Sophie Dupont*. Composed *circa* 1822 (on internal evidence it may have been composed much later). Published by *B. Schott's Sohne. Gebethner & Wolff*, Warsaw.

NOT RECORDED

1868.   Published after the composer's death without Opus number. *Valse*. In E minor. Published by *B. Schott's Sohne*. *Gebethner & Wolff*, Warsaw.

RECORDINGS

Alexander Brailowsky, Victor—18389, U.S.A.   Polydor—90174, France Germany, and Switzerland.   *Alfred Cortot*, His Master's Voice—DB 2316, Great Britain.   *Robert Goldsand*, Decca—23192, Great Britain, U.S.A.   *Edward Kilenyi*, Columbia—72070D, Great Britain, U.S.A. *Leonid Kreutzer*, Polydor—90034, France, Germany, and Switzerland. *Robert Lortat*, Columbia—LFX215, Great Britain, U.S.A.   *Serge Rachmaninoff*, His Master's Voice— DA1189, Great Britain.   *Solomon*, His Master's Voice—C3509, Great Britain.   *Raymond Trouard*, Odeon— 188951, Germany, Sweden, and France.

1872.   Published after the composer's death without Opus Number. *Polonaise*. In B flat minor. Composed *circa* 1826. Published by *Gebethner & Wolff*, Warsaw.

NOT RECORDED

1872.   Published after the composer's death without Opus number. *Valse*. In E major. Composed *circa* 1829. Published by *Gebethner & Wolff*, Warsaw.

NOT RECORDED